SELF-MANAGEMENT IN YUGOSLAVIA
AND THE DEVELOPING WORLD

SELF-MANAGEMENT IN YUGOSLAVIA AND THE DEVELOPING WORLD

Hans Dieter Seibel
and
Ukandi G. Damachi

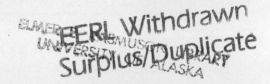

St. Martin's Press   New York

All rights reserved. For information, write:
St. Martin's Press, Inc., 175 Fifth Avenue, New York, NY 10010
Printed in Hong Kong
First published in the United States of America in 1982

ISBN 0–312–71237–5

Library of Congress Cataloging in Publication Data

Seibel, Hans Dieter.
  Self-management in Yugoslavia and the developing
world.

  Bibliography: p.
  Includes index.
  1. Works councils—Yugoslavia. 2. Underdeveloped
areas—Works councils. I. Damachi, Ukandi Godwin.
II. Title.
HD5660.Y8S4 1982   331′.01′12   81–21214
ISBN 0–312–71237–5   AACR2

Contents

List of Tables

Acknowledgements

I am particularly grateful to Dagmar Hasler, Christina Franz and Ulrike Backhaus for typing the manuscript.

For information on self-management in Algeria, I am indebted to Brigitte Lüchtemeier in Schwerte, to Werner Plum of the Friedrich Ebert Foundation in Bonn, and to Professor Dr Werner Ruf of the Gesamthochschule, Essen.

The authors and publishers wish to thank the following who have kindly given permission for the use of copyright material: Associated Book Publishers, for the extract from *The Unperfect Society: Beyond the New Class* by Milovan Djilas, published by Methuen & Co. and Harcourt Brace Jovanovich Inc. (1969); Mr Milan Bajec, for the extracts from *Yugoslavia: Self-Management in Action* published in *Yugoslav Review*, Belgrade; the International Institute for Labour Studies, for the extracts from *Workers' Participation in Management in Yugoslavia* by W. J. Burt, *I.I.L.S. Bulletin*, vol. 9 (1972); the McGraw-Hill Book Company, for the extracts from *The Human Organisation: Its Management and Value* by Rensis Likert (1967); the *Review of International Affairs*, Belgrade, for the extracts from *The Second Congress of Self-Managers of Yugoslavia* (1972); and the editor, *Yugoslav Survey*, Belgrade, for the data from *Changes in the Structure of Industrial Production 1952–1972* by Miodrag Nikolić, in *Yugoslav Survey*, vol. 14 (1973).

Every effort has been made to trace all the copyright-holders but if any have been inadvertently overlooked the publishers will be pleased to make the necessary arrangement at the first opportunity.

HANS DIETER SEIBEL

1 Introduction: Self-Management as a Third Way

Countries in search of a model for development see themselves confronted with a difficult choice: neither the capitalist nor the state-socialist model seem too attractive. In the Developing World, capitalism still bears the brunt of the blame of colonialism and continues to be identified with imperialism. State socialism, on the other hand, carries with it the danger of submitting to a superpower—not too exciting a prospect for those who just escaped the fetters of colonialism. It was in response to this dilemma that the Developing World went on its search for a third way. Africa discovered African socialism, a pragmatic approach to development rather than a specific ideology, appearing in quite different forms in each country that adheres to it. Asia, Latin America and Oceania, on the other hand, have been less consistent in their pursuance of any particular approach.

Many developing and developed countries face a similar problem: dissatisfied with capitalism, which is too ruthless, and disenchanted with state-socialism, which is too rigid, each one is groping for its own third way. Theirs is not a search for a particular ideology or model, but again a rather pragmatic response to day-to-day problems and pressures. Some of the most advanced countries are now discovering a new model in their search for a third way: the self-managing society, a system based on direct, participatory democracy in all spheres: in industry, other organizations and politics—in that order. The country that is being studied now with some interest is Yugoslavia, the only large-scale experiment in self-management, in progress for more than a quarter of a century.

The fact that highly developed countries are examining the Yugoslav system of self-management as a potential model for their own post-industrial future could easily be mistaken as an indication of the inappropriateness of this model for developing societies. But this conclusion would indeed be a mistake. For until very recently, Yugoslavia was a developing country. Moreover, it was under the system of self-management that Yugoslavia made the transition from an underdeveloped to a developed country. Today, Yugoslavia is one of the very few successful latecomers to modernization. As a potential vehicle for rapid development, self-management deserves particular attention among the developing countries.

In a study for ILO's International Institute for Labour Studies, Burt (1972, pp. 195–6) noted:

> Bearing in mind the underdeveloped state of the Yugoslav economy before the Second World War, and the damage suffered by the economy during the war, the growth and strengthening of the economy has been substantial. National income *per capita* at 1968 domestic purchasing power parity was US $600, compared with US $100 in 1939. In the period 1947–52, the average rate of growth of the social product of the economy was 2.35 per cent, and of physical volume of industrial production 6.5 per cent. The corresponding figures for 1953–64 (when self-management had been introduced) were 8.63 and 12.85 per cent.

At present, *per capita* income is approaching the US $1000 threshold, and it is even higher in some of the more advanced regions of Yugoslavia.

Adizes (1971, p. 222), a critical observer of *Industrial Democracy: Yugoslav Style*, found that:

> With all the dysfunctional behaviour . . . it should be borne in mind that self-management generally yielded amazing functional results in the long run.

And in a very carefully worded evaluation, Jenkins (1973, pp. 110–11) concluded:

> Even if we cannot prove that the self-management system is more efficient than some other system, we can certainly make the minimum claim that it does not interfere with satisfactory

economic performance. . . . Just as kibbutz industrial management in Israel seems to lead to acceptable economic results, so companies under self-management in Yugoslavia seem to survive in a satisfactory fashion—even though neither of these peculiar ways of running companies quite fits in with traditional beliefs about the omniscience of the men at the top of the pyramid.

Particularly for those developing countries which place a major emphasis on cooperative societies, the Yugoslav model of self-management may be found to be highly attractive. For self-management is ultimately nothing but the extension of the cooperative principle to other economic and political bodies. Applied to industry, hospitals, schools, communities and politics, the cooperative principle of course undergoes some transformation; but its basic tenet—democratic, direct participation—remains the same.

Self-management is a model of work organization and/or political structure that may be of greatest relevance as a model of development for both developing and developed countries. Yet, rather little is known about this model among development experts and scholars.

Self-management is a highly flexible system which is adaptable to very different circumstances. As Yugoslavia changed from an underdeveloped to a developed society, self-management did not remain the same.

It originated under state socialism, and during its inception it remained under state socialism, forming a system that may best be called paternalistic self-management. In the next phase, decision-making power was vested in workers' councils elected by the workers. These councils acted on behalf of the workers, the resulting system being one of representative self-management. While the material base of self-management, especially profit-sharing, was strengthened and decision-making power was farther moved towards the base, direct, or participatory, self-management emerged, with power vested directly in the workers who decide on major issues through referenda. Bearing in mind that the development of self-management was a very gradual process, we suggest the period of 1949 to 1952 for the first phase, the period of 1953 to 1962 for the second and the period of 1963 to 1973 for the third. The present, and latest, phase started in 1974 when a new constitution was passed, aiming at the proliferation of self-management into the political system.

Self-management has proved to be immensely adaptable to changing circumstances. This makes self-management a model for industrially underdeveloped, developing, developed and highly developed countries. It shows that industrial democracy is not a luxury that only rich nations can afford, as some rulers in developing countries try to make themselves and others believe. Nor is democracy a quadrennial act, relegated to a few seconds in the election booth once every few years. There is probably no single social sphere in which direct democracy could not be introduced to the benefit of all, systems and members.

Self-management is a system through which the human resources of a society are mobilized to the fullest—by activating everyone's participation. While this may be good for all, it may not necessarily be good for a few: those few presently at the top. One can be sure that in every society there are powerful vested interests directed against the introduction of self-management. But then, any major social change provokes such vested interests, and yet such changes do occur at times: sometimes through a long and gradual process, sometimes carried forward through a social movement, sometimes even introduced from the top. The Yugoslav experience is not there to be replicated in its exact shape; history does not repeat itself. Yugoslav self-management may serve as a guidepost. We hope that this book may contribute to a discussion about the feasibility of self-management as a model of development.

With regard to methodology, the following discussion of self-management in Yugoslavia and in the Developing World is based on interviews in Yugoslav companies, hospitals, cooperatives etc., during 1973 and on interviews with various entrepreneurs, government executives and union leaders from the Developing World between 1973 and 1978. The material for our discussion of the social-economic and political bases for self-management in the Developing World is derived from various research projects by the authors. We include of course the relevant literature on the subject.

We begin by examining the origins of self-management in a variety of countries, discovering a certain regularity in the circumstances leading to the emergence of self-management. A few vivid examples of self-management in action are given, presenting our first-hand experience from visits to Yugoslav companies. We then analyze the structure of self-management in its most refined form as existing in Yugoslavia. By presenting detailed statistical data on economic development in Yugoslavia, the reader may see for himself whether or not economic development and self-management are compatible. Subsequently, we present a systematic analysis of the question of the efficiency of self-management, using data mainly from Yugoslavia and the United States and adding a theoretical analysis. Next we enter into the equity debate: how much equality or inequality is desirable, justifiable or necessary under self-management? In the following chapter we examine industrial relations, showing how and why trade unions must continue to exist under self-management. We demonstrate how self-management, which first developed in industry, can be effectively transferred to other types of organizations. We finish our discussion of the Yugoslav system of self-management by presenting some of the core pieces of the constitution of 1974 which provides a model framework for self-management. We go on by examining the predispositions that may be present in the Developing World for the introduction of self-management. We first show that self-management and full participation of every individual form the very core of cooperatives and that such cooperatives are very widespread in the large majority of pre-modern cultures. In addition we show that a great many—particularly small-scale—traditional cultures practise grassroots democracy and full participation of every individual in the political and economic spheres, thus bringing along, as part of their traditional culture, a receptivity to self-management. Several brief case-studies are next included of approaches to self-management and worker-participation in the Developing World. These include Kenya, Tanzania, Zambia, Algeria, India and Chile during the Allende administration, which we feel are fairly representative of attempts made and problems encountered on the way towards worker-participation and self-management. In the final chapter we try to determine whether the successful story of Yugoslavia can be replicated in the Developing World, our conclusions being those of tempered optimism.

2 The Origins of Self-Management

Self-management is born out of crisis and resistance: economic, political, military or social crises; and resistance against crises, oppression by authoritarian organizations and by political forces from within or without, and economic disasters. Self-management emerges at times which require intensive mobilization of human resources. And this is what self-management ultimately amounts to: a drastic attempt at activating human work potential and creativity to the fullest. Self-management typically emerges when the survival of a society or of a subset of society is threatened or when its well-being is seriously endangered. Ideally, *self-management is a system in which all participants contribute their full potential cooperatively to a common cause and accordingly have the same rights and privileges.* In short, it is total and direct democracy, the conclusion of the domination of man by man.

DIVERSE EXPERIMENTS

Militarily, self-management frequently arises as an organizational form of guerilla resistance against a superpower in a seemingly hopeless situation, each individual acting as an independent freedom fighter. Examples are the resistance of Algerians against French colonialism during the Algerian war (Blair, 1969; Clegg, 1971), the Vietnamese resistance against US aggression during the Vietnamese war (Giap, 1962) and the Yugoslav resistance against the German occupation during the Second World War (Djonlagić *et al.* 1967). Politically, self-management is a system of grassroots democracy in which all members of society participate through their representatives who are directly responsible to the people and revocable at short terms. An example is the famous short-lived Paris Commune which emerged during the French civil war of 1870–1 as an attempt to save Paris from the power of a corrupt central government. In the words of Marx's (1921, pp. 30–1) description which has inspired many to try to free themselves from the domination of mighty powers:

> The Commune was formed of the municipal councillors, chosen by universal suffrage in various wards of the town, responsible and revocable at short terms. The majority of its members were naturally working men, or acknowledged representatives of the working class. The Commune was to be a working, not a parliamentary body, executive and legislative at the same time. Instead of continuing to be the agent of the Central Government, the police was at once stripped of its political attributes, and turned into the responsible and at all times revocable agent of the Commune. So were the officials of all other branches of the Administration. From the members of the Commune downwards, the public service had to be done at *workmen's wages*. The vested interests and the representation allowances of the high dignitaries of State disappeared along with the high dignitaries themselves. Public functions ceased to be the private property of the tools of the Central Government. Not only municipal administration, but the whole initiative hitherto exercised by the State was laid into the hands of the Commune. (cf. Bourgin, 1971; Schneider, 1971)

Economically, self-management is a system of vesting authority in the producers, i.e. the workers, who run their organization through councils elected by and responsible to the workers. In situations of total or near-total disaster, self-management may be the only method of keeping an economy running, as in the case of Algeria in 1962, for example:

> Thus in the moment of independence, Algeria was plunged into an almost unparalleled economic, social and political dissolution. The war had resulted in some one million deaths leaving at least 400,000 orphans. Half a million refugees were returning from Tunisia and Morocco. Two million peasants were in regroupement camps, their villages, crops and livestock abandoned or destroyed. Over a million hectares of the best

land had been abandoned by the *colons* and the time of harvesting and ploughing was approaching. Much of the machinery in agriculture and industry had been sabotaged by the owners before they left. Over two million agricultural, industrial and commercial workers were unemployed. The schools were closed and there were few teachers to staff them. The number of doctors had dropped from nearly 3000 at the beginning of the year to 600. Above all, there was no political authority capable of dealing with the immediate social and economic problems. It was in this situation that *autogestion* (self-management—HDS) made its appearance. During the summer and autumn *comités de gestion* (workers' councils), composed of workers, were set up in a large number of industrial and agricultural concerns. Their immediate role was to recommence production, provide employment and safeguard these national assets. Their long-term effect was to institute a practice of social and economic organization, which, with its concomitant theory, was to dominate Algerian national political ideology in the following years.

Nearly all commentators on the *comités de gestion* describe their emergence as spontaneous. (Clegg, 1971, pp. 44–5)

The spontaneous appearance of self-management in the economic and political sphere, organized in Workers' and Soldiers' Councils, also marked the revolutions of 1905 and 1917 in Russia. In 1917, Lenin returned to Russia with the slogan 'All Power to the Workers' and Soldiers' Councils!' and in November of the same year, workers' councils officially gained control over factories. To the revolutionaries, self-management meant freedom from the paternalism and authoritarianism of the centralized tsarist state and a transfer of power to the workers. Yet, 'institutionalizing a revolutionary movement appears to be the most critical phase in the revolutionary transformation of a people' (Rus, 1967, p. 201), and the Russian revolutionaries were not any more successful than later on the Algerians. The interests of the new elite which had gained power through the revolution soon loomed larger than their ideals of worker self-management and of freedom and participation for all. They set up a system of government and of bureaucratic control which was hardly less authoritarian than the Tsar's rule. The workers' councils, in 1918, were first turned into trade-union branches and then came increasingly under the control of the plant director and the party cell secretary, both political appointees. In protest, a movement emerged that upheld the ideals of self-management: the Workers' Opposition, recruiting its adherents predominantly from the base of the quickly-formed new hierarchy. As Kolontay (1921, p. 5) noted in a pamphlet on *The Workers' Opposition in Russia*:

> The higher we go up the ladder of the Soviet and party hierarchy, the fewer adherents of the Opposition we find. The deeper we penetrate into the masses the more response do we find to the program of the Workers' Opposition. This is very significant, and very important.

It was not some mythical 'Russian mentality to obey' that made the Russian workers submit to the new autocrats; it was by brute force that the Workers' Opposition was crushed, as was the Kronstadt Commune. This was the first act of what has been a continuing drama in the Soviet Union and in Soviet-dominated societies ever since: the continuous struggle between authoritarian Bolshevism and democratic socialism.

It was in the same vain attempt at democratizing political power and economic control that workers' and soldiers' councils arose in Hungary, Poland, Germany, Italy and Bulgaria during the revolutionary upheavals which shook Europe between 1917 and 1920. They were all crushed by the counter-revolution. Yet, the search for freedom and democratic control has not ceased. In Poland, for instance, councils akin to the Workers' and Soldiers' Councils that existed between November 1918 and July 1919 reappeared again for a short time during the next crisis situation, the Second World War, to be again forcibly disbanded when Poland went Russian. They sprang up for a third time by the end of 1955 with a twofold goal: in economic terms, they attempted to free themselves from bureaucratic and authoritarian control in order to increase production; politically, they tried to shake free from Russian domination and establish Gomulka, in 1956, as a representative of Polish nationalism. While they were economically successful (production did go up in 1957), they failed politically. The party did not allow its political hegemony to be challenged, and so their political failure eventually came to include economic failure, after the councils had been absorbed into the state bureaucracy (Babeau, 1960).

By 1964, little was left of self-management in Poland as a study in four engineering plants indicated:

> Elementary but basic aspects of the self-governing system, such as the relationship between workers and the administration, or attempts to increase workers' control, occupied the institution only to a minimal extent. This was the opinion of both manual workers and technical staff, both representatives of the work force and members of the KSR (Conference of Workers' Self-government) . . . Manual workers see the self-governing system as being chiefly concerned with discipline and with the plant's production schedule; engineers and technicians regard it as concentrating its efforts mainly on the production schedule, and also on the distribution of incentive rates and bonuses. (Owieczko, 1966, quoted in Matejko, 1973, p. 34)

At about the time when workers' councils emerged in Poland, they also made their appearance in Hungary—only to be smashed by Russian troops in 1956.

In Dubček's Czechoslovakia, workers who organized in councils to run their own factories became a challenge to the old regime and to the Soviet Union at the same time. With the rest of the country, they eventually crumbled under the boots of the Russian invasion.

In China, the existence of councils which had come to life between 1924 and 1927 ended with the military success of the right. In Spain, workers' councils lived for a similarly short span, from 1936 to 1939. Anna Louise Strong (1937, p. 71), who visited Spain during the Civil War, reported:

> Most of the larger corporation heads, hoping for and expecting a fascist victory, closed their factories and fled. But the economic life of Catalonia must proceed; the factories had to be opened. The workers of Barcelona opened them and organized them, and began to run them for the winning of the war. They ran them in the name of their shop committees and trade unions, not in the name of any government. For they had no trust in any kind of state.

In each case, it has been the very essence of self-management—democratic self-control—which has led to its destruction. It has become a symbol of democratic insubordination, a challenge to any autocratic, authoritarian rule by old or new elites. And as such elites gain power, they typically solve the problem of incompatibility between democratic self-management and authoritarian bureaucratic or political control by either eliminating or absorbing self-management and its organs.

In Germany, the idea of self-management can be traced back as far as 1848, namely in the form of works councils. It came forth again in the resistance movement against Hitler. In post-war Germany, self-management has been leading a kind of shadow existence in the form of so-called system of co-determination (*Mitbestimmung*) in industry which is in reality rather a system of worker consultation between the works council (*Betriebsrat*) and management. It became a legal reality through the Allied Control Council's Works Council Law of 1946, the Co-Determination Act of 1951, and the Works Constitution Acts of 1952 and 1972 (Wlotzke 1973)—gradually enlarging the influence of workers. So far, co-determination has provided a framework for industrial leaders in which they could co-opt the workers. Whether it is the seed from which genuine self-management will eventually develop is an open question. Pressures from workers in the direction of self-management seem to be mounting (Teutenberg, 1961; Schneider and Kuda, 1961; Tittel, 1971; Fürstenberg, 1969; Matejko, 1973, pp. 31–2).

One of the few highly successful examples of self-management has been the Israeli kibbutz which has escaped the fate of most other attempts at self-management for probably two reasons. On the one hand, it has provided for the larger Israeli society a bulwark against a very hostile environment—hostile in physical, political and military terms. On the other hand, kibbutzim have insulated themselves from the outside world, thus simultaneously protecting the larger society against the challenge—inherent to the kibbutz system of self-management—to hierarchical authority. Whether both types of social-economic organization can continue to coexist once the state of siege has ended, and, if not, which pattern will eventually predominate, cannot be safely predicted.

In many other countries there have been experiments with or trends towards self-management. The United States, however, has been left remarkably untouched by such developments. While there are some piecemeal attempts, usually very successful in economic terms, to give workers a small share of the big cake of decision-making power (Jenkins, 1973, pp. 188–245), self-management proper hardly exists even as an idea. To the large majority of workers, managers and executives, students and scholars, even the term is unfamiliar. David Jenkins (1973, p. 156) is one of the very few who think that self-management may, or wishfully must, eventually become the dominant pattern of American organizations:

> However, there is only limited interest in industrial democracy in America, and the implications of organizational studies for democracy are rarely discussed in business circles.
>
> This anomalous situation cannot be expected to endure for long, particularly in view of (1) the widespread and increasing dissatisfaction with industrial capitalism and its damaging effects on society and (2) the inescapably positive implications of the organizational studies for industrial democracy. It is difficult to see how a convergence of these two trends can be avoided—and when the converging takes place, the impact could be enormous. (cf. Clegg, 1971, pp. 7–22; Garson, 1973)

THE BEGINNINGS OF SELF-MANAGEMENT IN YUGOSLAVIA

Self-management in Yugoslavia grew out of a long history of resistance against domination from within and from without. The origin as well as the survival of self-management can only be understood before the background of that history of resistance. Besides furnishing a structure for economic and other types of organizations, self-management provides a system for coping with ethnic cleavages, which again have a long history to them.

The Yugoslav population originates from the Slav tribes who settled in the Balkan Peninsula during the first half of the seventh century. In the ninth century, Germanic tribes settled in the area of what is today Austria and Hungary and separated the southern Slavs from their western tribesmen. The southern Slavs occupied an area which recently has become known as Yugoslavia, 'Yugo-Slavia' meaning 'country of the southern Slavs'. Long and fierce struggles against various invaders like the Byzantines, Franks, Bulgars, Venetians and Hungarians, forced many of the tribes, which were too small by themselves to offer resistance, to form large tribal alliances and eventually organize in states. One alone survived the Middle Ages—Dubrovnik, an independent republic of the Croats since the fourteenth century, was the only state which lasted until the beginning of the nineteenth century. A tourist attraction today, this free city-republic presented a virtually impregnable bastion against any maritime aggressors, the southernmost position against the Turks for centuries and a flourishing centre of trade and cultural relations with other states of the southern Slavs.

Foreign invaders were an ever-present threat to the Slav tribes. The large-scale peasant uprisings in Slovenia, Croatia and Vojvodina; the armed rebellions and struggles against the Turks in Macedonia, Serbia, Croatia, Bosnia, Herzegovina and Montenegro; the struggles of the *hajduks* and *uskokos*, armed bands of outlaw-patriots, against the Turks and Venetians are but a few examples.

The large-scale revolutionary movements which shook Europe at the end of the eighteenth and during the nineteenth century, the emergence of nation-states and the expansion and development of capitalism had their impact on Yugoslavia. The struggle for national liberation and for economic and social development led to the formation of Serbia and Montenegro, which were recognized as independent states in 1878. In 1912, Turkey was forced to relinquish the last of its Balkan territories, which it had occupied for centuries: in the Balkan War, it was defeated by the allied forces of Serbia, Montenegro, Greece and Bulgaria. Macedonia, today one of the states in the Yugoslav federation, was divided between Serbia, Greece and Bulgaria. The rapprochement of the Balkan peoples during the Balkan War turned out to be a challenge to the German and Austrian-Hungarian hegemony; and when the Austrian Crown Prince was assassinated in Sarajevo in June 1914, Austria-Hungary had its pretext for declaring war on Serbia—and the Central Powers for starting the First World War. The war efforts of Serbia and Montenegro were supported by volunteer units from those Yugoslav peoples who lived on Austrian-Hungarian territory. Their military defeat only strengthened the demand for full liberation and unification and led to the same stubborn resistance against the Habsburg monarchy which had been characteristic of the relations between the Slavs and the Turks for centuries and was later to be repeated during the German occupation. With the end of the First World War, the idea of a common state for all Yugoslav peoples became at last reality. With its formation, however, problems and conflicts by no means ceased to exist. What previously had been resistance against domination by outside powers now turned into resistance against domination by inside forces. By advocating an ideology akin to the American belief in equality and in the melting-pot theory, the Serbian bourgeoisie and monarchy set up its hegemony over the other Yugoslav peoples, claiming that Serbs, Croats and Slovenes were in reality one and the same people and that the Macedonians and Montenegrins did not even exist as ethnic groups. Eventually, a Constitution was passed by Parliament in 1921, instituting a centralized system and legalizing, in effect, ethnic inequality.

One of the major challenges to the Serbian monarchy came from the left wings of the social-democratic parties. After the successful October Revolution in Russia, members of these groups formed the Communist Party of Yugoslavia which emerged from the elections for the Parliament in 1920 as the third strongest party. Shortly thereafter the Communist Party was declared illegal and went underground. Growing tensions between the regime and its underground opposition led to the introduction of overt dictatorship by the king in January 1929. Trade unions were banned and many communists and other opponents of Great-Serbian hegemony were prosecuted. While fascism spread throughout Europe, the Serbian king followed the general trend and introduced fascist methods of rule in an attempt to fight the mounting resistance. At the same time, he established friendly relations with the fascist powers.

In 1937, Josip Broz Tito, who had been Organizational Secretary of the Communist Party of Yugoslavia since 1936, assumed its leadership. The same year, the Communist Parties of Croatia and Slovenia were founded, milestones in the expansion and intensification of political activities throughout the country. Opposition against Serbian domination thus formed on two planes: ethnically, the Croats were the strongest opponents; politically, the Communist Party was the strongest anti-Government organization, cutting across ethnic lines and at the same time supporting any ethnic opposition. It was in part this Communist support of Croat nationalism which forced the government in 1939 into a compromise with the leaders of the

Croatian Peasant Party: the Province of Croatia (*Banovina Hrvatska*) was created, and the Croatian Peasant Party was represented in the government. By the time the Second World War began, the state was so hopelessly undermined from within and isolated abroad that even this agreement did little for its stabilization.

On 25 March 1941, the Yugoslav government signed an agreement under which it joined the Axis Powers Pact. On 27 March the government was overthrown. On 6 April German and Italian troops attacked Yugoslavia, meeting only nominal resistance from state and military leaders. The army capitulated, and the king and the government fled the country. Yugoslavia was divided among the Axis Powers: Germany annexed the northern part of Slovenia and occupied Serbia and the Banat; Italy occupied southern Slovenia, the Adriatic Coast, Montenegro, western Macedonia and Kosovo; Bulgaria annexed the greater part of Macedonia and the south-eastern part of Serbia; Hungary acquired the regions of Backa, Baranja, Medjumurje and Prekomurje. Croatia became the Independent State of Croatia under a quisling government.

Terror became the chief method of rule in Yugoslavia, forcing the population into compliance through concentration camps, mass deportations and executions, particularly of communists and other anti-fascists. The only political force that took it upon itself to organize a resistance movement for a national liberation struggle was the Communist Party. A month after the invasion, it decided to organize the resistance, and during May and June a network of military committees was established. In a country whose peoples had been fighting invaders for centuries, such action very quickly found widespread popular support. The first guerilla groups were formed in towns, where they sabotaged enemy operations. By the end of June, the Main Headquarters of National Liberation Partizan Detachments of Yugoslavia was set up, and Tito became its commander. On 4 July 1941, it was decided to start an armed uprising. Guerilla attacks were waged all over the country, totally unanticipated by the Axis Powers which had expected to find their battlefields elsewhere. Towards the end of 1941, the first regular army units were formed, numbering—together with the partisan detachments—about 80,000 men. On liberated territory, government bodies were set up to administer the area and organize supplies for the military units. Toward the end of 1942, a National Liberation Army of about 150,000 was formed, headed by a Supreme Headquarters. On 26 and 27 November 1942, an assembly was held at which a representative political body was elected: the Anti-Fascist Council of National Liberation of Yugoslavia (AVNOJ). Its basic task was the political mobilization of the people in both liberated and occupied territories and the organization of regular governmental functions. One of its first measures was to call elections for people's liberation committees, which are essentially the self-management bodies of the resistance. In 1943 and 1944, national anti-fascist councils were set up for Croatia, Montenegro, Bosnia-Herzegovina, Serbia, Macedonia and Slovenia. These were important steps towards a solution of the nationality question in Yugoslavia, for the creation and affirmation of national military commands and national political leadership enabled each of the Yugoslav peoples to organize its own armed struggle and to lay the foundations for its national independence. At the second meeting of the AVNOJ on 29 and 30 November 1943, it was decided to constitute the Anti-Fascist Council as the supreme legislative and executive body, to set up the National Committee as a provisional government and to organize the new state of Yugoslavia on the federal principle.

In November 1943, the Anti-Fascist Council for the National Liberation of Yugoslavia convened in Jajce, a small Bosnian town, and proclaimed a new state. To be sure, this was a socialist state of popular-democratic character, and it is interesting to note in the light of later developments that it must have been immediately clear to Stalin that this event posed a serious threat to Soviet hegemony: 'a knife in the back of the Soviet Union' (Bajec, n.d., p. 20) as he called it; for this socialist state was created without the assistance of Red Army bayonets and without the blessing of the Bolshevik Party authorities. Simultaneously, Stalin negotiated with the Western Allies on the demarcation of spheres of interest on the map of postwar Europe; Yugoslavia was to be divided equally between the Soviet Union and the Western Allies. *Divide et impera*! But Yugoslavia proved to be too strong for such manœuvres, and it became clear very soon to everyone that it would put up the same resistance against Soviet or Allied invaders as against the fascists. In 1942, the Axis Powers had to engage 32 divisions—or about 600,000 men—to fight the Yugoslav partisans, and throughout the war they were compelled to maintain in Yugoslavia about 25 divisions in addition to the local quisling units. And when they eventually capitulated in Yugoslavia during the last days of the war, they were confronted by a Yugoslav army which numbered about 800,000.

The strength of Yugoslav resistance was quickly realized by the Allies. They decided to recognize the National Liberation Army at the conference in Teheran in 1943 and to offer it military assistance. Subsequently, several offensive operations were launched by the Germans against the National Liberation Army, among them the abortive parachute drop of May 1944 which failed to accomplish its goal of destroying the Supreme Headquarters. By the end of 1944, major parts of Yugoslavia had been liberated: Serbia, Macedonia, Montenegro and Dalmatia. Stalin, too, had to recognize the military and political power of the new socialist state, and in agreement with the National Committee, his Red Army crossed into eastern Serbia, and they jointly liberated Belgrade, the capital, on 20 October 1944. When at the beginning of 1945 four army units were formed, the National Liberation Army became the Yugoslav People's Army, which liberated the rest of the country: Istria, the Slovene littoral and Trieste.

The anti-fascist resistance movement had been built on people's liberation committees founded in villages and towns in both liberated and occupied areas. These were the first forms of self-management. From its armed struggle against the superior forces of the German occupation, a new Yugoslav state emerged that was created by the people themselves. The task of organizing the people in the resistance movement, however, had been solely borne by the Communist Party. As the political establishment had fled the country and exiled itself, the Communist Party found itself firmly entrenched towards the end of the war as the only political force. On 7 March 1945, J. B. Tito was entrusted by the Anti-Fascist Council of National Liberation with the formation of a Yugoslav government. When the war had ended, the Third Meeting of the Anti-Fascist Council of National Liberation was convened in Belgrade in August 1945. The Anti-Fascist Council came to function as a provisional national assembly which included members of the last Parliament of pre-war Yugoslavia who had not discredited themselves by collaborating with the enemy. Elections for the Constituent Assembly were held on 11 November 1945. With the People's Front candidates winning an overwhelming majority, the social–political system of the new Yugoslavia which had evolved during the war was thus confirmed. At its first meeting, on 29 November 1945, the Assembly named the state the Federal People's Republic of Yugoslavia. Its constitution was passed on 31 January 1946. The constitutions of the Yugoslav republics of Bosnia-Herzegovina, Montenegro, Macedonia, Slovenia, Serbia and Croatia were promulgated within a year (Tomasevic, n.d., pp. 46–52).

In Article 6, the new constitution emphasized the continuity between the war time political system as it had emerged underground and the new polity:

> All authority in the Federal Peoples Republic of Yugoslavia derives from the people and belongs to the people. The people exercise their authority through freely elected representative organs of state authority, the people's committees, which, from local people's committees up to the assemblies of the people's republics and the People's Assembly of the FPRY, originated and developed during the struggle for national liberation against Fascism and reaction, and are the fundamental achievement of that struggle. (Constitution, 1946, pp. 6–7)

Twenty-eight years later, when the 1974 constitution was adopted and self-management had become the very essence of the Yugoslav socio-economic system, the origins of self-management were still traced back to the resistance movement during the Second World War. What has characterized 'the entire evolution of our political system from the establishment of people's liberation committees up to the present day, despite an uneven course, some wrong turnings and slowdowns', has been the idea of direct democracy, as Mijalko Todorović pointed out when he moved on 22 January 1974 to adopt the 1974 constitution (Mijalko Todorović, *Report on the Final Draft of the SFRY Constitution*, in The Constitution of the Socialist Federal Republic of Yugoslavia, 1974, pp. 28–9).

FROM STATE-SOCIALISM TO SELF-MANAGEMENT

At the end of the Second World War, Yugoslavia was about the most backward country in terms of level of economic development in Europe. It had not yet undergone its industrial revolution, and not even the euphemism 'developing country' would have been justified. It was simply underdeveloped. Before the war broke out, Yugoslavia occupied in economic terms the second-to-last place in Europe. During the resistance, it had lost 1.7 million lives, i.e. approximately 10 per cent of the population. It emerged from the war with only 23.4 per cent of its pre-war machinery and 16.1 per cent of its means of transportation. Two thirds of its industry and about 300,000 peasant holdings with their livestock and equipment had been destroyed.

Much of the capital in pre-war Yugoslavia was owned by foreigners. Many of them left the country during the war and did not return. Others collaborated with the enemy. Some of the capital was appropriated by the enemy. All in all, the destruction and the abandonment of capital left the newly formed Yugoslav state with a situation in which the amount of privately owned capital in industry, transportation, banking and wholesale and foreign trade was negligible.

This situation had been foreseen during the resistance by Moše Pijade, one of the leaders of the liberation movement, who later became president of the national assembly. In the liberated town of Foča, he worked out the so-called Foča instructions: a plan for the nationalization of all property of the enemy and of collaborators and its transfer to the people's liberation committees. Thus, when the war was over, industry, public transportation, banking, wholesale and foreign trade were quickly nationalized without meeting any opposition (Bajec, n.d., pp. 17–18). With this accomplished the newly formed state was effectively a socialist society. It is very important to realize that this was the logical outcome of the war and of the resistance against the fascist powers and that effective nationalization was virtually unopposed. Before the war, Yugoslavs had always felt exploited by foreign capital owners and by the small Serbian bourgeoisie; they therefore welcomed the opportunity to end *this* type of exploitation by nationalizing all major capital. Yet, this nationalization was by no means equal to the abolition of private property. Article 14 of the Constitution (1946, p. 9) of the newly formed state specified:

Means of production in the Federal Peoples Republic of Yugoslavia are either the property of the entire people, i.e.

property in the hands of the state, or the property of the people's co-operative organizations, or else the property of private persons or legal entities.

All mineral and other wealth underground, the waters, including mineral and medicinal waters, the sources of natural power, the means of rail and air transport, the posts, telegraphs, telephones and broadcasting are national property.

The means of production in the hands of the state are exploited by the state itself or given to others for exploitation.

Foreign trade is under control of the state.

Yet, the state reserved for itself the right to control the economy, leaving the extent of this control somewhat open:

Article 15

In order to protect the vital interests of the people, to further the people's prosperity and the right use of all economic potentialities and forces, the state directs the economic life and development of the country in accordance with a general economic plan, relying on the state and co-operative economic sectors, while achieving a general control over the private economic sector.

In carrying out the general economic plan and economic control, the state relies on the co-operation of syndicalist organizations of workmen and employees and other organizations of the working people.

Article 16

The property of the entire people is the mainstay of the state in the development of the national economy.

The property of the entire people is under the special protection of the state.

The administration and disposal of the property of the entire people are determined by law.

(Constitution, 1946, pp. 9–10)

The Constitution (1946, pp. 10–11) very carefully guaranteed the right to private property, including the right to private property of land, and simultaneously set up certain limits to this right:

Article 18

Private property and private initiative in economy are guaranteed.

The inheritance of private property is guaranteed. The right of inheritance is regulated by law.

No person is permitted to use the right of private property to the detriment of the people's community.

The existence of private monopolist organizations such as cartels, syndicates, trusts and similar organizations created for the purpose of dictating prices, monopolizing the market and damaging the interests of the national economy, is forbidden.

Private property may be limited or expropriated if the common interest requires it, but only in accordance with the law. It will be determined by law in which cases and to what extent the owner shall be compensated.

Under the same conditions individual branches of national economy or single enterprises may be nationalized by law if the common interest requires it.

Article 19

The land belongs to those who cultivate it.

The law determines whether and how much land may be owned by an institution or a person who is not a cultivator.

There can be no large land-holdings in private hands on any basis whatsoever.

The maximum size of private land-holdings will be determined by law.

The state particularly protects and assists poor peasants and peasants with medium-sized holdings by its general economic policy, its low rates of credit and its tax system.

While nationalization may be a prerequisite of a socialist society, it does not determine the type of socialism practised. In 1945, the Soviet Union was the only existing model of a socialist society. Impressed by the image of a society in which they had never lived, Yugoslavs thought it best to imitate the country which was then considered the pace-maker of socialist development: the Soviet Union with its system of central planning and administration through a state bureaucracy. It may also be that at this point Lenin's thesis of the importance of Red Army support in the liberation of a country played some role in that the minimal help received from the Soviet Union towards the end of the war influenced the Yugoslavs, at least for the time being, in their decision to adopt state socialism.

The immediate post-war years were characterized by a strongly accentuated role of the state in all major social transformations, particularly in the nationalization and in the management of the economy and of other social spheres. The state monopolized political and economic authority which furnished it with enormous power. All employees in the economy, in the civil service, in education, health, information and banking institutions were state employees, and the respective bodies were run by state administration bodies: by ministries through their departments, divisions and sections, general directorates and directorates, and by managerial staffs and directors who were appointed by the state organs.

A system of highly centralized state management emerged thus in Yugoslavia in which every enterprise was subject to strict administrative planning. State functionaries set concrete production tasks with narrowly defined specifications of quality, assortment, production costs and personal incomes. Under state administration, Yugoslav business was characterized by an authoritarian, centralistic structure, under the control of a general manager to whom all employees were responsible. Business was organized as a hierarchical system in which information went from the bottom upwards and orders were channelled from top to bottom. The general managers in industry, called directors, were civil servants who were responsible to a general or head directorate, and this in turn reported to one of various ministries for the economy. Thus there existed a well-organized bureaucratic hierarchy with the magnitude of power increasing towards the top.

During this period, business had no freedom of action, since it was fully controlled by the state. The state determined all business activity; fixed prices and controlled business relations with trade partners through state plans; and appropriated almost the whole of the sums earmarked for depreciation and accumulation and bore the commercial risk of their operations. All important decisions regarding the operations and development of a company were made outside, by some organ of the state administration. The role of business was confined to making proposals and observations. Income, annual leave, discipline etc., among workers and staff were regulated almost entirely by law and government orders. Neither workers nor management had any real say in the affairs of their companies.

Within companies, general managers had the most influence, however little it was *vis-à-vis* their superordinated state authorities. Workers had no direct influence on management. It was only through trade unions that workers could make themselves heard. Trade unions had the right to submit to the general manager proposals for increasing productivity and improving living and working conditions and to consult on production plans and their fulfillment (Bajec, n.d., pp. 17–18; Burt, 1972, p. 133).

Some of our discussants in Yugoslavia considered the introduction of a state-bureaucratic economic system as a result of a lack of theoretical and empirical alternatives, the Soviet Union representing the only model of socialism anyone could think of. It might also be that in the general euphoria of the victory over Germany and its allies, Yugoslavs felt some strong attachment to its Big Brother. Besides, some of the Yugoslav leaders might have thought that building a new socialist society was not an easy task, in peace possibly different from war times, and that some protection from Big Brother might not hurt. This was a wrong assumption, as it turned out. But at the time, the shortcomings and dangers of state-bureaucratic socialism were not yet visible to the Yugoslavs, and they embraced the new system wholeheartedly. Some writers however think there was more to it, that state socialism was in fact the most rational, if not the only possible thing to do. In the words of one of the defenders of state socialism for the immediate post-war era:

This mechanism, as was stressed at the time, was essential in the immediate post-war years because of the low level of industrial development, the meagre pre-war industry having been further set back by the wartime devastation, so that only by rigorous concentration of all material and manpower resources was it possible to take the first steps forward. (Bajec, n.d., p. 18)

Yet, this might only reflect a popular stereotype, namely a suspicion against the efficiency of self-management which has never succumbed in Yugoslavia and elsewhere despite all economic successes of this system.

We may add that once the Communist Party had gained power in Yugoslavia during the war, the introduction of state socialism surprised nobody in the country and abroad, as state socialism was considered a pleonastic synonym for socialism. What was much more surprising and initially meeting with almost total disbelief abroad, was the switch to democratic socialism, to a 'self-managing society', a hitherto virtually utopian system. It is true that the idea of workers' self-management is ever present in the works of all socialist writers from Saint-Simon, Charles Fourier, Louis Blanqui and Robert Owen to Marx and Engels. Their visions were not based on socialism as a state-organized economy; it was always conceived as an association of free producers in which, as stated by Marx and Engels in the *Communist Manifesto*, 'the free development of each is the condition for the free development of all'. This was, however, at best a concrete utopia, and all earlier attempts at introducing self-management had failed: crushed by more powerful forces whose survival or interests would have been threatened by a 'self-managing society'. Yugoslavia's job after the war was not only economic reconstruction. It also saw itself confronted with the formidable task of preparing for its industrial revolution, for the transition from an underdeveloped agrarian society to an industrial growth economy. In April 1947, the National Assembly approved the first five-year plan. Its main emphasis was on heavy investments in basic industry and in energy production to provide a basis for the industrialization of the country. The first step was the construction of about 200 enterprises in iron and steel, chemical and engineering industries, electric power and other key branches of production. Immediately after the passing of the plan, the trade unions initiated so-called production consultations. These consultations basically provided an outlet for grievances against the state apparatus, complaints being voiced against the various boards, directorates and ministries. These production consultations brought to light the mounting dissatisfaction with the workings of the central bureaucracy. Yugoslavs had successfully freed themselves from the Turks and Germans; now they found that they had placed themselves voluntarily under the guardianship of their own bureaucrats: a new form of domination.

The dissatisfaction of workers with bureaucratic socialism was, however, not the decisive factor that led to the introduction of self-management. For the state functionaries and politicians, i.e. the ones who held the power, were not so unhappy with a system which vested all power in them and worked reasonably well in economic terms. Under state socialism, the task of reconstruction was in fact accomplished and the foundations were laid for further industrialization.

The turning point came when the Stalin-controlled Information Bureau of Communist Parties, the *Cominform*, met in Bucharest on 20 June 1948, and passed a resolution condemning Yugoslavia for 'betraying socialism', 'counter-revolution' and the like. This was the beginning of a general exacerbation of relations with Yugoslavia on the part of all its former socialist allies. After Stalin's attack, Yugoslavia insisted on its independence from the Soviet Union. As a consequence, the Soviet Union imposed a blockade against Yugoslavia which was joined by all other Eastern European states. At that point, Yugoslavia had no relations yet with the West.

Frontier incidents and other forms of pressure from the East forced Yugoslavia into an enormous defence budget: up to 23 per cent of its national income went into military expenses. An added burden was of course the blockade which lasted for several years. It is estimated that the direct cost of the blockade alone to Yugoslavia was approximately US $430 million and that indirect losses amounted to a multiple of this figure.

After the break with the Soviet Union and its satellites, Yugoslavia had to find its own way, to invent its own brand of socialism in order itself to continue to be a socialist society. What else would have justified its opposition against the Soviet Union? Thus, the stigmatization gave rise to a comprehensive theoretical discussion of basic questions of socialism, and a new impetus to the desire to revive the country's revolutionary traditions, based on the concept of the democratic mobilization of the base. The conflict with Stalin awakened memories of the struggle for national survival: a few years earlier, it had been a military war against one superpower; now it was an economic and political war against another superpower, with the not too unlikely chance of a military encounter.

Left in an economic and political vacuum, the Yugoslavs started to question some of Stalin's hitherto unquestioned assumptions: of the inevitability of a fierce class struggle in socialist countries; of the consequent need to strengthen state control and its repressive apparatus; of state ownership as the highest form of capital ownership during the transition from capitalism to communism; of the need for 'iron discipline' in the party at the exclusion of anything resembling democracy; and of the 'transmissive function' of organs of the state bureaucracy, trade unions and youth and other mass organizations transmitting directives received from the party leadership. It now occurred to Yugoslavia that it might try to move away from messianic socialism in which socialism is perennially 'postponed' until its chiliastic arrival in the form of a pure model. 'In each phase of socialist development one lives as democratically and humanely as possible under the existing circumstances', ponders Bajec (n.d., p. 179), 'but one does not live "just anyhow" in the expectation of some remote ideal.'

At the Second Congress of the Communist Party of Croatia, Tito declared that the task of the Communist Party was not to command but to educate the masses and to learn from them, and that their aspirations and demands should be treated with the utmost respect. Such statements are frequently made by leaders and rarely mean much. The subsequent history of Yugoslavia, however, has shown that there was more than a grain of truth in this statement. It is also interesting to note that Tito was quite aware of the roots of self-management in the Yugoslav resistance. At the same meeting, when talking about the characteristics of popular government, he recalled the revolutionary experience of the people's liberation committees during the war. He specifically pointed out that the self-government traditions of those times should be further developed.

The introduction of self-management was a highly risky venture, an experiment with unpredictable results. The economy, and eventually the state, were to be thoroughly democratized at a point when the country's survival was threatened, economically, politically and militarily. Factory management was to be entrusted to the workers when the least risky move would have been to lend further strength to the system of centralized government administration. After all, regardless of its weaknesses, bureaucratic socialism had been quite successful in economic terms, growth rates being fairly high in the immediate post-war years. The state bureaucracy had become a reliable and well-oiled machine, demonstrably capable of directing resources towards the most important tasks of the five-year plan and the country's defence. Based on the actual experience with central planning and central administration, it would have been justified to heighten discipline, strengthen economic controls and perfect the administrative machinery. Bajec (n.d., p. 24) notes:

> Workers' councils, even without any particular powers, appeared to some like an alien body in a smoothly running machine, something anarchic and risky. What is gained, the sceptics asked, by all this waste of time on democratic discussions on enterprises at a moment when the whole country must turn into an armed camp?

It was apparently taken for granted by many that at this point central administration was the most efficient way of organizing production and that self-management was a kind of luxury one could not really afford. Bajec (n.d., p. 25) thinks:

> One would expect that in such a situation the existing centralized government administration of the economy would develop to the maximum, and there would be little scope for the growth of worker management and enterprise autonomy.

Besides, very few, if any, had a clear idea of what self-management actually meant. There was no country that could have served as a model for emulation. Yugoslavia started to go its own way, developing its own brand of socialism and making, at the same time, its own genuine contribution to the theory and practice of socialism.

After a consultation on local economies held in January 1949, the first decision was passed granting a certain amount of autonomy to the people's committees, the main local government bodies in the communes and districts. In economic terms, this autonomy meant that the committees were given the right to take a certain percentage of the profits of smaller enterprises on their territory for their own budgets and greater freedom in spending these amounts. At that time, there were some 150,000 people involved as members of such committees. Bajec (n.d., p. 23) writes:

> The whole of this democratic machinery, inherited from the wartime but grown rather rusty in the immediate post-war

years was given a strong impetus by the new law on people's committees.

To many, the new policy may have looked like a propaganda trick: an attempt by the Communist Party to involve as many sections of the population as possible in all spheres in order to win their support. Self-management might have turned out to be in reality just another form of worker consultation, similar to the existing production consultations, introduced in the expectation of favourable effects on worker morale. But the proof of the pudding is in the eating and, as it turned out, self-management was more than a trick; it was the beginning of genuine democratization in government, in business and in other organizations.

In retrospect, the introduction of self-management appears as a truly revolutionary act. It is highly questionable, however, whether those who first introduced and implemented self-management felt that. The actual process of developing the idea of self-management and of translating it into reality seems to have been a very gradual one. The various laws and constitutional amendments may today appear as new beginnings, but in actuality they were something like syncopes in a sonata, rather than the beginning of a new movement.

The first workers' council predated the passing of the self-management law of 27 June 1950. At a meeting in 1949, it was decided to transform the workers' right of consultation into a right of decision-making. Boris Kidrič, a member of the government, and Djuro Salaj, chairman of the trade unions, were instructed to draw up a document about the specifics of workers' councils and of election procedures. This document was approved on 23 November 1949 and sent to 215 large enterprises selected for an experimental introduction of workers' councils.

When analyzing the goals stated in the document, it appears that the introduction of workers' councils was, in fact, primarily a means of supporting existing government plans. It did not signify the abrupt beginnings of a new era. Self-management was meant to reinforce the efforts made at fulfilling the plan by means of direct worker participation in management and control of enterprises. Specifically, the functions of the first councils were: to work out production plans for the enterprise; to propose measures to increase output and productivity; to raise quality and reduce costs; to discuss measures of further training; to strengthen work discipline; to submit proposals about work norms and the systematization of jobs and the like.

Workers' councils were to be elected annually by secret ballot of all employees. They were to comprise from 1 per cent to 5 per cent of the employees of a company. Council membership was not to be remunerated, and meetings were to be held after work. The general manager of a company was automatically to be a member of the workers' council, an indication of the roots of self-management in the system of state socialism in which the general manager was a state functionary. The transitional character of this phase becomes obvious when one examines the relationship between general manager and workers' council and the procedures to be followed in case of disagreement. The general manager was to take into consideration all conclusions approved by vote of the workers' council. If he disagreed, he was to submit them to a higher organ of the state administration, i.e. the director of the main or general directorate of the appropriate economic branch. The decision of this higher organ was binding; but the workers' council had the right to appeal against it at the highest level, the ministry. The vestiges of the centralized state-administrative system, 'birthmarks of the old society', are clearly visible. For all practical purposes, the self-management law might not have made any difference in terms of actual decision-making power at all. But in actual development it turned out to make an enormous difference. The first workers' council was formed on 31 December 1949, in the Dalmatian town of Solin, a suburb of Split. In its 9 January 1950 issue, the Yugoslav news agency, Tanjug, announced:

> The workers of the *Prvoborac* Cement Factory in Solin have elected a workers' council of 13 members. The council will devote most attention to the training of personnel, checking the fulfillment of annual and monthly targets, lower production costs and other matters concerning production. Through the council, members will be able to play a more active part in settling all the enterprise's problems. The best workers in the enterprise have been elected to the council.

Prvoborac was actually one of the companies selected for the self-management experiment. When the government and trade-union instructions were received informing the workers that they had been selected for an experiment, some of those present proposed to hold elections immediately, and a commission to nominate candidates was formed on the spot. The proposed list of 13 candidates comprised 7 workers, 5 department heads and the general manager. Those present approved of them as the workers' council by acclamation. As president they elected carpenter Ante Gabelić, a well-known strike leader and Communist Party member in pre-war Yugoslavia (Bajec, n.d., pp. 28–9).

During the first few experimental months it became clear that the powers of the workers' councils would have to be expanded, both at the expense of the general manager and his technical-managerial apparatus and of the state machinery for managing the economy. The first workers' council expressed their desire for an increased share of the responsibility for management.

Tito responded immediately. On 7 February 1950, the Presidium of the National Assembly, upon a proposal submitted by Josip Broz Tito, passed a decree on the reorganization of the state administration, particularly in the economic sphere, whereby several federal economic ministries were abolished and their jurisdiction transferred to the republics, while various economic directorates were merged or had their powers reduced.

However, doubts were raised if one could really entrust the management of industry to workers. So, somewhat later, general and main directorates were reorganized as associations of enterprises in a particular branch, headed by their own workers' councils composed of delegates of member enterprises. But this attempt was soon abandoned as it was incompatible with the essence of self-management which demanded full enterprise autonomy. Thus, the last vestiges of the former hierarchy of the state management machinery shortly disappeared.

The self-management experiment in 215 companies turned out to be successful: worker management justified itself in practice. The next step was its legalization. Government, trade-union and party bodies jointly prepared the draft of the first law on workers' councils, and it was subsequently discussed by a broad circle of economists, lawyers and other experts.

By June 1950, before the law was passed, most companies had already sought the right to form workers' councils and all such requests were approved. Thus when the law was passed, 520 councils in all parts of the country had resumed functioning, with a total of 14,382 members, of which almost 10,000 were workers engaged in production, about 4000 were office workers and nearly 400 engineers and technicians. All these enterprises elected new workers' councils after the passing of the law, since their composition and election methods had to be brought into line with it (Bajec, n.d., p. 32).

On 27 June 1950, the Yugoslav Parliament passed the self-management law, transferring enterprise management from state bureaucracy to workers. This law stipulated that enterprise would be administered, in the name of the community and in accordance with the economic plan, by their personnel 'work collectives', normally through an elected workers' council and elected board of management. This was the official blessing for the increasing number of rapidly developing experiments in workers' management.

'I shall vote for the proposed law with the greatest pleasure, for this law gives us rights such as no other working class has ever had . . .', stated one of the deputies during the six-day debate at the June 1950 session of the National Assembly (Bajec, n.d., p. 32).

On 27 June 1950, the law passed unanimously. On that day, Josip Broz Tito explained the historical significance of the event:

> The law handing over the management of factories and other enterprises to their working collectives is a logical consequence of the course of socialist construction in our country. It is a continuation with the series of measures our government has introduced on its unwavering path to socialism. (Bajec, n.d., p. 33)

Edvard Kardelj, chief ideologue and Tito's closest associate, declared when the self-management law was presented to the Parliament for debate, expressing the new official self-management philosophy:

> It should never be forgotten that no perfect bureaucratic apparatus, however brilliant the people at the top, can build socialism. Socialism can grow only from the initiatives of the masses of the people, with the Communist Party playing a correct leading role. Consequently, the development of socialism can take no other course but that of steadily expanding

socialist democracy in the sense of increasing self-government by the working people, their ever-broader inclusion in the work of the state machinery from the lowest organs to the highest, their increasing participation in direct management in every enterprise and institution . . . (Bajec, n.d., p.23)

The self-management law of 1950 legalized the existing workers' councils. The law included the following innovations:

(1) Provision was made for *a managing board*, an executive body which was to be elected by the workers' council from among its members.

(2) It was stipulated that the workers' council should have from 15 to 120 members, depending on the size of the company.

(3) In enterprises with less than 30 employees, all employees should form the workers' council.

(4) And, most importantly, the workers' council was granted autonomous powers to approve the company's production plan and annual financial report: to formulate company policies, to approve measures of the managing board and general manager and, with the confirmation of the competent organ of the state administration, to draw up and pass the internal rules and regulations.

(5) Companies were given the right to spend part of their profits as they wished and the workers' council was given the authority to decide on the allocation and distribution of this portion of profits. (Bajec, n.d., p. 33)

After the self-management law was passed, all companies were instructed to hold elections for workers' councils between August and October 1950. The electoral procedure was laid down in the government instructions. The trade unions in each enterprise were to organize electoral meetings and to ensure democratic procedures in the nomination and election of candidates, secrecy of the ballot, etc. The regular conduct of the election was being supervised by the courts.

Many party and trade union officials suggested to their higher committees that they should draw up the lists of candidates. They claimed this would prevent the infiltration of workers' councils by so-called Stalinist undercover agents. However their real motives seem to have reflected, as Bajec (p. 35) suggests:

. . . the tendency to continue copying the methods of Stalin's 'transmissive democracy', whereby the party authorities selected persons for various functions in society, and formal elections of these previously selected persons were then arranged in the 'transmissive' organs (the soviets, trade unions and elsewhere).

The first council elections ended with a special ceremony which caught on in all parts of the country. At a gathering of all employees, the general manager handed over the factory keys of the president of the new workers' council. Some factories had a hand made extra large key while others used their ordinary gate keys (Bajec, n.d., p. 35).

Today, the introduction of workers' councils may seem like a heroic deed not quite justified by the economic situation, a humanistic attempt at democratization. But to those introducing and implementing the new policy, the pragmatic orientation of the venture was in no way doubtful. Ten years after the introduction of the first workers' council, carpenter Ante Gabelić, who remained a popular figure in Yugoslavia until his retirement, explained in an interview what had led him and his colleagues to speed up the elections:

> Even earlier we had been thinking about a council of workers which would run our factory. It was something which seemed to be needed. Building was going on in all parts of the country, and every day we were being pressed for more cement.
>
> We did our best, using every available man and machine, but, still, we knew we could achieve more. But this called for further effort from every single man, from the entire collective. (Bajec, n.d., p. 29)

And Bajec's interpretation (pp. 29–30) lends additional support to this efficiency theory of self-management:

> This statement touches on the basic motive which at that time led the workers to adopt and support the idea of self-management. In a period of general poverty and national peril, when all thoughts were turned to the five-year plan and the country's defence, the workers' councils were expected to accelerate still further the already exhausting tempo of work and life.

The minutes of the first meetings of the 215 experimental workers' councils point to the psychological impact of self-management. They reveal a general desire to solve all production problems at one swoop and to move forward as quickly as possible. Self-management did mobilize resources. That at least was the conclusion of the Central Committee of the Trade Unions after the first few months of experimentation with workers' councils. It was emphasized that workers everywhere took great interest in the activity of their elected organs and were given full support (Bajec, n.d., p. 31).

Resistance and a strong sense of independence prepared the ground for the growth of self-management. But its actual introduction seems to have originated from the top of the political hierarchy. Self-management was not introduced through self-management. It is difficult if not impossible to trace a movement or a structural innovation back to all its beginnings, the main problem being that there simply are too many roots out of which it has grown. We have a tendency to attach events, innovations, inventions and the like to names which then become great names to be printed in history books. But it is rarely great names to which historical changes are really attributable. Who introduced self-management in Yugoslavia? Milovan Djilas, once second in command and later fallen from grace into the purgatory of Yugoslav prisons, claims it was his idea. We do not doubt that he may in fact have had the idea; nor that he, a powerful politician, was instrumental in the introduction of self-management. But it is highly questionable that it was any single person's fiat which created self-management. However, Djilas' (1969, pp. 220–3) account of his contribution to the origin of self-management which he gives in *The Unperfect Society* should be an interesting historical document throwing some light on the thinking and acting of those people who were in power when self-management first developed:

The idea of self-management was conceived by Kardelj and me, with some help from our comrade Kidrič. Soon after the outbreak of the quarrel with Stalin, in 1949, as far as I remember, I began to reread Marx's *Capital*, this time with much greater care, to see if I could find the answer to the riddle of why, to put it in simplistic terms, Stalinism was bad and Yugoslavia was good. I discovered many new ideas and, most interesting of all, ideas about a future society in which the immediate producers, through free association, would themselves make the decisions regarding production and distribution—would, in effect, run their own lives and their own future.

The country was in the stranglehold of the bureaucracy, and the party leaders were in the grip of rage and horror over the incorrigible nature of the party machine they had set up and that kept them in power. One day—it must have been in the spring of 1950—it occurred to me that we Yugoslav Communists were now in a position to start creating Marx's free association of producers. The factories would be left in their hands, with the sole proviso that they should pay a tax for military and other state needs 'still remaining essential'. With all this, I felt a twinge of reservation: is not this a way for us Communists, I asked myself, to shift the responsibility for failures and difficulties in the economy onto the shoulders of the working class, or to compel the working class to take a share of such responsibilities from us? I soon explained my idea to Kardelj and Kidrič while we sat in a car parked in front of the villa where I lived. They felt no such reservation, and I was able all too easily to convince them of the indisputable harmony between my ideas and Marx's teaching. Without leaving the car, we thrashed it out for little more than half an hour. Kardelj thought it was a good idea, but one that should not be put into effect for another five or six years, and Kidrič agreed with him. A couple of days later, however, Kidrič telephoned me to say that we were ready to go ahead at once with the first steps. In his impulsive way he began to elaborate and expound on the whole conception. A little later, a meeting was held in Kardelj's cabinet office with the trade union leaders, and they proposed the abolition of the workers councils, which up to that time had functioned only as consultative bodies for the management. Kardelj suggested that my proposals for management should be associated with the workers councils, first of all in a way that would give them more rights and greater responsibilities. Shortly there began the debates on the issues of principle and on the statutory aspects, preparations that went on for some four or five months. Tito, busy with other duties and absent from Belgrade, took no part in this and knew nothing of the proposal soon to introduce a workers council bill in the

Parliament until he was informed by Kardelj and me in the government lobby room during a session of the National Assembly. His first reaction was: our workers are not ready for that yet! But Kardelj and I, convinced that this was an important step, pressed him hard, and he began to unbend as he paid more attention to our explanations. The most important part of our case was that this would be the beginning of democracy, something that socialism had not yet achieved; further, it could be plainly seen by the world and the international workers' movement as a radical departure from Stalinism. Tito paced up and down, as though completely wrapped in his own thoughts. Suddenly he stopped and exclaimed: 'Factories belonging to the workers—something that has never yet been achieved!' With these words, the theories worked out by Kardelj and myself seemed to shed their complications, and seemed, too, to find better prospects of being workable. A few months later, Tito explained the Workers' Self-Management Bill to the National Assembly.

Djilas's account of his contribution to the introduction of self-management has never been officially questioned. It may very well be that he was the first one to mention self-management in official circles.

The beginnings of self-management in Yugoslavia are still very much alive in the memory of most middle-aged men and women. To illustrate these beginnings, we will report an interview with the president of the workers' council and the head of administration at Ognjen Prica, a printing company in Zagreb.

Ognjen Prica was founded in 1917 by a Mr Rožankowski as a lithographic printing plant. Later on it became a joint-stock company. During the Second World War it was occupied by the Germans. In 1945 it was nationalized, and so were many other small printing plants. Several of them were fused into one large enterprise, among them Mr. Rožankowski's company as the biggest. The new company Ognjen Prica, which employed about 150 workers, used the whole range of printing techniques. It expanded to about its present size in 1947 when it became the official printing plant for Marxist literature in Croatia. The parent company was in Zagreb; several subsidiaries were located in other parts of Croatia. Today its workers number about 670, 52 per cent of them women.

Franjo Čuješ who is presently president of the workers' council has been with the company since 1950. When the first workers' council was introduced in Ognjen Prica in 1950, Mr Čuješ became a member. Belimo Marenić, administrative manager, suggested they might still have some files from this time. After a brief conversation with Mr Čuješ, he left and returned a few minutes later with the minutes of that first meeting. Examining the minutes, we found they were signed by Mr Čuješ. He had served as a secretary at that first meeting.

Mr Čuješ remembered that 'All factories to the workers !' was then a very popular slogan. He considers the introduction of self-management a result of intense opposition among the workers to the centralized bureaucratic system of state ownership and management of industry. He said:

In 1945 we followed the Russians because theirs was the latest model of socialism. But it did not work here: we were too different. There were no great landowners, and our peasants have a different mentality of 'I am not going to be told'. The old factory hand did not like the system either. They were for efficiency, and the state ownership system was very inefficient. We were all for socialism, but we didn't like the way it was put into practice. When we found out we disliked it, we started to look for a new form. Then we invented self-management.

Out of approximately 400 workers, 94 were nominated and 70 were elected into the first workers' council. As the minutes indicate, 57 were present at this first meeting, eleven were absent with an excuse, and two absent without an excuse. The agenda listed the following items:

(1) Report of the president of the election committee;
(2) Choosing a verification committee;
(3) The election of a president of the workers' council;
(4) Report of the general manager;
(5) Deciding on the number of members of the managing board;
(6) Electing the managing board; nine members and nine substitutes were elected.

While the first meeting of the workers' council apparently

centred very much on its own affairs, i.e. mainly on elections, the second meeting moved toward self-management. The agenda of the 10 October 1950 meeting shows the following items:

(1) Production contracts with the state for 1951;
(2) Production problems;
(3) Establishing a canteen;
(4) Rationalization and Innovation;
(5) Miscellaneous.

Item (4) deserves some attention. 'Rationalization and innovation were two catchwords in those days', Mr Čuješ explained. 'We were cut off from Russia, and had hardly any connections with the West yet. Therefore it was very important to start with what we had: to use, improve and protect the existing machines in the best possible way.

'There was a real *rationalization and innovation movement,*' Mr Čuješ continued, 'everybody talked about *racionalizacija* and *novatorstvo.*' During the next workers' council meeting of 6 October 1950 three suggestions came up:

(1) to rearrange machines spatially in order to save transportation time;
(2) some specific changes concerning technical details of machines; and
(3) the installation of some protective devices.

All three suggestions were put into practice, and the three innovators received a bonus representing a percentage of the amount of money saved in one year. Such bonuses were very high, ranging from the equivalent of a two-week wage to a six-month wage.

Innovators became heroes in the company and some of them even became national heroes. The rewards, money and prestige, represented, of course, strong incentives for innovations.

On 17 July 1951 it was realized that the company was far ahead of its production plan. As a considerable amount of additional income resulted from that overproduction, a number of awards were given to those who had made the most outstanding contributions to this success:

10 workers received 5000 dinars each;
26 workers received 4000 dinars each;
60 workers received 3000 dinars each; and
35 workers received 2000 dinars each.

The total sum paid amounted to 404,000 dinars. To make this figure meaningful, Mr Čuješ explained that his annual salary was then about 15,000 dinars.

In a meeting on 19 December 1952, it was again discovered that there was a considerable surplus—a total of 3 million dinars, which corresponded to the annual amount of wages in Ognjen Prica. It was decided by the workers' council to distribute 50 per cent of this amount among all workers. Franjo Čuješ thinks that self-management has been of greatest benefit for the economy as well as for the workers' income and their satisfaction.

The introduction of self-management in 1949/50 was the starting-point of a long series of reforms designed to transform Yugoslavia's structure. Since then, self-management has permeated all spheres of work. It is the central organizing principle of Yugoslav society. It is identical with the democratization of social, economic and political life.

Until today, the world public has hardly taken notice of the Yugoslav model. While TV, radio, journals and newspapers in countries like Sweden or the Federal Republic of Germany occasionally devote some of their time or space to a presentation and discussion of self-management in Yugoslavia, the United States is prominent among those countries who ignore self-management. The attitude of neglect or disbelief towards the self-managing society goes back to the very beginnings of self-management. It took the world press more than a full year to take notice of the events in Yugoslavia. The delay in reactions abroad indicates that the introduction of workers' control was first thought of as a communist propaganda trick that was not to be taken seriously.

For the *New York Herald Tribune* (21 April 1951), self-management was an interesting communist experiment which originated in the head of a single man at the top of the hierarchy:

The withering away of the state seems to be an unrealistic cause in a period of world crisis. But in Yugoslavia it is now in the forefront of attention, together with the war threat. It began like this: two days after the outbreak of the war in Korea, Tito made an impressive speech in the Assembly in which he said that Marxist–Leninist teaching would be put into practice in Yugoslavia, and that the first step in this direction would be the decentralization of state power, and the second, the creation of workers' councils for the purpose of handing over the factories to the workers. At the time, the Marshal's speech was thought to be primarily propaganda. It seemed ridiculous to talk about the withering away of the state. However, recent events have made it possible to study the value of the programme as a serious experiment to create a new system which is not simply communist propaganda.

Around the middle of 1951, however, many more newspapers started to take the development in Yugoslavia for a 'serious experiment', if not more, as the following excerpts show. The *Neue Züricher Zeitung* (25 May 1951) reported with some enthusiasm:

> Marshal Tito's regime is at the present moment undertaking a really revolutionary reorganization of the economic system built up after 1945. The aim of this reorganization is far-reaching. The bureaucratic economy, i.e. an economy based on centralized state planning, is to be abolished. It is to be replaced by an economic system in which, it is true, there will be no place for private ownership of major means of production, but in which principles of the private-enterprise economy, such as the free play of the law of supply and demand and the principle of profitability will again operate.

The Times (13 June 1951) wrote in a similar vein:

> The setting up of workers' councils is merely the latest, though the most striking phase of the process of decentralization which has changed the state's entire economic organization.

And the *Frankfurter Allgemeine Zeitung* (28 June 1951) stated:

> The taking over of factories by the working collectives has not remained just a slogan; it has actually happened, for the workers' share in the enterprise profits, and competition is developing among the individual enterprises.

Morgan Phillips, General Secretary of the British Labour Party, mused:

> If this experiment really succeeds, then every socialist party in the world will be forced to review its stand on industrial democracy, taking into consideration the experience of Yugoslav workers.

And while self-management was for the *New York Herald Tribune* just another experiment in communism, Morgan Phillips saw its relevance for any socialist party in both East and West. And the *New Statesman and Nation* even looked with some envy up to the new model:

> Tito's courage in taking this risk may finally prove wiser than our exaggerated caution when we entrusted our nationalized industries to managements headed by appointed directors. (Quoted in Bajec, n.d., pp. 36–7)

Yet, after a quarter century of experience with self-management in Yugoslavia, one can no longer reasonably speak of a risk. If other countries in East and West have chosen not to adopt the model of self-management, this must have other reasons than fear of risk.

3 The Development of Self-Management in Yugoslavia

Legally, self-management was introduced on 27 June 1950. At that point, the economy was under the authority of the state administration. From there to the 'self-management society' was still a long way, its realization being a gradual process extending both ways: before and after that specific date. For more than a decade, self-management remained more a 'revolutionary vision in the process of realization' than an accomplished fact (Gorupić and Paj, 1970, p. 6).

The development of self-management in Yugoslavia took place in three major phases. In phase I, *Paternalistic Self-Management under State Socialism,* self-management organizations continued to be supervised in essential spheres by state functionaries and organs. This was a dualistic and inherently contradictory system in which the old hierarchical managerial organization under state direction was intertwined with the newly emerging democratic structure. The contradiction rested mainly in the fact that power and authority were simultaneously vested in both the base and the top.

In phase II, *Representative Self-Management*, decision-making power was vested in workers' councils elected by the workers as organs acting on their behalf. This system resembles representative democracy in the political system of some Western societies.

In phase III, *Direct or Participatory Self-Management*, power was vested directly in the workers who decided on major issues through referenda and delegate decision-making power in matters of lesser importance to the workers' council, to various commissions formed by the workers' council and to the professional management including the general manager. All these organs and individuals to whom power has been delegated remain ultimately responsible to the workers.

Bearing in mind that the development of self-management was a very gradual process and that delineation of a certain period for each phase must be somewhat arbitrary, I suggest the period of 1949 to 1952 for phase I, of 1953 to 1962 for phase II and of 1963 to 1973 for phase III.

There are indications that, seen in a long-term perspective, 1974 might mark the beginning of a new phase, characterized by direct self-management in *all* spheres, i.e. being no longer limited to business, other organizations and the communal administration but including the political system in all levels.

PATERNALISTIC SELF-MANAGEMENT

The economic system under which self-management was introduced in Yugoslavia was that of state socialism: a centrally planned economy in which decisions were made at the top of the political–administrative hierarchy and handed down to the base of the pyramid. Workers were but recipients of orders.

The introduction of the first workers' council in December 1949 signalled the abandonment of central planning and of political–administrative management. Yet this was only a signal, and the 520 workers' councils which existed by the end of 1950 were consultative bodies without full, if any, decision-making power. They did have the right to propose measures on all matters concerning the management of a company, and the general manager was bound to take their view into account. He could not simply overrule the suggestions of the workers' council. Matters in dispute between the workers' council and the general manager were arbitrated by organs of the state. During this phase, the state continued to be responsible for the 'administrative–operational management' of the company, and the general manager was its direct representative. This gave the general manager of course considerable power. At the time when self management was introduced, most general managers may not have felt any reduction in their power at all. Yet they soon realized that the new law did make a difference, even though the state arbitration agencies may have been inclined to judge cases of disagreement in favour of their representative, the general manager, rather than the workers' council in which they had only very limited confidence. But every case of arbitration involved a certain amount of publicity, and a general manager who did not get along with his workers' council was likely to meet the disapproval of his administrative superiors who at least felt bothered by too much litigation or feared to be reprimanded by their higher-ups for industrial unrest, and industrial peace was important during a period of economic reconstruction, industrialization and military rearmament. Thus, at the end, the general managers found their powers greatly reduced: simultaneously controlled by workers' councils and by the state. In the long run, the dualism in industrial organization, the conflict between democratic institutions in the company and authoritariam state management, began slowly to disappear in favour of direct democracy on the company level.

A similar dualism characterized the structure of the economy which started to change from central planning to a *free market economy*. In 1951, prices in key branches of production and consumption like power, transportation, basic industries, cereals and other staple foods continued to be government-controlled. But at the same time, the prices of many general consumer goods were freed and became subject to the interplay of supply and demand.

The next step in the development of a self-managing society was marked by a new economic and social development plan. To underline the fundamental difference from former plans and to signal the beginning of a new economic era, the new plan was called the *Social Plan*, rather than a state plan. The major novelty of the *Social Plan* was that, within certain limits set by the plan, companies were given the right to draw up their own production plans, to establish relations with other companies, to determine the direction of their economic development and to spend a significant proportion of their income as they wished. To be sure, the major share of investments were still in the hands of the state, and the plan determined proportions of production in the various branches of the economy, but the plan no longer specified what and how much each company was to produce. Moreover, the choice of production methods and the determination of prices became the prerogative of each company.

Of course, bureaucratic socialism did not disappear overnight, and vestiges of central planning and administration continued to be visible in the form of indirect economic coercion: to finance its regular budget and its investments in key branches of industry, the state imposed a heavy tax which progressed with the increasing profitability of a company.

In spite of popular dissatisfaction with state socialism, the introduction of self-management was not the result of popular, 'self-management' initiatives; self-management was introduced *under* state socialism—and *by* state socialism. It was the top of the party hierarchy, not the workers, that created self-management. In that respect, the party acted as a 'vanguard of the working class', and it has continued to play this role. Until today, the development of self-management in Yugoslavia has been in the hands of this 'vanguard'. Self-management did not, in an act of parthenogenesis, create itself. For some, this may appear paradoxical; for others, this may simply be dialectics: direct democracy has been initiated and nurtured by and through hierarchical channels.

REPRESENTATIVE SELF-MANAGEMENT

'Self-management under state socialism' is, properly speaking, a contradiction in terms. One cannot have both at the same time. It is either workers who manage their companies or it is state functionaries who run them on behalf of the workers or, more frequently, on their own behalf, i.e. in the interest of a bureaucratic political ruling class. State functionaries are appointed from above, not elected or delegated from below. State socialism is, therefore, incompatible with the self-managerial system of direct democracy.

For self-management to become a reality, state socialism with its administrative hierarchy and its central planning structure had first to disappear. One could even say that the growth of self-management and its expansion through all spheres of society correlates with the withering away of the state.

The shape which self-management first assumed during this process was that of *representative self-management*. Authority was vested in the workers' council. This council was elected by the working collective; it represented the workers and it ruled *on behalf of the workers*. The fact that someone ruled on behalf of someone else remained the same during this transition from state socialism to self-management; but the difference was that it was no longer the state but workers who ruled on behalf of workers.

Through the constitutional amendments of 1953—the Magna Carta of Yugoslav citizens as Moše Pijade, President of the Assembly, called it—self-management became an 'inalienable right' of the working people. The state tied its own hands by protecting self-management constitutionally against any violation including that by the state.

The construction of self-management coincided with the emergence of a market economy. With the abandonment of central planning, the market provided now the framework within which a company was to experience success or failure. The goal of plan fulfillment was now replaced by profit maximization. Companies continued of course, to have certain tax obligations to the state which at first were quite high. But once they had met these obligations, it was their right to determine the allocation of their net income and the distribution of profits. The economic performance of a company ceased to be under the control of the state and became the sole responsibility of its workers. This of course implied that differences in business success and in the level of company earnings as well as personal incomes became more marked. Maybe for the first time in the history of any socialist state, the idea of the *withering away of the state* was given some concrete meaning:

> The working class should organize a democratically constituted state, founded on self-management in the basic units of society, which will begin to be transformed from below into a modernly organized and integrated community. Thus, the withering away of the state means only its gradual transformation into something essentially different from the traditional state—an equally efficent mechanism, but maintained and regulated from below, not above. (Bajec, n.d., p. 47)

In 1957 several laws were passed increasing the freedom of business to dispose of its income. During the debates preceding these bills, the fear was repeatedly expressed that '*the workers will eat up their factories*'.

One of these laws was of particular importance in giving a new impetus to worker management. The law on the distribution of the total income of companies specified that no taxes be imposed on an amount equal to the fixed minimum income of all employees.

All earnings above this sum were subject to a progressive scale of taxation. Taxes were still very high, and a large proportion of these taxes was being used by the state to alleviate regional disparities in economic development in the federation. In 1958, for instance, the total income of manufacturing and mining industry totalled two billion dinars (billion = a thousand million). One and a half billion dinars were spent on material and running costs, depreciation, debt payments and special taxes. Of the remaining 500,000 million dinars, 39 per cent went into direct taxes, 52 per cent into personal incomes and 9 per cent into company funds.

While the new laws of 1957 increased the companies' control over their income, the workers still considered this a far cry from what they really wanted, and criticisms were voiced almost immediately. A new catchword came up around that time: *the material base of worker management*. It was alleged that the heavy taxation severely limited this material base of worker management and presented a serious obstacle on the way towards genuine self-management.

Most of these taxes went into the investment funds of the federation, republics, provinces, districts and communes. For the change from a central planning economy to a decentralized state meant, during this phase, that the administration of these funds was to be transferred from the centre to the lower levels of the state. All investment decisions were passed by the assemblies on each of these levels.

Unlike the former period of state socialism, when such decisions were administrative acts, they were now political in nature. For worker management, this difference did not solve the fundamental problems that they, the workers, did not have full control over investment in the economy. The former conflict of authority between the producers and the central administration had now turned into a conflict between the producers and the politicians on all levels of the political structure. But while the former conflict had been largely silent, the present conflict came out in the open. The politicians' right to decide over investment and to control business began to be publicly questioned.

For industry this was much more than a political fight over power; it was simultaneously an economic struggle. It was one of the legacies of state socialism that capital continued to be controlled by the state through a credit system of investments. New companies borrowed their capital from a federal, republic, provincial or communal investment fund and repaid this amount, with interest, to the fund. In this way, 'state capital' was self-perpetuating on all levels of the state bureaucracy. Later, these funds were abolished and their capital was transferred to the newly founded commercial banks. A chief consequence of this system has remained virtually unaltered until very recently: Investment credits carried exceedingly high interest rates. Because of their monopoly over investment credit, state funds could easily impose their own terms, given the pressure of demand for credits and the ubiquitous shortage of capital. Many companies ran into financial difficulties because of these unfavourable credit terms. Meanwhile, the economic power of the state funds and of their administrators continued to rise. In the mid-fifties, the conviction started to grow that investments would eventually have to be transferred to the competence of a self-managing economy.

Self-management was first applied to business, but as a structural model it is applicable to almost any organization or institution, and a self-managing society is doubtless one in which all major institutions, including government and administration, are structured along the lines of self-management principles. The general dismantling of local government bureaucracies thus accompanied the development of self-management as a gradual process. More and more powers were transferred from districts to local communities and communes. At the same time, communes expanded territorially and grew economically. In 1956 there were 107 districts and 1479 communes in Yugoslavia. The breakthrough occurred in 1957 when districts were abolished. Today Yugoslavia comprises 500 communes. This change was accompanied by alterations in the political structure of the commune. Before 1957, local government functions were in the hands of a people's committee, a single representative body composed of deputies elected by all citizens of voting age on the territory of a commune or district. In practice however, Bajec (P. 48) says, 'it was the president of the commune and his apparatus who held the real power in their hands'. This changed with the transformation into two-chamber assemblies which included separately elected representatives of the economy and other public sectors in all assemblies. This was an important step in the further elaboration of the self-management system and in the transformation of the traditional state into self-managing communities. An important meeting took place in 1957 from which the development of self-management received some strong impulses: the First Congress of Self-Managers from 25 to 27 June. It was attended by 1782 delegates from companies and communes all over Yugoslavia.

Another important meeting, during the same year, was the Seventh Congress of the Communist Party, by then renamed the League of Communists of Yugoslavia. This Congress adopted a new ideological programme on which the entire social system of Yugoslavia was to be founded, a programme of immediate socialism in the form of a self-managing society abdicating state socialism with its messianic vision of 'true' socialism in some remote 'higher' stage of socialist development. The new programme was founded on the idea of democratic socialism *hic et nunc*: 'Socialism cannot subordinate the personal happiness of man to any higher objectives, for the highest goal of socialism is man's personal happiness.'

During the Fifth Congress of the Socialist Alliance of Working People of Yugoslavia in April 1960, these goals became more specific about the material base of worker management: The workers should be given complete freedom from state interference and be allowed to decide independently on the distribution of their business income. In the following years, several laws were passed to the effect of abolishing the state's right to tax business profits. Taxes were limited to a certain percentage of a company's fixed assets. This tax was first fixed at 6 per cent of the value of fixed assets and then reduced to 4 per cent and eventually to 2 per cent.

The philosophy behind new tax laws was that of *distribution according to work*, applicable to the entire national economy, including the so-called socially owned sector. At the same time, workers had the social responsibility to operate the means of production that had been placed under their management, with a certain minimum of efficiency—hence the fixed-assets tax.

How well did self-management work economically? Did it fulfil the hopes of those who had initiated it in the interest of rapid economic growth? Or was a slow-down in the rate of growth the price for the new humanistic socialism? In 1960, by the end of the first decade of self-management, Yugoslavia had begun to catch up with the European countries of a medium level of economic development. Industrial production was about four times greater than in pre-war Yugoslavia. With an annual growth rate between 10 and 12 per cent, Yugoslavia emerged as a country with one of the highest growth rates in the world. Between 1953 and 1959 industry doubled its output, while the consumption of electric power increased threefold. Unlike development in the Soviet Union, economic growth in Yugoslavia did not take place at the expense of the consumer. Personal consumption rose at an average rate of about 10 per cent annually. Every year an additional 150,000 workers entered the wage sector. At the end of the period, over 1.5 million people had migrated from rural to urban districts. 700,000 people, or one in every ten adults, had by then participated in self-management through membership in a workers' council.

DIRECT SELF-MANAGEMENT

Self-management and state socialism are incompatible. It is either the workers or the state that is in charge of an organization. The emergence of representative self-management—workers managing on behalf of workers—brought the idea of self-management a great deal closer to its realization. The fact that workers could elect a workers' council from among themselves and keep in close touch with its members certainly increased the power of workers to control their companies immensely. Yet, it was always a select few who ruled, and the mass of workers had to submit to their rule, awaiting their own turn, if it ever came. Criticism of 'elitism', of 'bureaucratization' was voiced. At the same time, the economic results of self-management had been overwhelmingly positive. Gradually, Yugoslavia became ready for the next step in its gigantic experiment of self-management: its direct-democratic phase. To be sure, genuine self-management is always *direct* self-management. But this is the outcome of a long process of development; it is not created by fiat. A representative democratic structure is a form of incipient self-management before it comes to maturity.

Formally, direct self-management was grounded in Yugoslavia's new constitution of 1963, an exceptional document in that it is based on self-management as the organizing principle of Yugoslavia's social, economic and political system. The working man as the manager of the socially owned means of production is the fundamental unit of the new society. This direct democratic right to manage production and all public affairs is a new addition to the traditional civic rights proclaimed during the French Revolution.

The widest possible participation, the backbone of direct self-management, was actively sought and implemented in the process of discussing the new constitution before its enactment. The draft constitution was submitted to public discussion early in 1962. For about a year, the population involved itself in the debate of the details; over six million, a third of the total population, participated. Bajec (p. 150) reports:

About 300,000 different views, proposals, suggestions and objections were stated. Tens of thousands of proposals were submitted to the Constitutional Commission directly. The Social Science Institute in Belgrade and the daily paper *Borba* conducted a special inquiry and found that over 80 per cent of citizens over 18 years stated they had read or had otherwise become acquainted with the contents of the draft Constitution.

The political structure did not remain unaffected by the new system of economic relations grounded in the constitution. Rotation and limited re-election to all public office became a novel principle on the political scene. As a consequence, the majority of the men and women in the various assemblies today are no longer professional politicians.

The basic principles of the new self-managing society are: (1) All Yugoslavs are free and equal. (2) They own, control and plan their own affairs, be it in business, politics, or any other public sector. (3) They distribute the fruits of their labour according to labour input.

The preamble of the new constitution spells these principles out:

The socialist system in Yugoslavia is based on relations among people acting as free and equal producers and creators, whose labour serves exclusively for the satisfaction of their personal and common needs.

Accordingly, the inviolable foundation of the position and role of man lies in:

Social ownership of the means of production, which precludes reversion to any system of exploitation of man by man, and which, by eliminating man's alienation from the means of production and other conditions of labour, ensures conditions for self-management by working people in production and the distribution of the proceeds of labour, and for social guidance of economic development;

Emancipation of labour by the gradual transcendence of historically conditioned inequality and dependence of people at work, which is assured through: The abolition of wage-labour relations, the exercise of self-management by the working people, the allround development of the productive forces, the reduction of socially necessary labour time, the development of science, culture and technology, and the continual expansion of education;

The right of man, both as an individual and as a member of a work community, to enjoy the fruits of his labour and of the material progress of the community, in accordance with the principle 'From each according to his abilities; to each according to his labour', provided he contributes to the development of the material foundations of his own and social labour and to the satisfaction of other social wants;

Self-management by the working people in work organizations; free association of working people, work and other organizations, and socio-political communities for the purpose of satisfying common needs and interests; self-management in communes and other socio-political communities with a view to ensuring as direct a participation of citizens as possible in the guidance of social development, the exercise of power, and decision making concerning all social affairs;

The democratic political relations which enable man to realize his interests, the right of self-management and other rights and mutual relationships, to develop his personality through direct participation in social life, especially in the bodies of self-management, in socio-political organizations and associations, which he himself sets up and through which he influences the development of social consciousness and the expansion of conditions for his activity and for the attainment of his interests and rights;

. . .

Being the common inalienable basis of social labour, socially owned means of production serve to satisfy the personal and common needs and interests of the working people and to develop the material foundations of the community and socialist social relations. Socially owned means of production are managed directly by the working people who work with these means both in their own interest and in the interest of the community, and who are responsible to each other and to the community.

Since no one has the right of ownership over socially owned means of production, nobody—socio-political communities nor individual working men—may appropriate on any legal basis the product of social labour, or manage and dispose of socially owned means of production, or arbitrarily determine the terms of their distribution.

Man's labour is the only ground for the appropriation of the product of social labour and the basis for the management of social resources.

. . .

In order to assure the realization of the individual and common interests of the working people and to attain self-management, encourage their initiative, and create the most favourable conditions for the development of productive forces, equalize the working conditions, achieve distribution according to labour input, and develop socialist relations, the community shall guide and coordinate, by planning economic development and the material foundations of other social activities. Planning shall be done in work organizations by the working people as the agents of production and social labour, and by socio-political communities in the performance of their socio economic functions.

Social Plans of Yugoslavia shall coordinate the basic relations in production and distribution. Within the framework of these relations and a unified economic system, the working people in work organizations and socio-political communities shall autonomously plan and develop the material foundations of their activities.

. . .

Social ownership of the means of production shall be the basis for personal property acquired by personal labour and used for the satisfaction of the individual's personal needs and interests.   (The Constitution, 1969, pp. 8–13)

What self-management specifically means, i.e. beyond the general principles laid down in the preamble, is spelled out in article 9 of the 1963 constitution:

Self-management in work organizations shall include in particular the right and duty of the working people:

(1) To manage their work organizations directly or through bodies of management elected by themselves;

(2) To organize production or other activities, to promote the development of their work organizations, and to lay down working and development plans and programmes;

(3) To decide on the exchange of products and services and on other matters relating to the operation of their work organizations;

(4) To decide on the use and disposition of social resources and to employ them with economic efficiency, so as to ensure the highest possible returns for work organizations and the community;

(5) To distribute the income of their work organizations and provide for the development of the material base of their work; to allocate income among the working people; to fulfil the work organizations' obligations towards the community;

(6) To decide on the admission of working people into their work organizations and their dismissal, and on other labour relations; to determine working hours in the work organizations in conformity with general working conditions; to secure internal supervision and make their work public;

(7) To regulate and promote their working conditions, to organize industrial safety measures, and rest; to provide conditions for their education, and to advance their own and the general standard of living;

(8) To decide on the split-up of their work organizations and on turning parts of them into separate organizations, and to decide on merger and association of their work organizations with other work organizations.

Exercising their self-government rights, the working people in socio-political communities shall decide on matters concerning the guidance of economic and social development, the distribution of the social product, and other affairs of common concern.

Citizens directly concerned, representatives of the organizations concerned and representatives of the community may participate in the management of work organizations regarding matters of special concern to the community.

(The Constitution, 1969, pp. 25–7)

The primary emphasis of the 1963 constitution was on *direct* self-management. But how do you implement direct self-management? In small companies, direct management through the workers is feasible. But how can a thousand workers manage their company directly? The answer is: they cannot, as long as the whole company is the unit of self-management. But if the company is broken down into smaller entities and if these smaller entities are made units of self-management, then workers in their totality can in fact exercise direct self-management rights.

In the economic reform of 1965, companies were restructured into smaller units of self-management. These work units were frequently identical with departments, but not always as indicated in article 9 of the basic law of 1965:

Members of the work collective exercise self-management rights in the work unit excepting those which, in the interests of the whole enterprise, must be exercised by the whole collective of the enterprise, directly or through management bodies.

(Burt, 1972, p. 136)

This law further specified that small units may be combined into 'work units' in various ways to be determined by the statutes of a company as approved by the workers' collective. Major decisions concerning a work unit were to be made by all workers through a referendum. Less important decisions would be made by the workers' council and its various committees, and each work unit would have its own workers' council in addition to the one general workers' council of the company as a whole. Under direct self-management, the role of the workers' council changed: major decisions were taken out of its hands altogether and taken by the workers directly. In minor decisions, the workers' council was responsible to and held accountable by the workers' collective. Under representative self-management, the workers' council was in theory responsible to the workers' collective too, but in reality, it was an independent and practically the ultimate decision-making body. Under the new system of direct self-management, the workers' council lost that independence and became in theory *and practice* responsible to the workers in their totality.

The legal position of these work units as self-managing bodies was further strengthened by constitutional amendments, especially by Amendment XXI and Amendment XXII which made the 'Basic Organization of Associated Labour' (OOUR) the basic economic units in charge of all decisions concerning the OOUR including income allocation, profit distribution and the like.

Many of the novelties introduced during the economic reform of 1965 and grounded in the basic law of 1965 and in subsequent constitutional amendments were subtle yet important. For instance, organizations and the constituent OOUR were now to be considered as free associations of responsible *work partners*—as opposed to wage-earners—managing the organization directly and through delegated bodies.

The economic reform of 1965 also marks an important turning point in the economic history of Yugoslavia. Before 1965, the password was growth, and all productive efforts were directed towards the attainment of high growth rates. To an outside observer it might appear as if the emphasis on growth was second only to the emphasis on self-management. But I think the priorities are in the reverse order: self-management was second only to growth; and, more specifically, the self-managerial organization of work was a means to achieve higher growth rates.

1963 marked the beginning of a new liberal trend in Yugoslav economics and politics, a trend which met the administration largely unprepared. The administration was well trained in centralism but quite unfamiliar with decentralized economic policy. On the whole, the new policy was one of *laissez-faire*, the only tool of economic policy being monetary intervention. The result was economic chaos, which expressed itself in rapidly declining growth rates for 1964 and 1965. The economic reform of 1965 was thus first of all a reaction to pressing economic problems, and the new developments in self-management structure represented an attempt to deal with these problems.

On the whole, the struggle for economic growth through self-management was wholly successful. During the seven-year period 1958–64, the *per capita* income increased to approximately US $500. The average growth rate of industrial production was 12 per cent per year, among the highest in the world. Agricultural production grew at a rate of 5 per cent annually, which is also exceptionally high. During that seven-year time span, personal consumption increased by 70 per cent. Exports rose by 120 per cent and imports by 100 per cent.

When self-management was introduced, the fear that 'workers will eat up their factories' was repeatedly expressed. The impact of self-management was just the opposite: it provided an incentive to make an enormous effort at production on the part of the workers without demanding—from themselves, that is—wage increases equivalent to increases in production.This enabled Yugoslav industry to continue over an extended period to make heavy investments. The result was a very large increase in productivity. During the period 1948 to 1952, an annual investment of 8.29 dinars in fixed assets was required to obtain a 1-dinar increase in the national product. During the period 1953 to 1956, 4 dinars were required for the same increase. From 1956 to 1964, 2.5 dinars sufficed. An American journalist observed in 1964: 'Yugoslavia is in a position to manufacture whatever it wants in whatever quantity' (Bajec, n.d., p. 156).

In 1946, Yugoslavia was an underdeveloped country. In 1964, i.e. in less than two decades, Yugoslavia had successfully gone through its industrial revolution and become an industrial nation. One cannot emphasize strongly enough the importance and magnitude of this achievement. In less than 20 years, Yugoslavia had made it into the ranks of the select few successful 'latecomers to modernization'. Today, Yugoslavia is a modern industrial country, not as advanced as West Germany or the United States, but definitely on its way. It has accomplished this feat through its own work, through the labour of its workers. Not only did it not enjoy the support of any foreign aid, it was even embargoed and constantly menaced by one of the world's superpowers, the Soviet Union.

With its industrial revolution won, Yugoslavia was ready for a reversal of priorities: self-management and its development became now the first, and growth the second priority. This shift in priorities was the object of the economic reform of 1965. The foundation for this shift was laid by the constitution of 1963 which made direct self-management a *legal* reality. But what about the *material base* of self-management, the economics of direct democracy? This was the specific object of the economic reform. While the problem of capital formation and economic growth continued to be crucial, it had lost some of its urgency. Hence, the growth of personal incomes could now become a primary concern of the economic reform.

One of the most dramatic aspects of Yugoslav society is its dynamism and its ubiquitous readiness for experimentation with representative self-management. With economic growth hardly accomplished, it shifts the emphasis to income distribution. And with *income distribution according to the results of work* hardly envisaged, the next goal to move to is already taking shape: *income distribution according to work*.

Income distribution according to the *results* of work ties personal incomes to the business results of the company as realized on the free market. Disparities in individual incomes between companies, branches of the economy, regions and even within companies, particularly between the OOUR, or work units, are of course inevitable. But the crucial question is whether these income disparities are due to differences in work input, including work input during preceding periods which may have resulted in higher investments and consequently in higher efficiency—in short, differences in work—or whether these disparities are due to extraneous conditions like geographical location, i.e. difference in the *results* of work rather than work alone. The pivotal point of the economic reform of 1965 was for the state to ensure market relations that would provide for at least roughly equal conditions of economic activity and the acquisition of income. To the extent that such equal conditions would be approximated, income from the *results* of one's work would become identical with income from one's *work*.

After the 'take-off into self-sustained growth' (Rostow, 1952)—a period characterized by exceptionally high growth rates, ending around 1964 and 1965—growth rates dropped to 6 or 7 per cent which is still quite high compared with other industrial countries. During the preceding period, increases in industrial employment had made a major contribution to economic growth. After 1965, a strong effort was made to *modernize* the economy, i.e. to base further growth of output on an increase in productivity rather than employment. In fact, most of the expansion in gross national product from 1966 to 1970 was based on higher productivity, which rose at an annual rate of 5–6 per cent. Employment during that period gained by only 165,000: less than in any single year preceding the economic reform. The modernization of industry, i.e. the transition from labour-intensive to capital-intensive production techniques, reduced of course the demand for labour. Many companies not only did not hire additional workers, they even found themselves confronted with redundancies. The problem of 'technological redundancies' put self-management to a test: will workers dismiss themselves? No workers were laid off. The problem was solved in various ways: by expansion, by establishing new companies and by the natural decline in employment—workers who retired or left for other reasons of their own were not replaced. In addition, special funds were established by the communities and republics to train or retrain workers for new skills that were in short supply.

All in all, the contrast between self-managing Yugoslavia and the United States in a comparable situation is most drastic. In the United States, workers are laid off by the thousand or by the hundred thousand, and no company, corporation, or communal, state or federal government considers itself responsible for policies to avoid such lay-offs.

4 Self-Management in Action: Examples from Yugoslavia

There is something to be gained from a scholarly presentation and something different from a first-hand account of one's observations and reactions. I will, therefore, begin with relating to the reader some of my experiences and first reactions to self-management, a system I gradually discovered as I interviewed my way through from one company to another. I also visited other organizations, such as hospitals, cooperatives, trade unions, etc., on which I will report later when I present a more thorough analysis. I should point out that the system of self-management has gone through a process of gradual development extending over a quarter century. All major changes were initiated or legalized by constitutional amendments. Some companies were quicker than others to introduce these changes. Some of the more recent changes have, therefore, not yet been universally implemented. It will be noted in the reports below that some companies are still being run by *workers' councils* as the ultimate decision-making body while others have already progressed to the more recent system of direct democracy in which major decisions are made by the *workers' collective*. A change which has, in larger companies, accompanied this process of democratization is the transformation of a company into *basic organizations of associated labour* (OOUR): economically independent work units with their own independent self-management structure.

ŠKOFJA LOKA

My first visit to a Yugoslav company was on Friday, 3 August 1973. Shortly after 7 a.m., I went to see Bogomil Babnik of the

Secretariat of Information of Slovenia, in Ljubljana, Prešernova 8. Mr Babnik had been most helpful in providing me with various materials on Yugoslavia, among them an expensive volume on Yugoslav culture, with colour plates, and on self-administration in Slovenia, of which Ljubljana is the capital. For this day, Mr Babnik had arranged a visit to Škofja Loka, a very pretty small town which that year happened to be celebrating its thousandth anniversary. We first went to the town hall of Ljubljana where we picked up an interpreter. We then departed, leaving behind Bogomil Babnik, who had better things to do— namely to spend the weekend in his summer home in Bled, supposedly one of the most beautiful places in Yugoslavia, at least in the eyes of President Tito who, like Bogomil Babnik, had a summer home there, though his is probably more a summer palace.

Half an hour later we arrived at Škofja Loka, located between two rivers and surrounded by mountains. Had I not known I was in Yugoslavia, I might as well have guessed that this was a small medieval town anywhere in Austria or southern Germany. At the town hall, *skupščina občine*, we met Lojze Malovrh, vice-president of the community, who had been expecting us. Besides being vice-president of the community, or, more precisely, of the council of the community, he was director of the gymnasium of Škofja Loka and president of the committee for the celebration of the one thousandth anniversary of Škofja Loka. In that capacity, he felt obliged to give a brief account of the history of the town in which he was born and where he had risen to a respectable position.

In A.D. 973, the German Emperor Otto II gave the land which is today Škofja Loka as a present to the bishops of Freisingia. The document of this transaction can still be seen in the museum of Škofja Loka. The name is documented since 1274, *škof* meaning bishop and *loka* locality at the water. On a hill the Freisingian bishops built a tower, the first part of the castle of Škofja Loka, which still exists. It was below that tower where the first houses were built. When a wall was built against the Turks during the fourteenth century, the houses moved back behind the wall, giving the place its character which it has preserved till today: houses very close to one another and very narrow streets. Until 1803, Škofja Loka belonged to the Freisingian bishops. After that, it became part of the Austrian-Hungarian monarchy, until the First World War when Yugoslavia became independent. When looking down from the thick walls of the castle onto the red roofs of the town, the picture is about the same as 500 years ago, not even distorted by TV antennas, telephone cables or electric power lines. For the anniversary, all antennas were removed from the roofs and installed inside and all cables were put underground. During the time of my visit, the remodelling of the façades of the houses was still in progress: all houses in the medieval part of the town were to be given their medieval appearance. With a broad smile, Mr Malovrh pointed to one of the larger houses: 'This building shows you the continuity of power. The Freisingian bishops lived there, the Nazis made it their headquarters and look at the sign now.' The sign indicated that the building now housed the Communist party of Škofja Loka.

Today, the community comprises 511 square kilometres, with approximately 31,000 inhabitants, of whom 14,300 were gainfully employed in March 1971, 55 per cent being men and 45 per cent women (Polajnar, 1973, pp.1–3). Škofja Loka is a wealthy town and most of its inhabitants find work locally. The majority work in local industries; only 18 per cent are still in agriculture. There are several major enterprises: Alpina-Žiri, a shoe factory; Tovarna-Predilnica, a spinning factory; Jelonica and Alples, both saw mills and furniture factories; LTH which produces refrigeration equipment; Elra, an electronics factory; Kroj, a textile factory; Šešir, a hat-manufacturing company which dates back to the nineteenth century; Odeja, a quilt factory, and a branch of Iskra which produces electric motors. All major companies export part of their production to a large number of countries. It is estimated that in 1973 Škofja Loka's enterprises export commodities worth approximately US $18 million.

The *per capita* income was estimated to be about US $1298 in 1973, which was well above the *per capita* income of Yugoslavia. Škofja Loka's *per capita* income has steadily risen from US $617 in 1967 to over US $697 in 1968, US $858 in 1969, US $980 in 1970, US $1018 in 1971 and US $1088 in 1972 (Polajnar, 1973, p. 42).

Škofja Loka has five elementary schools with 18 branches; a high school of which comrade Malovrh is director; three technical schools, one each for the metal, shoe and furniture industries; and a workers' university which trains adults employed in Škofja

Loka's industry in evening courses. Every year, three to four thousand people take courses at the workers' university, which means that over the years, almost every adult undergoes additional training and for a great many, formal education is a process which never stops.

KROJ

From Škofja Loka, we drove up one of the valleys which are part of the commune, accompanied by Mr Malovrh who, in his dark suit, white shirt and tie, gave the expedition a very official look. After a few miles we arrived at Konfekzija 'Kroj', a garment factory which produces eight to ten thousand coats every month. Approximately 20 per cent of its production is exported, mainly to Switzerland and West Germany.

We were received by the general manager, Vinko Primožič, a stout man in his late fifties who had very much the looks and self-assurance of an entrepreneur, which he in fact turned out to be. He led us into his office, equipped with modern furniture and in no way extravagant, not too different from the other rooms occupied by the administration.

If companies are owned by the workers, or by the state in an earlier phase, how do new companies emerge then? Under capitalism, individuals or groups of individuals accumulate enough capital, get some loans and start a company on their own initiative driven supposedly by the profit motive. In a centrally planned economy like the Soviet Union, the establishment of a new industry is the outcome of a decision-making process centred in the bureaucracy. How about Yugoslavia where companies are 'socially owned', i.e. by the workers? This was my first question.

Kroj started in 1946, shortly after the war. Mr Primožič was then a tailor, and the enterprise that he founded was little more than a tailor's shop, comprising himself and five other employees. Initial capital was so minute that the problem of how to raise the initial capital did not arise: a few sewing machines, scissors, some tables and a room or two in which to work, that was about all that was needed.

Who owned the company then? Not Mr Primožič because this was the period of bureaucratic socialism, i.e. the state owned Kroj. That meant for Mr Primožič and his co-workers that not they, but the state, received the profits. In 1952, workers' councils were introduced, and the system of self-management began. Kroj was no longer state owned, but socially owned, placed under the trusteeship of its workers. They now received the profits, rather than the state, or some remote group of capital owners, or the general manager.

Through self-financing and short-term credits, Kroj gradually grew to an industrial enterprise. In 1958, it gave employment to about 50 workers and started to be big enough to accept large commissions to produce uniforms for the Yugoslav railways, the military etc.

Today, Kroj has 310 workers, 85 per cent of whom are women. More than 100 have been with the company for more than 15 years. For 10 years of uninterrupted service, they are rewarded with the obligatory watch.

Labour turnover is fairly low. Over the last two and a half years only 30 employees left the company. This was when a new company opened up in the area. They were not dissatisfied; they left because the distance to their new site of employment was considerably shorter. During the same period, about 100 additional workers were hired, an indication of the continued expansion of the company.

At first glance, a visit to the plant gives a picture in no way different from companies of the same type in West Germany or the United States. Yet there are fundamental differences. Kroj is owned and run by the producers, i.e. workers, not by outside capital owners or their executives.

What does it mean that the company is run by the workers? Being raised in a capitalist economy and having worked myself in capitalist companies, it appeared obvious that the company couldn't possibly be run by all 310 workers. However, it turned out that it was.

The highest organ of decision-making was the workers' council, *delavski svet*, which comprised 15 members during the time of my visit. I immediately suspected that this was an elitist group which nominally represents the workers but in reality is not different from the management board elsewhere. Again I was wrong. The members of the workers' council are elected by the workers for one or two years. In order to prevent the formation of an élitist group and to ensure at least some rotation, immediate re-election is not possible after the expiration of the terms of office but only after a minimum of two years. Mr Primožič estimates that at most 20 per cent of the workers were never elected to the workers' council. As almost everybody has his turn, it seems justified to say that the company is indeed run by the workers.

Women make up 85 per cent of the workforce of Kroj. Is the proportion of women in the workers' council equally high? Smiles on the faces of my informers, an animated discussion in Slovenian following for a few minutes. The women's question was apparently of concern in Yugoslavia too. No, I was told, the proportion of women in the workers' council is somewhat lower: 'only' about 70 per cent. Why?

The workers' council meets after work and its members are not compensated for their work. Many women simply do not have the time for that additional work input as they have two jobs: one in the factory and one at home. That means men do not do their share of housework even though their wives work?

This is changing, Mr Primožič explained: The older men do not help their wives, but the younger ones do. Among the younger generation, equality among the sexes is not only becoming a reality in terms of equal work opportunities and equal pay for equal work, but also in terms of equal shares of housework.

I did not give up yet, however, in my attempt to discover sexism. Who is president of the workers' council: a man or a woman?

A man now, but the preceding president was a woman. That satisfied me, at least for the time being.

Back to my question about leadership in the company. How can a workers' council with more or less rotating membership run a company, i.e. manage a company in its daily details?

There are four organs in which special leadership functions are vested:

the workers' council, *delavski svet*;
the managing board, *poslovni odbor*;
the management, *izvršilni organi*;
the general manager, *direktor*.

While the collective of all workers, from the lowest paid unskilled worker to the general manager, acts as a kind of trustee of the company, which is 'socially' owned and shares the profits, it vests the highest and ultimate decision-making power in its representative body, the workers' council, *delavski svet*. The 15 members of the workers' council meet as need arises, usually monthly or bi-monthly. The range of topics discussed and decisions made is almost unlimited, prominent issues being decisions about one- and five-year plans, investments, bye-laws and personal incomes. As the workers' council meets too infrequently to take care of all business details and as it may in fact not be technically competent to do so, it elects a managing board, *poslovni odbor*, of seven members from among those it judges technically most competent and trustworthy: be they members of the management, the workers' council, or 'ordinary' workers. Workers from production are most likely to be elected as they are more familiar with the daily business routine. The general manager is a member *ex officio*. President of the managing board is presently the technical manager who is elected for two years. His terms as president of the managing board can be extended to a maximum period of four years. The managing board is in charge of all routine decisions concerning production planning, personnel, discipline, accounts etc., and of preparing resolutions to be discussed by the workers' council—which is, of course, in no way limited in the range of its decisions by the suggestions of the managing board. Any details the managing board needs are to be supplied by the management.

The management, *izvršilni organi*, is the executive organ; it carries out the decisions of the workers' council and of the managing board. In Kroj, the management consists of four members: the general manager, the sales manager, the technical manager, and the controller. They all may be present at the meeting of the workers' council though they cannot vote unless they are members. The general manager cannot be a member of the workers' council, but the other three executives can. As a matter of fact the sales manager and the technical manager are presently members of the workers' council. All three managers are professionals with long experience and special training. The sales manager has been in leading sales positions for thirteen years. Before he joined Kroj, he was in charge of national sales in another company in the neighbourhood. He has a degree in economics and an advanced degree in administration. The technical manager has a degree in economics and an advanced degree in textile engineering. He was previously textile engineer in another company. The controller, a woman incidentally, has a diploma in economics and is presently studying toward her M. A.

in economics. She was controller for the Škofja Loka commune before she came to Kroj.

The management meets weekly or bi-weekly; when necessary more frequently. It is of course in very close contact with the managing board, communication between the two being greatly facilitated by the fact that the general manager and the technical manager are members of both bodies.

The present general manager of Kroj has been in that position since 1946 when he founded the company. This is however not a lifelong position. Every four years, his position is declared vacant and advertised in the new media. The advertisement specifies of course what qualifications prospective applicants must have. The workers' council selects a search committee which chooses the two or three applicants it judges most competent and presents a list to the workers' council. The workers' council elects the director then by secret ballot. This procedure is the same for the other managers, except that the vote is not by secret ballot. If the present general manager is not re-elected, he receives his salary for an additional six months even if he chooses to leave the company, which most general managers who fail to be re-elected, prefer to a lower position in the same company.

In case of conflict or dissent between these various bodies, the workers' council has the highest authority. If the managing board and the management disagree on some issue, however, the workers' council normally does not step in as it does not consider itself technically competent to solve problems of a purely technical nature. In such a case, the workers' council forms a committee which re-examines the issue and brings it to a final decision. The same procedure is followed whenever the managing board, the management, the general manager, or the workers' council makes use of its right of veto.

In its organizational structure, Yugoslav industry is apparently highly democratic. Power is not vested in a few who have inherited that power, or who have monopolized it on account of their political influence, or of their special training. Rather, power is vested in the collective, in all workers, who delegate their power to their representatives who may delegate it further to more specialized bodies. The effectiveness of all these bodies and their members is in some aspects constantly, and in others periodically, controlled and re-assessed. Is it not very dangerous however, to vest all power in the workers? Will they not 'eat up' their factories as they have the right do distribute profits and may, in fact, chose not to re-invest?

Is there a contradiction between efficiency and democracy? One may assume that conventionally industry is founded on the assumption of the inherent inefficiency of democratic procedures in industry and that this is the reason for the powerlessness of workers and the basically autocratic, or at least hierarchical, power structure of industry in most parts of the world. Yugoslav industry has a democratic structure. Is it, therefore, inefficient?

For an answer to that question, one may look at the statistics of profits and of growth and they are quite impressive. One certainly cannot infer from these statistics that industrial democracy in Yugoslavia is inefficient. But how is it possible for a system of industrial democracy to be efficient?

Mr Primožič suggested six reasons:

(1) It is the whole collective of workers that votes, and they elect only those in whom they have confidence, whom they trust to be qualified to take care of the interests of all. As workers know their fellow workers and their competencies better than anyone else—because they observe each other daily in all aspects pertaining to work—they have a good chance of selecting those who are qualified.

(2) In an enterprise with continuity, workers are trained by daily experience; everyone has the problems of the company 'at his fingertips'. Work experience is an exceedingly important factor.

(3) From elementary school on, workers are prepared for their roles of responsibility. As adults, they receive continuing training in self-administration at workers' universities.

(4) The workers' council may invite experts to its meetings whenever it feels itself not sufficiently competent to judge on an issue;

(5) The real decision making structures are extremely flexible and take into account that leadership is a highly diffuse phenomenon. Depending on each one's relative competence, contributions to the decision-making process may be elicited from all quarters. This flexibility, together with the built-in system of mutual controls as expressed in the various veto-rights, tends to make maximum use of the diverse talents and competencies in all major and minor decisions.

(6) The fact that profits are redistributed is a strong incentive for every individual and every council, board and committee to seek for efficiency, i.e. to let those who are most competent rather than those in rigidly defined positions contribute to decisions. The income and security of every worker depend directly on the efficiency of the company, and all decisions pertain ultimately to their own company. Hence their interest in the rationality of decisions, an interest that is frequently absent in centrally administered economies as in the Soviet Union, where the capital is owned by the state, and in privately owned companies as in the United States, where the capital is owned by remote shareholders.

In Mr Primožič's company, these arguments may explain its economic success. In 1972, the personal incomes of the workers increased by 29 per cent.

In the first years of self-administration, distributable profits were determined two or four times a year and then paid to each worker in a lump sum. Today, profits are computed monthly and added to each pay cheque.

Choosing June 1973 as an example, the average base wage was 1750 dinars (net) that month. In addition to his base wage, each worker received the 60 dinars as food allowance.

All except new employees received an allowance of 10 dinars for continued service, and an additional 50 dinars were paid to those who were always on time and never missed a day during that month. These allowances may thus bring the average base wage up to 1870 dinars. In June 1973, the rate of distributable profits, which of course varies from month to month, was 16 per cent. This brings the wage of the average worker up to 2170 dinars.

All jobs in the company are evaluated by the REFA system. A point value is assigned to each position in the company, which is then converted into dinars.

By Western standards, the range of wages is relatively small in Yugoslavia, the national average being approximately 1:4 for the ratio between highest and lowest income.

Kroj is very close to that national average. The lowest-paid worker, a janitor, has a monthly wage of about 1100 dinars; the highest-paid worker, the general manager, 5500 dinars.

The general manager indicated that there has been a recent

trend towards more equality and that there is a tendency for the ratio between lowest and highest wage to change towards 1:3.

ALPLEZ

We left Kroj and continued our trip up the valley. The road became narrower and narrower, winding through little hamlets and densely wooded mountains. After about twenty minutes, the valley widened and made room for a large complex of factory and office buildings: Alplez, a furniture factory with its own saw mill.

Alplez was originally a cooperative enterprise. Its beginnings date back to 1937 when some of the owners of the surrounding woods joined together and formed a forestry cooperative with the purpose of buying a saw, hiring four to five workers to saw their logs and marketing the wood cooperatively.

With the German invasion in 1941, business came to a halt. In 1945, the cooperative was re-established, this time on a much larger scale and with some difference in structure. The new cooperative comprised now about 300 forest-owners and about 150 workers; in the pre-war cooperative, the workers were not members of the cooperative. Later the cooperative started to process its own wood, and eventually, the production of furniture became its main activity. With the new law on self-administration, the workers started to take things into their own hands and decided they were better off with separating the cooperative of forest-owners from manufacturing and formed an independent industrial company: Alplez.

Today Alplez has about 700 workers of which half are women. In terms of finished products, it produces mainly living-room furniture. In terms of half-finished products, it manufactures loudspeakers, radio and television boxes and the like, some of which are used by an electronics company next door. When I visited Alplez, it had just finished a major consignment of loudspeaker boxes for export to the United States.

At Alplez I was to talk to the president of the workers' council. We had to wait for a few minutes as he had to be called from his work-place in the plant. Meanwhile we chatted with our host, a woman in her fifties who was in charge of one of the departments in the administration.

Alplez is ruled by a workers' council with 31 members, eight of whom are women; by a managing board of nine; a management of six, including the general manager. Of the nine members of the managing board, four are also members of the workers' council, three are members of the management and two are outside experts who are employees of another furniture factory. Of the six members of the management, none is in the workers' council. The management is not elected. Vacant management positions are publicly advertised. The applicants are screened by a search committee determined by the workers' council. The search committee comes up with a list of candidates and the workers' council chooses one, by secret ballot in the case of the general manager, in an open vote in the case of other executives. If a member of the management proves to be incapable, he may be asked by the workers' council to resign. This, however, has never happened yet as the candidates are most carefully selected, as our host pointed out. Contracts for the general manager are for four-year periods, contracts for other managers for two. If managers perform satisfactorily, the advertisement of the position every two or four years, respectively, seems to be a formality; the advertisement does in fact specify whether the position is really vacant or whether it is a matter of re-appointment. The members of the management in Alplez have been in their present positions for periods of between nine and fourteen years.

This process of periodical re-appointment through the workers' council puts considerable power into the hands of the workers, and I wondered if the longevity of the present management was because of proven competency or because of good personal relations with the members of the workers' council. And, more precisely, how important is it for managers to be popular? I was told that good 'human relations' between individual managers and workers or members of the workers' council are important, but that competence and skill—in short, achievement—are pivotal.

Suppose a manager is highly qualified and does an excellent job technically speaking, I hypothesized, but is at the same time unpopular. How will the workers' council act when his re-appointment is up? How much weight will it give to each of the two dimensions? Put in such terms, my informant was quite sure that only competency would matter and that popularity would be irrelevant in this case.

The door opened and Lovro Gajgar, president of the workers'

council, *predsednik delavskega sveta*, came in: a tall man, lean but muscular, half bald, the remaining hair greyish, a wide-open, teasing grin on his face. Just as any other worker, he was wearing a blue overall that showed clearly visible marks of manual labour. If anyone may be called the most powerful man in Alplez, it is Lovro Gajgar, yet no status symbol of any kind indicated that power, and in his own eyes there is, in fact, no 'most powerful man' in the company. His presidency does not confer any monarchical power, unlike some democratic systems in other societies.

Lovro Gajgar is 46 years old, married, 'of course', as he said, with three children. His oldest son, who is 24, works also for Alplez. He worked during the day and went to the workers' university at night where he took technical courses and recently got a technical degree. Mr Gajgar also has a 20 year-old daughter, who is enrolled in a teachers' training college, and an 18 year-old daughter who is becoming a trained saleswoman. We saw her later when we toured the plant: thin as her father, with big glasses, she had a vacation job with Alplez, I was told. Mr Gajgar's wife is at home; she makes lace, for which the area is famous.

Mr Gajgar has been with Alplez for 21 years. He received his elementary school education before the war. He joined the army and remained active as a non-commissioned officer until 1952. In 1952 he joined Alplez where he was a boilerman for 10 years. During that period, he took courses at the workers' university, and when he obtained his diploma as a mechanic, he became head of the heating plant. He continued to take courses, and since 1964 he has been in charge of machine maintenance. His career seems to have been based on hard work, job-related training, skill and experience: a typical 'achiever'.

Since November 1971, Mr Gajgar has been president of the workers' council. His term expires this year (1973) in November, and he cannot be re-elected. He has been president of the workers' council once before, namely from 1967 to 1969. He became a member of the workers' council for the first time in 1956, four years after he had joined the company. Since then he has been a member on and off, serving for a total of about eight years on the workers' council. Continued service is of course not possible because of the law on rotation.

I wanted to know why Mr Gajgar thought he was elected president of the workers' council. He had always been socially and politically interested, he explained, and he had been active in Alplez and in other organizations. For instance, he was a member of the town council of Škofja Loka, of the Veterans Association, from 1958 to 1962 he was trade union secretary for Alplez and after that secretary of the trade union federation of Škofja Loka until he became president of the workers' council. The fact that he had been with the company for a long time and knew it inside out was of some importance too but it was not decisive. What was more important is that he was outspoken at meetings, came up with convincing arguments, was reliable, honest and hard-working.

What is the most important of all these criteria? 'His work, the quality of his work and his competence in all matters pertaining to the work process', he replied immediately, and the other informants added that this was, generally speaking, the most important criterion for such a position.

How influential is the workers' council president? How much power does he have? Mr Gajgar thinks he does not have more power than the other members; he is a *primus inter pares* who prepares and organizes meetings, coordinates and moderates. Technical information may be elicited from any member as well as from non-members, and any member may contribute to the final decision. If he has any extra power, it is quite informal and based on his objective competence rather than on the authority of his position.

Decisions are taken by vote. The mode of election is specified by the statutes of the company; if left unspecified, it depends on the problem whether a simple majority is sufficient or whether a two-thirds majority is necessary. In most cases, however, issues are decided by simple majority.

As the working hours are from 6 a.m. to 2 p.m. for production workers and from 7 a.m. to 2 p.m. for office workers, my first day of interviews ended shortly after 2 p.m. It was concluded by a sumptuous dinner in a small cosy inn further up the valley, surrounded by densely wooded mountains once the centre of resistance against the German occupation, as Lojze Malovrh proudly pointed out.

TOZ

TOZ is a company in Zagreb, the capital of Croatia, which produces pens, pencils and similar utensils. It took Ivan Šifter, the general manager of TOZ, a while to warm up when I visited the company on 9 August 1973. It turned out later that this was apparently a model factory. He had seen some fifty delegations and seemed somewhat tired, but as the discussion carried on and the customary libations of Turkish coffee, soda water, cognac and fruit juice were served, he apparently forgot his fatigue.

TOZ has a gross income per man of 95,000 dinars per year, and the net personal income per employee averages, presently, 2380 dinars per month. The value of the production per man and year was 30,000 dinars in 1965 and is projected to be 230,000 dinars in 1973—compared to an average of 90,000 for Croatia in 1973. The annual growth rate of TOZ has been 31 per cent, about six times the federal average. The company has accumulated 26 million dinars in funds. In 1970, TOZ moved into new premises which had been built entirely through self-financing, without any credit.

On 1 December 1958, the system of basic organizations of associated labour was introduced, i.e. the factory was divided into self-contained departments or production units, each with its own workers' council (OOUR).

'This system was introduced', Mr Šifter said, 'because we had production and sales problems. There was a real crisis. The new system did what it was supposed to do: it increased production and lowered prices.'

The company consists now of seven OOURs: OOUR I to VII.

The total company has 523 workers, 65 per cent of whom are women. The units of associated labour differ in size and so do their workers' councils: Each has between 10 and 30 members.

The workers' council of the company has 50 members, 70 per cent of whom are women. Out of eight presidents of the workers' council, five are women. Each OOUR has its own workers' council. Professionally, it is run by its manager and the section heads. Each unit is economically independent and calculates its own results, profitability etc. Five criteria have to be fulfilled before an OOUR can be formed:

(1) it has to be a technological whole;
(2) an economic whole;
(3) a self-management unit;
(4) an organizational whole; and
(5) a personnel unit with its own functional hierarchy.

The company is run by:

(1) a general manager;
(2) the management, consisting of 11 members, including the general manager;
(3) the workers' council; and
(4) the workers' control committee.

There is no managing board as the workers' council decided that its existence was superfluous.

Most of the power is vested in the OOURs, and within these in the workers' collective. As it is too large to be effective in detail, it delegates most of its functions to the workers' council.

The workers' collective in the OOURs decides on purchasing, planning and other major issues. All major decisions are made by the workers' collective. It meets every three months, as a rule, though more often when there is need for it. During the last six months actually it met 10 times.

The workers' council meets at least once a month; in fact, it met 15 times during the last six months.

In Western opinion, meetings are a waste of time, but this is a matter of attitude. Mr Šifter explained:

First of all, our workers are well-prepared when they come to meetings. Technical details are submitted by professionals. Final decisions are made by the workers' council, except in the case of major issues when the workers' collective is called upon. We found out that the sales department is the most crucial of all, therefore we give a 7.5 per cent commission on all sales to the sales department as an incentive.

In 1972, 34 suggestions for innovations and rationalizations were submitted and accepted. This saved us 1,770,000 dinars and we paid about 100,000 dinars as incentives. This does not cause any envy: on the contrary, everyone realizes that these innovations are for the benefit of all. The largest amount we paid to any one individual last year was 15,000 dinars, plus a car. We have an annual competition: the worker who contributes the biggest saving with the longest-lasting value receives a car as a special prize: a Fiat 750. The car arrives by the end of August, sits on a stand for several months tempting the workers to be innovative, and is eventually turned over in

January. The car is actually given for a composite achievement: for the biggest saving, originality, its lasting value and for technological innovativeness.'

Pay in TOZ is according to work and the director says: 'We fight hard against the egalitarian system.'

There are some other amenities for workers: a restaurant where two meals are served—one for two and one for three dinars—and a swimming pool.

While piped music comes through the door from the next room flooding at the same time the office block and the whole company with 'O happy day . . . ', Mr Šifter analyzes some of the main dimensions of productivity in TOZ.

Human relations: In the West, human relations are built on the authority of management or on capital. Here, authority is based on work. This puts certain requirements on the management: the improvement of human relations without petty privileges.

'As a general manager, I have been here for 23 years, every single day from six to two, without ever being late. Everything as public as the company is run by the collective of workers. This applies of course also to the salary structure. We have achieved very much with self-management.'

'*Being informed* is one of our main principles. We have about 12 to 14 major communications channels, among them a factory newspaper and a loudspeaker system where everyone, the general manager as well as any worker, can go on the air at any time and make an announcement, express a complaint, or talk about anything he wants to.'

The general manager recalls how once a group of workers had decided to go to the centre and make an announcement, among them a stammerer. He was teased by his fellow workers that he would never get his message out considering the way he stammered. As a matter or fact he concentrated very hard and brought his message out without stammering and, as a result, he had lost his stammer. The miracles of self-management!

Production is stimulated in a number of ways:

(1) The output of a worker is evaluated in points.
(2) The value of these points becomes known when the product is sold.
(3) There are incentives for technical innovation.

(4) The level of income and of liquidity of the company influences the worker's income.

(5) The best worker in each unit gets a special bonus, e.g. 100 dinars, which may be only symbolic, plus a flag, which certainly is purely symbolic. In addition, he is interviewed by the factory newspaper and his picture appears in it: he becomes a star.

(6) There is a vacation allowance of 50 dinars per day.

(7) If a worker is disabled within six years of his retirement date, he continues to receive his full pay.

(8) The worker is stimulated to continue to stay with the company as long as possible, by receiving a 5 per cent increase after 5 years etc.

(9) There is a retirement bonus, equal to 6 months' salary.

(10) Retired workers receive an annual allowance of up to 1000 dinars, plus 400 dinars as a vacation allowance.

Mr Šifter does not think highly of sociologists, but he thinks the more developed an economy, the more important is sociology.

'If an economist would prove to you that capitalism is more profitable than self-management, would you change to capitalism?'

'No.'

About the new constitution which was to go into effect in October 1973 (and actually did in the spring of 1974) he said:

We are fighting for the "productive attitude". There still prevails a political attitude of giving people rights without duties. The social-economic attitude is to make workers think both how to produce and how to use the money.

In that respect, the new constitution represents a great step forward. This company has progressed already very far towards the new constitution: that's why we are considered a showpiece.

BRATSTVO

Bratstvo is a machine factory in Zagreb which I visited on Thursday, 9 August 1973. It started its operation in 1935. Today it has about 500 workers. It consists of three semi-independent parts, each known as a 'unit of associated labour': machine

production, service department and administration and marketing. Each of these units is run by its own workers' council.

The company as a whole is run by five organs:

(1) The general manager.

(2) The management, consisting of the general manager and
an additional six managers who are all professionals; each is the
head of a department.

(3) The managing board, which consists of six members, two
from each unit of associated labour. No managers are represented on the management board though they may sit in without
voting rights.

(4) The workers' council, which comprises 21 members,
seven from each unit of associated labour.

(5) The workers' control committee, *radnička kontrola*, with
three members, one from each unit of associated labour.

A sixth body has to be added to the list which is in fact the most
important: the workers' collective which is the ultimate authority
and makes decisions of a major scope.

Of these organs, the workers' control committee is of recent
origin; it was introduced in 1972. The three members are
delegated by the workers' council to which they report. Their
main function is one of control, mainly over the director.

One of the members of the workers' control committee is an
assembly worker, one is an electrician and one is an office worker
in the supply department. They are chosen for their personal
independence, for their ability to have their own standpoint and
fight for it, for their honesty and discipline, for their good
relations with fellow workers and for their ability to
communicate. When elected they may not be qualified for their
new function as 'controllers'; but once on the job they learn it.
They start with areas which they understand—production, the
plan and discipline—and from there they will expand their area of
competence.

Why was workers' control introduced? The workers in this
company felt that management had too much influence over
issues decided by the workers' council and by the managing
board. They introduced, therefore, an additional body whose
only function was to check that influence.

The general manager feels they are, in Yugoslavia, in a

situation in which the influence of those in bureaucratic power is still too strong.

'For such key people in managerial positions, in the party, or in trade unions, we use the word *vrhuška* which is Russian for "president": being Russian indicates that it stands for something negative. In this company, we had not really broken their influence. Therefore we created this additional committee: to break that influence.'

It did not seem to bother the general manager that he was talking about himself simultaneously as someone whose influence was too strong and was to be broken, and of someone who was engaged in the attempt to break it. But then he added: 'But I believe we won't break it. It is too deeply engrained in our culture, our civilization, or state of mind, our consciousness.'

I asked him about the efficiency–participation dilemma. He explained: 'Yes, management usually knows best, but it is nothing without the cooperation of the workers. It may understand things better, but then it is just like war: if someone runs out alone, he will be killed. All have to run out at the same speed.'

In most companies in Yugoslavia, the work week is five days. In Bratstvo, it is six days. The workers decided to work without additional compensation for six days a week to be able to afford some new investments that would of course give them higher incomes in the future. When the matter came to a vote, only the six managers were against the six-day week. But now they come on Saturdays too, out of solidarity. With reference to the managers and others who may have dissented, the general manager added:

In the mass, nobody has enough courage to be against something good.

By law every factory must reward innovators. In the olden days people were envious of innovators because of their higher income. As a consequence, many people held back not to arouse envy. The assumption was if someone got a bigger piece of the cake his neighbour would get a smaller one. But this notion is changing now. We all know that we can make the cake bigger, and everyone gets bigger pieces. As a consequence, the attitude to innovations has been changing.

We in this factory also realize that we badly need certain types of experts. We have changed our statutes so that some experts now receive higher wages than the general manager. This is not opposed by the workers because they realize they will ultimately gain from it.

The system of seniority allowances is not strongly developed. After a total number of 10 working years, both inside and outside this company, a worker receives one *average* monthly wage, i.e. the general manager and an unskilled worker receive the same amount. After 15 years, the allowance is one-and-a-half times the monthly wage, after 20 years twice and after 25 years two-and-a-half times.

The ratio between lowest and highest monthly income is about 1:4. In June, the lowest wage was 1150 dinars net; the general manager received 4600 dinars, which was slightly less than the amount that some experts were paid.

The general manager thinks wages are relatively low in this company. He explains that this is because of their fight for modernizing and expanding the plant. I asked if the brain drain was any problem. 'No, it is no problem for this company. About five years ago, some workers left for Germany.' But the general manager sees some positive aspects. They will learn something; they will make enough money to build a house or solve some of their other economic problems so that we don't have to do that and they will eventually return. Nobody is irreplaceable, anyway.

ALHOS

Alhos is a garment factory in Sarajevo, the capital of Bosnia Herzegovina, one of the less-developed republics of Yugoslavia. I was received by the general manager, the president of the central workers' council and the presidents of the workers' councils of the seven basic organizations of associated labour.

Alhos started in 1948 as a small workshop in a rented building. Today it has 1600 employees, 70 per cent of which are women, in five units of production—three in Sarajevo and two outside Sarajevo. An additional textile factory with about 600 workers had been acquired early in 1973. This brings the total number of workers to 2200. In addition, there is a tailoring shop and a trade unit with 70 retail stores all over Yugoslavia and several wholesale stores.

Today, the Combine Alhos comprises seven OOURs, excluding the newly purchased textile factory which will add an additional four OOURs when integrated.

The central workers' council has 32 members, 13 of whom are women. The same reason was given for the relatively small number of women in the workers' council: as workers and housewives, they have relatively little time to spend on extra commitments like membership in workers' councils or committees.

All major issues are decided upon by the workers' collectives in each one of the OOURs. The central workers' council deals mainly with general policy questions. There is also a business board with two members from each OOUR and one from the central workers' council, i.e. with a total number of 15 members.

Three months before the interview, a workers' control committee was introduced which consisted of seven members, one delegate from each of the OOURs' control committees. The presidents of the OOURs' workers' councils are present at the meetings of the workers' control committee, but they have no voting rights. On the level of the basic organizations of OOUR, all major issues are decided upon by the workers' collective. Less important questions are dealt with by the workers' council of each OOUR. Each workers' council has between five and seven members. In addition, there are several committees, like the workers' control committee, a standard of living committee, a recreation committee.

Basic personal incomes average approximately 1500 dinars per month. The lowest income is 1200 dinars, the highest 5500. The head of a basic organization of OOUR makes approximately 3000 dinars. Through hard work and extra hours, a worker may greatly increase his basic personal income. It was pointed out, for example, that a worker whose base income is 1500 dinars may earn actually more than 2500 dinars.

Profits are calculated on a monthly basis and add approximately 5 per cent to the monthly income. In previous years workers received a vacation allowance. No such allowance was paid in 1973 because profits were too low.

Workers may receive seniority allowances of between 50 and 200 dinars per month. After five years of service, a worker receives a salary increment of 0.5 per cent, after ten years of 1.0 per cent and so on, up to a maximum increment of 2 per cent which he reaches after twenty years of service.

There is a solidarity fund for those who have worked at least twenty years and have become less productive because of advanced age. Through what is being called norm correction, a worker may receive up to 40 per cent of his income as a compensation for his loss of income due to advanced age.

There is a medical recreation programme through which workers may be sent at the company's expense to a recreation home, with salary payments continued. In the company canteen, food can be purchased for six or seven dinars. Workers with monthly incomes up to 1200 dinars receive allowances of 3 dinars per day; workers with incomes above 1200 and up to 1700 dinars receive allowances of 2.50 dinars.

There is a standing disciplinary commission which is elected for two years. It operates on two levels. On each level there are three members elected by the workers' council. A worker may be reported by the head of his basic organization of OOUR to the disciplinary commission for offences that are classified as slight, such as being late; medium, for fighting; or serious, for physical damage to factory property, or unexcused absence for three or more days. The commission summons the worker and two witnesses and passes judgement. A worker may appeal and have his case referred to a second-level disciplinary commission which reports to the basic organization of associated labour which then has the final word.

'Yugoslavia's model is the first of its kind', one of the workers' councils' presidents reports, 'so we have no one to look to for guidance. We are trying hard. We have a critical view, and so we are improving our model'. The Workers' Amendments to the Constitution have brought several improvements: each OOUR has now its own council, trade union, youth organization and Communist Party units.

'About 75 per cent of the production goes to West Germany; we supply department stores.'

Alhos has its monthly newspaper. 'All the workers controllers' is the title of a recent article in that paper introducing the workers' control committees.

A number of questions were asked by the presidents of workers' councils. They focused on workers' power in the US, not about income and money.

Although Yugoslav companies are on a five day week schedule, workers at Alhos work six days a week, seven hours a day: a decision of the OOURs. Only the administration works five days a week, eight hours a day. As the majority of workers are women, it is more convenient for them to have a shorter working day.

What was most striking in these interviews was the gradual discovery of a system of distributing authority in industry which is the reverse of the conventional system. In both cases, the distribution of authority can be illustrated by a pyramid. At the bottom of the pyramid are the workers; at the top is the general manager, director or president. In the United States or West Germany, all authority is vested in the top of the pyramid; some of that authority is then delegated towards the bottom of the pyramid, being more and more diluted as it approaches the base, until it is virtually nil when it actually reaches the base. In Yugoslavia, all authority is vested in the base of the pyramid; some of it is then delegated up towards the top of the pyramid. These are, of course, *formal* models of distributing *authority* in a company. This means they tell a great deal about the structure and the decision-making processes in a company, but not everything. In the United States, e.g. workers acquire and exercise *power* by organizing in unions. In Yugoslavia, the general manager has *influence* (or 'bureaucratic authority' as Max Weber would have put it) by virtue of his professional competence. We will discuss this in much more detail later.

But what was almost as striking as this discovery was the virtually total openness and frankness with which questions were answered and detailed data about income, investments, profits, terms of loans, production plans, etc. were revealed. I have done research in dozens of companies in other countries: in the United States, in West Germany, in Nigeria and in Liberia. In all these companies and countries, there were certain issues that were taboo: 'business secrets'. I did not encounter a single business secret in Yugoslavia. Whenever I cared to know I was given, for example, wage lists with the incomes of every single employee, from the janitor to the general manager—including information about any additional allowances they received and their share of profits.

'We have nothing to hide', explained a discussant once when I expressed surprise about this openness. In an interview with a group of presidents of workers' councils, one of them who had visited companies in the United States apparently felt he had to explain to his colleagues that this frankness was not universal.

'In America, these would be business secrets', he said, 'but we are open, maybe too open. We want to demonstrate to the world that there is nothing to hide. We want them to come and learn as much about our system of self-management as they want to learn.'

5 The Structure of Self-Management

Under self-management, the organizational set-up of business has become very complex. Vertically, the number of steps and levels of decision-making and of authority have been increasing; at the same time, lateral divisions have been expanding. The structure of self-management is contingent upon the size of a company; there are one-tier, two-tier and three-tier structures. In small and simple companies, self-management is organized on one single level; in medium-size companies on two levels and in large companies on three levels (Table 5.1).

TABLE 5.1 The structure of self-management

Level	Small companies	Medium Companies	Large companies
First level	Workers' council Board of management General manager	Workers' council Board of management General manager	Workers' council Board of management General manager
Second level		Workers' council of work units Boards of management of work units	Workers' council of plants Boards of management of plants
Third level			Workers council of plant work units Boards of management of plant work units

SOURCE
Burt (1972, p. 143).

In companies with up to 30 workers, self-management is carried out on one level: directly and exclusively through the work collective, i.e. the whole body of workers. Every member is a worker, representative and manager. In 1972, there were 1611 companies in which workers managed directly. Self-management in these companies involved 42,123 workers, 11,687 of them women. There were 7617 workers active in various self-management committees, so-called collegial organs (Statistical Yearbook, 1973, p. 77).

In two-tier companies, self-management is carried out on the first or company level and on the second or work unit (basic organization of associated labour) level. On the company level, the structure of self-management comprises:

the work collective;
the workers' council;
auxiliary bodies of the workers' council; and
the board of management.

On the work unit level, self-management is carried out by:

the workers' assembly;
the work unit workers' council;
the board of management of the work unit.

TABLE 5.2 Self-management in basic organizations of associated labour (OOUR)

	Two-level companies	Three-level companies	All companies
Number of companies	1120	113	1233
Number of work units	8823	3423	12246
Number of work units which elect councils	6310	2480	8790
Council members	72179	32332	104511
Number of work units in which workers manage directly	2513	943	3456
Members of working communities	75859	51736	127595

SOURCE
Statistical Yearbook (1973, p. 78).

In 1972, there were 6130 companies (including three-tier companies) in which workers elected workers' councils. The total number of members of workers' councils during that year was 135,171, of which 22,775 were women. An additional 54,156 workers were active in collegial organs, 6817 of them women (Statistical Yearbook, 1973, p. 77).

Self-management is decentralized in work units, the so-called basic organizations or OOUR; each of them is a relatively independent economic unit, interrelated with all other units of course to form the larger entity, the company. In 1972, there were 1233 companies that were structurally divided into work units. The total number of work units in these companies was 12,246 (Table 5.2).

The primary institution through which direct self-management is carried out is the work collective, i.e. the entirety of the workers of an organization. This was the result of changes initiated during the economic reform of 1965. Only two years earlier, the organs of self-management were certain bodies representing the workers, as specified in Article 90 of the constitution of 1963:

In exercising self-management in their work organizations, working people shall entrust . . . certain managerial powers to the bodies of their work organization: the workers' council, the board of management and the director, or to some other body of management.

To be sure, 'Members of the workers' council shall be elected by the working people directly' (Article 92), and in that respect, the workers' collective did have power, but only the power to delegate. It was left to the workers' council to 'adopt the bye-laws and other general rules of the work organization, lay down its work and development plans, and decide on other general matters', and it was up to the board of management, to 'be elected by the workers' council and/or the work community', to 'decide on matters concerning the running of the work organization' (Article 92). The general manager of a work organization, called director, was supposed to 'run its business, execute the decisions of the workers' council and other bodies of management, and . . . represent the organization' (Article 93, The Constitution, 1969, pp. 69–71). After the economic reform of 1965, all these provisions were changed, and in 1967 these changes became part of the Constitution as amendment xv:

> Exercising self-management in work organizations as a whole and in organizations of associated labour making part of the former, working people shall determine matters on which they can decide directly, and shall entrust specific functions of management to workers' councils or, according to the nature of the activity of the work organization concerned, to another appropriate organ of management, and shall entrust specific executive functions to bodies and individuals responsible to this organ of management and elected by the workers' council.
>
> Working people in work organizations shall determine the organs of management of their work organizations, specify their province of work and tenure, and shall lay down conditions for and the mode of their election and removal.
>
> A special procedure and mode of appointment and removal of individuals entrusted with executive prerogatives in organizations conducting affairs of special social concern may be laid down by statute. (The Constitution, 1969, pp. 188–9)

Major decisions concerning the whole company or the basic organization of associated labour as a whole are now made by the workers' collective. Decisions about medium-level business matters are entrusted by the workers to the workers' council. For all practical purposes, one may say that the workers' collective largely operates through the workers' council.

In companies with up to 30 employees, there is no workers' council and all managerial decisions are made by the workers as a collective. Companies with 31 to 70 employees may decide not to elect a workers' council and run their business affairs in the same direct manner as in smaller companies. The workers in such companies have to lay down in their company statutes whether or not there should be a workers' council.

The workers' council is elected by universal suffrage through secret ballot. Any member who is on the electoral roll, except the general manager, may stand for election. Each company lays down in its statutes the terms of office of the members of its workers' council. Most statutes provide for a two-year term, and half the members of the council are elected each year. The workers' council decides on matters which have been placed under its competence by the statutes of the company. The council drafts the statutes and other general regulations, prepares development plans and programmes, adopts decisions on basic questions concerning business policy and the use of company funds, prepares the company balance-sheet, takes any decision concerning the amalgamation of companies and takes decisions on statutory matters—unless these, or some of these, decisions are made by the workers' collective by referendum.

The workers' council usually appoints auxiliary bodies which make decisions within a framework set by the council. Such auxiliary bodies are recruitment commissions for certain positions like general manager, or a discipline and complaints commission. In addition, the council may appoint expert committees for professional advice on important matters before the council. Examples for such matters are development plans, financial, commercial, personnel and social policies (Burt, 1972, p. 140).

The workers' council appoints a board of management as its executive body. The board of management is elected by the workers' council from among the members of the workers' collective. The workers serving on the board of management may, but do not have to be, members of the workers' council. Its size varies with the size of the company and the workers' council; it usually ranges between five and eleven. It is the general function of the board of management to direct the operation of the company. It prepares draft proposals for the statutes and other company regulations, it works out business plans and programmes and submits them to the workers' council. In some companies, the workers have decided to allocate certain functions to the board of management independently of the workers' council (Burt, 1972, pp. 140–1).

The *general manager*, usually called the director, of a company may be its most powerless and its most powerful worker. The theory of direct self-management vests all power in the workers and makes the general manager the executive organ of the workers, with no power of his own. With his direct access to information processes, however, and the technical-managerial staff, he may very well possess a considerable amount of *actual* power, or influence and turn out to be a genuine 'technocrat': a descriptive term—usually meant as an epithet in Yugoslavia— which mostly indicates that its bearer should be regarded with much suspicion. But this suspicion may in actuality be considerably reduced if that 'technocrat' turns out to be highly efficient in earning profits to be distributed, in part, among the workers.

The general manager is the only one in a company who participates in self-management *ex officio*. He is obliged to participate in the work of the workers' council but he has no vote in the council. The general manager runs the business of the company, executes the decisions of the workers' collective, the workers' council and the board of management, represents the company to the outside and performs any functions specified by the company statutes. While he is independent in his work, he is personally responsible to the workers and their organs of representation.

The general manager is elected by the workers' council every four years. The vacancy is publicly advertised. Reappointment is possible and frequent (Burt, 1972, pp. 134, 141).

Day-to-day business administration is in the hands of professional managers. Their daily routine is probably hardly different from that of their American colleagues. Under self-management, however, this managerial work is carried out in accordance with policies formulated and/or approved by the work collective and its representative organs, and the professional staff remains under their authority.

An important aspect of self-management is the adoption of general regulations like bye-laws or statutes. They are worked out by the workers' council or a special commission appointed by the council, discussed with the workers' collective and adopted by the workers' council. The statutes specify the rules and criteria for the apportionment of the company's total income between investment, reserves, workers' personal income and social overheads. They lay down the rules for the allocation of personal incomes, including the distribution of profits. They further contain provisions concerning vacation, disciplinary procedures, safety, health etc.

The most important components of a company are its work units, the basic organizations or OOUR. The essential criterion for the separation of a company into such work units is independence of cost-benefit analyses. Examples are production units like plants, workshops, design offices, auxiliary departments; examples for professional service units are research and development (R & D), book-keeping, marketing, personnel and social services.

The importance of these basic organizations of associated labour within the Yugoslav system of self-management cannot be emphasized strongly enough. They are the basic units of self-management. A lengthy constitutional amendment (Amendment XXI) has been devoted to these OOURs. They exist of course only in larger and more complex companies. Small companies may consist of just one unit, i.e. one OOUR. The most complex companies are those organized on three levels of self-management. According to Table 6.2 below, there are 113 such companies with a total of 3423 work units or OOURs; this amounts to an average of 30 work units per company. In 2480 of these work units, workers elect workers' councils; in the remaining 943 basic organizations of associated labour, workers manage directly.

As an example of such a three-tier organization, I will describe the structure of BOR, a copper mine in Serbia. (Interview with Neca Jovanov, trade union secretary, in Belgrade, on 14 August 1973.) BOR employs approximately 12,000 workers in three plants which are about 200 miles apart. Vertically, there are three levels of self-management:

the level of OOUR;
the level of *communities of associated labour* of which each
    comprises several OOURs; and the so-called *combinat*, i.e.
    the whole company.

On the first level, there are 29 OOURs (*radnički savet osnovne organizacije udruženog rada*), introduced in 1972. They are independent units of self-management, which in terms of the 'material base of self-management' means that they independently acquire and distribute income. Each OOUR has between 150 and 1500 members.

The most important bodies of decision-making are the workers' collective, the workers' council, several auxiliary commissions and the general manager.

The major decisions in each basic organization are made by the workers' collective. All major organizational decisions are made, if possible, by the workers in the OOUR; only decisions concerning the whole company are made by the workers' collective of the company as a whole.

The workers in each OOUR elect a workers' council which comprises between 11 and 25 members. According to the company statutes, the terms of office are two years, and nobody may be elected consecutively more than twice, i.e. for a maximum continuous period of four years. An individual may be re-elected after the expiration of his first two-year term, but the possibility of being re-elected is limited by the rule that two-thirds of the membership of the workers' council have to be newly elected in order to assure a certain magnitude of rotation of office.

By the company statutes, each OOUR could have an executive committee, but the workers decided they did not want one.

The workers' council forms several auxiliary commissions, the members of which are elected by the workers' council. In each OOUR there is a personnel commission, a work organization commission, a planning commission and a distribution of personal income commission.

Each OOUR has its director. His task is the execution of the decisions of the workers and of the workers' council to which he is responsible. His position is publicly advertised every four years, and a director is chosen from one of the applicants. A director in office may reapply when his position is advertised and there is no limit to the number of times he may be reappointed.

The second level of self-management is that of communities of associated labour (*zajćdnice osnovnih organizacija udruženog rada*). The 29 OOURs of BOR form three communities of associated labour of unequal size: one comprises 8, one 16, and one 5 OOURs. Each community deals with matters which are of relevance to the aggregate of basic organizations. The rights and tasks on that level, compared with the level of basic organizations, are considerably reduced.

Each community of associated labour has a workers' council to which each basic organization sends three delegates. The executive committee comprises delegates from the basic organizations, one from each. The director of the community of associated labour is elected for a four-year term. He cannot be a member of the workers' council, but he may be a member of the executive committee.

The third level of self-management is that of the combinat (*radnički savet kombinata*), i.e. the company as a whole. The highest degree of power is vested in the OOUR. The combinat deals only with matters that are of concern to the organization *in toto*.

The combinat's workers' council is based on the councils of the basic organizations which sends delegates to the combinat's council. These delegates do not have to be members of the workers' councils of the basic organizations. The combinat's workers' council comprises 83 members.

The executive committee consists of 29 members, one representative from each basic organization. An additional member is the general manager of BOR; he has full voting rights but cannot be chairman of the committee. No other members of the management are represented.

There is a so-called expert collegium without decision-making power. It is an executive body which exists only as an informal, not legally instituted, group.

There are two very important internal institutions. The first is the arbitration committee with seven members which deals with conflicts between basic organizations. This is an *ad-hoc* committee to which each one of the two disputing parties delegates three members; the seventh member is the chairman, chosen from a neutral basic organization.

The second internal institution is an internal bank: an expert service which circulates finances through the organization. Basic organizations may deposit funds in this internal bank and borrow money from it at the moderate rate of 3 per cent. Contacts between the company and outside monetary institutions are handled by the bank.

The general manager of the combinat is elected for a four-year term. Neither he nor his deputy can be a member of the workers' council. The general manager is directly responsible to the workers' council.

I have pointed out that under direct self-management the basic tendency is for decisions to be made on the level of OOUR and not on the company level. In a conventional company decisions are made at the top on the company hierarchy, and decision-making authority may be delegated towards the base of the pyramid; seldom if ever, is decision-making authority delegated all the way down to the bottom, i.e. the workers. The reverse is true for a typical Yugoslav company. Decision-making power is vested in the base, i.e. the workers of the OOUR, and may be delegated from there up towards the top of the pyramid. While much more of that delegated power reaches the top of the hierarchy in the Yugoslav company than the bottom in the American company, a major portion of the delegated decision-making authority is placed by the workers in the middle rung of the self-management structure: the workers' council and its organs. I have emphasized elsewhere that self-management is not just a particular formal type of the decision-making system; rather, there is a 'material base' which corresponds to the decision-making structure. One may hypothesize that if a three-tier company in fact practises direct self-management, that one should find the 'material base' to be vested in the OOURs.

There are three continuous funds in BOR: one for the personal incomes of workers, one for housing and other social expenditures and an investment fund. These funds exist in fact only on the level of OOURs, *not* on the level of communities of associated labour nor on the level of the combinat. On the combinat's level, only *ad-hoc* funds may be established, for example, for the construction of a new plant. The decision over the establishment of such an *ad-hoc* fund is made by combinat's workers' council, the members of which are accountable to the workers and workers' councils in the OOURs to which they belong.

It is interesting to note that this 'material base' of self-management is indeed related to the structure of self-management. Before the constitutional amendments were passed, BOR's system of self-management was *representative*. Consequently, all continuous funds were established on the level of the combinat while *ad-hoc* funds existed on the level of basic organizations. This was reversed when the company changed from representative to direct self-management.

6 Economic Development under Self-Management

A crucial question concerning the viability of any alternative form of industrial organization is that of its economic feasibility. Is the alternative mode productive and efficient enough to warrant our attention and a more serious scrutiny? And, more specifically in the context of this book, is self-management economically efficient?

For a precise answer, one would need a sufficiently large number of countries that would fall into two groups: countries with and without self-management. However, we have only Yugoslavia as a self-managing society, and this is certainly not sufficient to come up with a final answer. We can of course do some other things: we can group companies in Yugoslavia by the *extent* to which they have introduced self-management and compare those which are high in participation with those which are low in participation in terms of productivity. This is one of the things we will do in another chapter. Another thing we can do is simply to look at the economic development of Yugoslavia since the inception of self-management. This will certainly not allow us to conclude that whatever economic development took place is due to self-management. But one exceedingly important question we may be able to answer by this method is: Are economic growth and economic efficiency *compatible* with self-management? To be sure, we may find out in the next chapter whether self-management is more efficient than other methods of management. But even if we did not, there may be other reasons for the introduction of self-management than purely economic ones. Such reasons could, for instance, be humanistic ones, though we have little doubt that any organizational pattern that has 'only' humanitarians speaking for it is most unlikely ever to emerge into reality. For the time being, let us then examine the economic development of Yugoslavia under self-management. If we find that Yugoslavia has developed rapidly, then we will know at least that economic growth and efficiency and self-management are not necessarily mutually exclusive.

POPULATION AND EMPLOYMENT

A few general data about the geographical and population size of Yugoslavia should be useful in providing background for the following data on economic structure and development. Yugoslavia is probably never going to be one of the industrial giants of the world, with an area of 255,804 km² (98,766 square miles) and a population of approximately 21 million in 1974. The last census was in 1971 when 20,522,972 people were counted. Population growth rates have been decreasing from a high of 1.77 per cent in 1954 to below 1 per cent now; the growth rate was 0.95 per cent in 1971 and 0.91 in 1972. From 1921 to 1974, the population of Yugoslavia developed as shown in Table 6.1.

TABLE 6.1 Population growth in Yugoslavia from 1921 to 1974 (million inhabitants)

Year	Population
1921	12.5
1931	14.5
1948	15.8
1953	17.0
1961	18.5
1971	20.5
1974	21.0 (estimated)
1982	22.6 (projected)

SOURCES
Statistical Pocket Book of Yugoslavia (1973, pp. 21–2).
Statistički Godišnjak Jugoslavije (1973, p. 82).

Yugoslavia comprises six republics: Bosnia and Herzegovina, Montenegro, Croatia, Macedonia, Slovenia and Serbia; and two autonomous provinces: Vojvodina and Kosovo, which are ethnically part of Serbia (Table 6.2).

During the 10-year period from 1963 to 1972, employment rose in Yugoslavia from 3,320,000 to 4,115,000, or 23.9 per cent, in the

TABLE 6.2 Basic population structure of Yugoslavia (1971 census) (million inhabitants)

Area	Total population	Active population	Persons with income of their own	Dependants
Yugoslavia	20.52	8.89	1.24	10.39
Bosnia and Herzegovina	3.75	1.37	0.15	2.22
Montenegro	0.53	0.17	0.04	0.32
Croatia	4.43	2.02	0.37	2.04
Macedonia	1.65	0.63	0.06	0.96
Slovenia	1.73	0.84	0.20	0.70
Serbia	5.25	2.73	0.26	2.29
Vojvodina	1.95	0.83	0.16	0.90
Kosovo	1.24	0.32	0.03	0.90

SOURCE
Statistical Pocket Book of Yugoslavia (1973, pp. 28–9).

social sector and from 70,000 to 95,000, or 35.7 per cent, in the private sector. While these statistics seem to point to a more rapid expansion in the private sector, a closer look at the employment trend in the social and private sector reveals a different picture. In the social sector, employment rose from 3,320,000 in 1963 to 3,535,000 in 1964; the last year of a long trend of rapid increases in employment—during the 5 years from 1958 to 1963 employment had risen by approximately 34 per cent. During the economic reform of 1965, employment levelled off at approximately the same level as 1964. The economic reform of 1965 aimed at the modernization of the economy as I have pointed out in Chapter 5, i.e. further growth was to take place on the basis of increases in capital rather than employment. When these attempts took effect, employment not only levelled off, it even went down: it dropped from 3,583,000 in 1965 to 3,491,000 in 1966 and to 3,466,000 in 1967 and remained approximately on that level during the following year, increasing very slightly by 0.6 per cent. During the following years, employment rose by 100,000 or 200,000 annually, or rates of 3–5 per cent: 3.9 per cent from 1968 to 1969, 3.9 per cent from 1969 to 1970, 4.8 per cent from 1970 to 1971 and 4.3 per cent from 1971 to 1972. In brief: employment in the social sector has been increasing steadily up to the economic reform of

1965 and, after a 3-year 'employment recession' following the economic reform, it has continued to grow.

Employment trends in the private sector have been quite different. From 1963 to 1966, when growth rates in the social sector not only went down but eventually even reached a negative value, growth rates in the private sector went up by 4.3 per cent; during the following year by 8.2 per cent; and from 1965 to 1966, precisely during the slump in the social sector, the private sector saw its biggest increase: employment went up by 15.2 per cent. The rates of increase slowed down during the following 2 years but still were as high as 4.4 per cent during 1966/67 and 5.3 per cent during 1967/68, the years of stagnation in the social sector. But from 1968 to 1969 when employment in the social sector started growing again, the private sector had its biggest employment cut: 16 per cent. From 1969 to 1972 employment in the private sector grew again, but only to be subsequently reduced to the level of 1966 in 1974 and 1975 (Tables 6.3 and 6.4).

Dramatic as some of these differences in employment trends between the social and the private sector may appear, one has to bear in mind that the size of the private sector is very small relative to the social sector. The private sector comprises only little more than 2 per cent of total employment. From 2.06 per cent in 1963, it dropped to 2.02 per cent in 1964 and increased to 2.16 per cent in 1965, 2.54 per cent in 1966, 2.67 per cent in 1967 and to a peak of 2.79 per cent in 1968. In 1969, it slumped to 2.27 per cent and has continued to fall ever since (Table 6.4).

Structural changes in employment clearly indicate the phases of economic growth Yugoslavia has gone through. Employment in the primary sector rose until 1961 and decreased subsequently, not only proportionally but also in absolute numbers. Employment in the secondary sector went up steadily until 1965, accompanied by a moderate growth of the tertiary sector. The retrenchment during the following three years was largely due to employment cutbacks in the secondary sector, the tertiary sector remaining fairly stable. After 1968, the bulk of employment gains have to be accredited to the tertiary sector, indicating that Yugoslavia had entered a phase of economic development in which the other industrial nations had been for some time.

Table 6.4 summarizes the employment trend for a longer period, namely from 1952 to 1976. During the first decade, from 1953 to 1962 total employment rose by 1,482,000 employees or

TABLE 6.3 Employment in the social and private sector by type of activity from 1966 to 1975 ('000)

	1966	1967	1968	1969	1970	1971	1972	1973	1974	1975
					SOCIAL SECTOR					
Total	3582	3561	3587	3706	3850	4034	4210	4306	4514	4758
Economic activities	2979	2960	2974	3074	3193	3345	3490	3559	3728	3931
Manufacturing	1358	1352	1349	1399	1454	1531	1614	1665	1757	1852
Agriculture	295	276	255	248	243	242	246	249	258	270
Forestry	77	69	66	68	67	68	68	67	69	71
Construction	313	312	323	339	355	365	370	363	386	420
Transport & communication	246	249	255	260	269	280	292	298	306	321
Trade and catering	351	366	379	408	439	480	514	541	571	602
Arts and crafts	239	237	242	248	254	263	266	254	256	264
Public utility	100	99	105	104	112	116	120	122	125	131
Non-economic activities	592	589	603	627	652	683	714	742	780	822
Culture & social welfare	423	428	440	458	477	501	525	545	570	598
Social & govern. services	169	161	163	169	175	182	189	197	210	224
					PRIVATE SECTOR					
Total	91	95	100	84	85	90	95	93	91	91
Agriculture	2	2	2	2	1	1	2	2	2	2
Construction	4	6	8	7	8	9	9	10	12	13
Trade and catering	2	4	5	6	6	7	8	9	9	10
Arts and crafts	39	42	46	39	41	44	48	46	43	42
Housemaids	33	29	29	25	24	23	22	21	19	19
Other	11	12	10	5	5	6	6	5	6	5

SOURCE
Statistički Godišnjak Jugoslavije (1976, p. 112).

TABLE 6.4 Employment in the social and private sector in Yugoslavia from 1952 to 1975 (annual average)

Year	Social sector (000s)	Employment Private sector (000s)	% of total employment	Total
1952	1684	50	2.88	1734
1953	1784	52	2.83	1836
1954	1952	53	2.64	2005
1955	2159	56	2.53	2215
1956	2161	55	2.48	2216
1957	2332	60	2.51	2392
1958	2485	67	2.62	2552
1959	2664	66	2.42	2730
1960	2903	69	2.32	2972
1961	3170	72	2.22	3242
1962	3250	68	2.05	3318
1963	3320	70	2.06	3390
1964	3535	73	2.02	3608
1965	3583	79	2.16	3662
1966	3491	91	2.54	3582
1967	3466	95	2.67	3561
1968	3487	100	2.79	3587
1969	3622	84	2.27	3706
1970	3765	85	2.21	3850
1971	3944	90	2.23	4034
1972	4115	95	2.26	4210
1973	4213	93	2.16	4306
1974	4423	91	2.01	4514
1975	4667	91	1.91	4758
1976[a]	4838	92	1.87	4930

NOTE
[a] Estimated.

SOURCE
Statistički Godišnjak Jugoslavije (1964, p. 177; 1973, p. 171, 1976, p. 187).

80.8 per cent. During the second decade, growth was remarkably slower: from 1963 to 1972, employment rose by 820,000 or 24.2 per cent. The percentage increase from 1953 to 1972 was 129 per cent. Table 6.4 also indicates that the decrease of the relative importance of the private sector in terms of employment is not a recent phenomenon: it has been steadily going down from 2.8 per cent in 1952 to 2.02 per cent in 1964, and, after a 4-year increase to 2.79 per cent in 1968, it has been falling constantly to 1.87 per cent in 1976.

FEMALE EMPLOYMENT

Employment of women has increased from 1,096,000 in 1967 to 1,699,000 in 1976: an increase of 55 per cent. During the same period, total employment has gone up by only 38.4 per cent. These gains in female employment have mainly taken place in manufacturing, trade and catering, and culture and social welfare, in that order. The private sector has not only not contributed to this trend: female employment in the private sector has been going down (Table 6.5).

TABLE 6.5 Female employment from 1967 to 1976 ('000s)

	1967	1968	1969	1970	1971	1972	1973	1974	1975	1976
Total	1096	1097	1144	1207	1283	1371	1446	1532	1625	1699
Social sector	1053	1053	1106	1169	1245	1332	1407	1494	1586	1660
Private sector	43	44	39	38	38	39	39	38	39	39
Economic activities	779	775	809	855	911	976	1029	1089	1154	1202
Manufacturing	413	407	427	450	478	508	539	573	603	628
Agriculture	49	44	44	44	45	41	44	47	51	51
Forestry	5	5	5	5	5	5	5	5	6	5
Construction	24	24	25	27	29	29	30	32	36	40
Transport & commun.	31	32	33	35	37	40	42	44	47	50
Trade & catering	159	165	179	195	214	249	266	284	303	320
Arts and crafts	54	54	57	59	64	65	63	65	67	67
Public utility	44	44	39	40	39	39	40	39	41	41
Non-economic activities	317	322	335	352	372	395	417	443	471	497
Culture & social welfare	245	250	261	274	289	307	323	341	360	376
Social & govern. services	72	72	74	78	83	88	94	102	111	121

SOURCE
Statistical Pocket Book of Yugoslavia (1973, p. 36; 1977, p. 33).

Women have a relatively strong position in the private sector where they represent somewhat less than half the labour force. In 1967, the proportion of women in the private sector was 45 per cent; in 1968 it was 44 per cent; in 1969 it went up again to 46.4 per cent and fell to 44.7 per cent in 1970. Since then the proportion of women in the private sector has been declining; in 1976, it was 42.4 per cent.

In the social sector, the proportion of female employees has steadily increased from a plateau of 30.4 per cent in 1967 and 30.2

per cent in 1968, to 30.5 per cent in 1969, 31.0 per cent in 1970, 31.6 per cent in 1971, 32.4 per cent in 1972, 33.4 per cent in 1973, 33.8 per cent in 1974, 33.98 per cent in 1975 and 34.3 per cent in 1976. Combining the private and the social sector, women constituted 34.5 per cent of the Yugoslav labour force in 1976.

This trend towards increased female employment paralleling the process of industrial development in Yugoslavia is also reflected in the proportion of women in the labour force in the various republics and provinces: the more developed a republic or province, the higher the proportion of women in the labour force. Taking the proportion of the agriculture population in the total population as an indicator of economic development (the lower the proportion of the agricultural population, the higher the level of economic development), it is interesting to note that Slovenia, which is the most highly developed republic (with an agricultural population of only 20.4 per cent) has by far the highest proportion of women in the labour force, namely 41.5 per cent in 1971. The second-lowest proportion of agricultural population is found in Croatia which, at the same time, has the second-highest proportion of women in the labour force: 35.5 per cent. At the other end of the scale is the province Kosovo which has, with 51.5 per cent, the highest proportion of agricultural population and, simultaneously, with 17.8 per cent, the lowest proportion of women in the labour force (Table 6.6 below).

TABLE 6.6 Female and agricultural employment by republic and province in 1971

Republic or province	Persons employed (000s)	Agricultural population in % of total population, 1971	Employed women	
			(000s)	% of total employment
Bosnia and Herzegovina	546	40.0	138	25.3
Montenegro	85	35.0	23	27.1
Croatia	1003	32.3	356	35.5
Macedonia	274	39.9	71	25.9
Slovenia	573	20.4	238	41.5
Serbia	1022	44.1	303	29.6
Vojvodina	424	39.0	135	31.8
Kosovo	107	51.5	19	17.8

SOURCE
Statistical Pocket Book of Yugoslavia (1973, pp. 32–6).

ECONOMIC GROWTH

Table 6.7 summarizes the overall economic development of Yugoslavia from 1955 to 1974. In terms of 1972 prices, the social product grew from 81 million dinars in 1955 to 280 million dinars in 1974, that is an increase of 245 per cent over 20 years. During the same period, personal consumption grew from 46 million to 151 million dinars, that is an increase of 228 per cent. Collective and public consumption grew from 9 million to 24 million dinars, that is an increase of 167 per cent. In percentages, capital formation showed the largest expansion: gross fixed capital formation rose from 20 million dinars in 1955 to 83 million dinars in 1974, that is an increase of 315 per cent.

Table 6.8 gives a broad survey of economic development from 1956 to 1975 for a variety of indicators. While the population grew during that 20-year period from 17.7 million to 21.4 million, employment in the social sector of the economy increased from 2.2 million to 4.7 million. The proportion of persons employed in the social sector in terms of total population thus almost doubled; it was 12.2 per cent in 1956 and 21.8 per cent in 1975. Fixed assets of economic organizations grew from 37.4 billion dinars in 1958 (data for earlier years are not available) to 908.7 billion dinars in 1975 at purchase value. The gross national product (the so-called social product in Yugoslavia) grew during the 20-year period from 16.1 to 497.8 billion dinars at current prices and the national income from 14.4 to 449.5 billion dinars at current prices. At constant prices, the growth of the national income was less spectacular but still remarkable. In terms of 1972 prices, the national income was 70.5 billion dinars in 1956 and 259.7 billion dinars 20 years later. Table 6.8 also shows the development of net personal incomes, of personal consumption, of collective and public consumption, of investment (gross fixed capital formation), of exports and of imports.

Table 6.9 below gives another broad survey of economic development from 1956 to 1975 through different indices. 1955 serves as a base, i.e. the 1955 value of an indicator is set at 100 and all other years are expressed as a proportion of the 1955 value. The national income at constant prices rose from an index of 95 in 1956 to 349 in 1975. *Per capita* income during the same 20-year period increased from 94 to 286. The physical volume of manufacturing industry has gone up from 110 in 1956 to 613 in

TABLE 6.7 Social product, personal consumption, collective and public consumption and investment from 1952 to 1971 (1966 prices)

Year	End use of social product (in '000 dinars)				Structure of the end use of social product (social product = 100)				Chain indices (each previous year = 100)			
	(1)	(2)	(3)	(4)	(1)	(2)	(3)	(4)	(1)	(2)	(3)	(4)
1955	81 087	45 571	9 082	19 704	100	56.2	11.2	24.3	113.5	110.1	92.8	102.2
1956	76 996	46 275	8 932	19 480	100	60.1	11.6	25.3	95.0	101.5	98.3	98.9
1957	92 781	51 772	8 535	22 824	100	55.8	9.2	24.6	120.5	111.9	95.6	117.2
1958	94 527	54 258	8 980	26 089	100	57.4	9.5	27.6	101.9	104.8	105.2	114.3
1959	109 909	59 571	9 782	29 675	100	54.2	8.9	27.0	116.3	109.8	108.9	113.7
1960	118 283	65 883	11 237	35 958	100	55.7	9.5	30.4	107.6	110.6	114.9	121.2
1961	125 086	70 674	12 384	40 027	100	56.5	9.9	32.0	105.8	107.3	110.2	111.3
1962	129 383	71 678	12 809	42 308	100	55.4	9.9	32.7	103.4	101.4	103.4	105.7
1963	145 026	78 749	13 343	45 828	100	54.3	9.2	31.6	112.1	109.9	104.2	108.3
1964	161 607	87 914	14 706	52 522	100	54.4	9.1	32.5	111.4	111.6	110.2	114.6
1965	164 658	93 196	14 654	46 598	100	56.6	8.9	28.3	101.9	106.0	99.6	88.7
1966	177 511	94 791	15 443	50 058	100	53.4	8.7	28.2	107.8	101.7	105.4	107.4
1967	181 520	101 288	17 063	50 826	100	55.8	9.4	28.0	102.3	106.9	110.5	101.5
1968	188 173	104 624	18 065	55 323	100	55.6	9.6	29.4	103.7	103.3	105.9	108.8
1969	206 339	112 042	19 602	58 807	100	54.3	9.5	28.5	109.6	107.1	108.5	106.3
1970	217 947	120 960	20 269	67 346	100	55.5	9.3	30.9	105.6	108.0	103.4	114.5
1971	235 540	130 960	20 256	71 839	100	55.6	8.6	30.5	108.1	108.3	99.9	106.7
1972	245 567	137 026	21 364	74 161	100	55.8	8.7	30.2	104.3	104.6	105.5	103.2
1973	257 684	140 695	22 160	76 017	100	54.6	8.6	29.5	104.9	102.7	103.7	102.5
1974	279 685	151 030	23 774	82 787	100	54.0	8.5	29.6	108.5	107.3	107.3	108.9

NOTES
(1) Gross fixed capital formation; (2) Collective and public consumption; (3) Personal consumption; (4) Social product.

SOURCE
Statistitčki Godišnjak Jugoslavije (1973, p. 120; 1976, p. 136).

1975; the physical volume of agricultural production from 83 to 179; and the physical volume of construction industry from 83 to 275. Retail trade developed in terms of physical volume, from 102 in 1956 to 523 in 1975. Between 1956 and 1975 the physical volume of exports rose from 123 to 573 and the physical volume imports from 109 to 643. Producer prices of manufactured goods went up from 101 in 1956 to 385 in 1975 and of agricultural products from 105 to 1104. Construction prices rose from 103 to 1213 and retail prices from 105 to 806. The cost of living index went up from 100 in 1956 to 980 in 1975. The index of nominal income of persons employed in the social sector of the economy was 110 in 1956 and 2833 in 1975; real income was 102 in 1956 and 289 in 1975.

INDUSTRIAL GROWTH

The following two tables of index numbers of industrial production provide a summary of overall industrial growth in Yugoslavia. Table 6.10 gives the data for 1939 to 1975 on the basis of 1939, 1946, 1952, 1955, 1960 and 1962 to 1975 = 100. Table 6.11 provides a survey of annual growth rates of industrial production in percentages of industrial production of the preceding year from 1947 to 1975.

In 1946, the first post-war year, the Yugoslav economy had not yet fully recovered from the wounds of the war; industrial production reached only 79 per cent of its pre-war (1939) level. 1947 was then the year of recovery: from 1946 to 1947, industrial production rose by 52 per cent. The growth rates for the subsequent 2 years were 25 per cent and 11 per cent. After 1949, the economic embargo by Moscow hit Yugoslavia. In 1950, industrial growth slowed down to a meagre 3 per cent: the beginning of the recession. During the following 2 years, industry not only failed to grow, it shrunk: in 1951 by − 4 per cent and in 1952 by − 1 per cent. During these years, desperate attempts to recover were made on two fronts: to mobilize all internal resources and to find new trade partners. The latter were eventually found outside the Eastern bloc. As to the former, the principal effort was the introduction of self-management: an inducement for everyone to work their hardest and give their utmost. During the following 8 years, growth rates of industrial

TABLE 6.8 General data on the development of the economy, 1955–75 (million dinars)

Year	Total population (in '000)	Employment in the social sector (in '000)[a]	Fixed assets of economic organis-ations[b]	Social product at current prices	National income Current prices	National income Constant prices[c]	Net personal income[d]	Personal consumption	Collective and public consumption	Gross fixed capital formation Total[e]	Gross fixed capital formation In productive funds	Exports[f]	Imports[f]
1956	17 685	2161	—	16 123	14 441	70 479	6168	8640	2209	4605	3640	5496	8060
1957	17 859	2332	—	19 909	18 294	85 099	7762	10 280	2227	5501	4010	6717	11 241
1958	18 018	2485	37 350	19 888	18 337	86 384	8093	10 960	2418	5869	4250	7502	11 646
1959	18 214	2664	40 370	24 463	22 691	100 501	9551	12 690	2714	7500	5510	8103	11 682
1960	18 402	2903	46 940	28 868	26 859	107 764	11 226	14 920	3138	9362	6690	9524	14 048
1961	18 612	3169	54 667	33 653	31 099	113 800	13 114	17 550	3629	11 660	8010	9670	15 475
1962	18 819	3250	71 608	37 726	34 704	117 406	14 636	19 500	4000	13 331	8580	11 738	15 091
1963	19 029	3320	78 991	45 804	41 992	131 470	17 356	23 050	4392	15 848	10 050	13 435	17 962
1964	19 222	3535	89 630	61 001	55 878	146 471	23 729	29 005	5183	20 378	13 074	15 183	22 494
1965	19 434	3583	97 810	79 515	73 573	148 911	33 001	40 168	6079	21 788	13 094	18 556	21 894
1966	19 644	3491	179 744	99 052	91 740	160 683	44 088	50 510	8137	26 616	17 124	20 741	26 782
1967	19 840	3466	186 804	103 710	94 426	164 183	46 877	56 897	10 008	30 283	21 911	21 278	29 024
1968	20 029	3487	200 975	111 973	101 573	169 985	50 126	61 921	11 639	35 044	25 289	21 482	30 545

1969	20 209	3522	185 250	131 960	119 690	186 409	59 173	71 706	13 409	41 049	30 021	25 065	36 274
1970	20 371	3765	206 416	157 207	142 835	196 554	70 798	86 305	14 689	51 723	36 304	28 514	48 857
1971	20 572	3344	357 180	204 476	186 138	212 210	89 229	110 514	17 508	64 651	45 684	30 845	55 283
1972	20 772	4415	393 910	245 395	220 959	221 147	107 113	137 025	21 285	73 977	50 455	38 033	51 957
1973	20 956	4213	436 536	306 326	275 549	231 986	128 304	168 877	26 708	85 502	57 563	48 494	76 689
1974	21 155	4423	486 615	407 221	363 281	251 385	166 050	220 187	35 972	117 387	79 620	64 678	27 837
1975	21 352	4567	908 705	497 838	449 592	259 657	204 315	—	—	—	—	69 228	130 844

NOTES

a Persons employed in economic and non-economic organizations.

b Only active fixed assets at purchase value. Data are not fully comparable by years due to partly different coverage. From 1966 fixed assets are shown at revalorized value of 31 December 1966.

c Data at constant prices were calculated for the whole period by application of 1972 prices.

d Data derived from the computation of national income of productive industries, thus they cover net personal incomes and other receipts of the employed in economic organizations and also that part of income of individual producers available for personal consumption after allotting resources for accumulation.

e Total gross fixed capital formation out of social and private resources.

f Data on exports and imports are shown at the rate US$ = 17.00 dinars. Data are provisional and obtained partly by estimate.

SOURCE
Statistički Godišnjak Jugoslavije (1976, p. 142).

TABLE 6.9 General economic indices[a], 1956–75 (1955 = 100)

Year	Total popu-lation	Employment in social sector	National income at constant prices		Index of physical volume[a]			Commodity turnover			Prices					Income[e]	
					Production				External trade		Producers'						
			Total	per capita	Manufac-turing	Agricul-ture	Construc-tion	Retail trade[b]	Exports	Imports	Manufac-turing	Agricul-ture[c]	Construc-tion	Retail	Cost of living[d]	Nomi-nal	Real
1956	101	100	95	94	110	83	83	102	123	109	101	105	103	105	108	110	102
1957	102	108	114	112	129	120	101	121	145	142	100	115	111	106	111	133	120
1958	103	115	116	113	143	105	111	130	164	154	101	117	117	109	117	140	120
1959	104	123	135	130	162	139	130	148	184	158	101	114	123	110	118	164	139
1960	105	134	145	138	187	125	153	168	212	187	104	122	140	118	130	188	145
1961	106	147	153	144	200	121	166	188	211	205	108	140	174	127	140	204	156
1962	107	151	158	147	214	125	166	196	248	195	108	161	180	136	155	224	145
1963	109	154	176	162	247	138	185	223	279	225	108	177	192	141	163	264	162
1964	110	164	197	179	286	145	204	252	296	271	114	220	223	154	182	335	184
1965	111	166	200	180	309	132	182	265	337	249	131	314	270	200	246	464	189
1966	112	162	216	192	323	153	173	280	365	303	146	369	336	246	302	642	213
1967	113	161	220	195	322	151	183	300	373	328	149	351	360	262	323	729	226

1968	114	162	228	200	342	146	192	321	384	344	150	329	381	274	339	798	235
1969	115	168	250	217	381	160	209	350	429	389	154	372	411	294	366	917	251
1970	116	174	264	227	416	154	228	392	448	485	168	444	478	323	405	1086	268
1971	117	183	285	243	458	164	237	435	463	530	195	556	574	372	467	1326	284
1972	119	191	297	250	494	162	237	465	544	497	216	709	660	429	543	1552	286
1973	120	195	311	260	524	173	228	479	580	577	244	911	754	510	649	1794	276
1974	121	205	335	279	580	184	243	508	586	660	315	998	970	641	787	2294	291
1975	122	216	349	286	613	179	(275)	523	573	643	385	1104	1213	806	980	2833	289

NOTES

[a] Indexes of physical volume of national income and prices are not completely mutually comparable since they have unequal coverage of some constituent elements of the value of production. The price indexes have not been constructed for the purpose of deflation of indexes of nominal values. At comparison of these indexes one should seek only general agreement of presented tendencies and not the exact coincidence of their results.

[b] It covers only retail sale of commodities in trade economic organizations including shops of producing enterprises and establishments.

[c] Indexes of producers' prices of agricultural products show movement of purchase prices from individual producers.

[d] Costs of living index is a special form of the retail prices index of articles and services of personal consumption which have been computed according to definite consumption structure of urban households.

[e] Indexes of nominal receipts have been calculated on the basis of average net personal receipts per one employed person in the social sector (in the economy and institutions). Indexes of real receipts represent the ratio between the indexes of nominal receipts and costs of living index.

SOURCE

Statistički Godišnjak Jugoslavije (1976, p. 142).

TABLE 6.10 Index numbers of industrial production for 1939, 1946, 1952, 1955, 1960 and 1963–75

1939	1946	1952	1955	1960	1962	1963	1964	1965	1966	1967	1968	1969	1970	1971	1972	1973	1974	1975
100	79	164	242	451	516	596	692	748	780	778	827	921	1005	1108	1195	1126	1402	1480
126	**100**	207	305	569	651	752	873	943	983	980	1043	1161	1266	1397	1506	1596	1767	1866
61	48	**100**	147	274	314	363	421	455	474	473	503	560	611	674	727	770	853	901
41	33	68	**100**	187	214	247	286	309	323	322	342	381	416	458	494	524	580	613
22	18	37	54	**100**	115	132	154	166	173	172	183	204	223	246	265	281	311	328
19	15	32	47	87	**100**	116	134	145	151	151	160	178	194	214	231	245	271	286
17	13	28	41	76	87	**100**	116	125	131	130	139	154	169	186	200	212	245	259
14	11	24	35	65	75	86	**100**	108	113	112	120	133	145	160	173	183	203	214
13	11	22	32	60	69	80	93	**100**	104	104	111	123	134	148	160	169	188	198
13	10	21	31	58	66	76	89	96	**100**	100	106	118	129	142	153	162	180	190
13	10	21	31	58	66	77	89	96	100	**100**	106	118	129	143	154	163	180	190
12	10	20	29	55	63	72	84	90	94	94	**100**	111	121	134	144	153	169	179
11	9	18	26	49	56	65	75	81	85	84	90	**100**	109	120	130	138	152	161
10	8	16	24	45	52	59	69	74	78	77	82	92	**100**	110	119	126	140	147
9	7	15	22	41	47	54	63	68	70	70	75	83	91	**100**	108	114	127	134
8	7	14	20	38	43	50	58	63	65	65	69	77	84	93	**100**	106	117	124
8	6	13	19	36	41	47	55	59	62	61	65	73	79	88	94	**100**	111	117
7	6	12	17	32	37	43	49	53	56	56	59	66	72	79	85	90	**100**	106
7	5	11	16	31	35	40	47	51	53	53	56	62	68	75	81	86	95	**100**

NOTE
Data to be read horizontally only.

SOURCE
Statistički Godišnjak Jugoslavije (1976, p. 187).

TABLE 6.11 Annual growth rates of industrial production (% of preceding year) 1947–75

Year	Growth rate (%)	Year	Growth rate (%)
1947	52	1961	7
1948	25	1962	7
1949	11	1963	16
1950	3	1964	16
1951	−4	1965	8
1952	−1	1966	4
1953	11	1967	0
1954	14	1968	6
1955	16	1969	11
1956	10	1970	9
1957	17	1971	10
1958	11	1972	8
1959	13	1973	6
1960	15	1974	11
		1975	6

SOURCE
Statistički Godišnjak Jugoslavije (1964, p.177; 1973, p.171; 1976, p.187).

production varied between 10 per cent and 17 per cent, which is exceedingly high by comparison with other countries. During the following 2 years, 1961 and 1962, growth slowed down somewhat: to 7 per cent each year, to skyrocket to 16 per cent for 2 years in a row, in 1963 and 1964. In 1965, the year of the economic reform in Yugoslavia, the decision was made to modernize the economy, i.e. to shift from the pattern of growth primarily on increases in employment which characterized the period until 1965, to a pattern of growth based primarily on increases in capital during the subsequent years. The price for this shift in economic policy was paid for in terms of a slowing-down of growth rates to 8 per cent in 1965 and 4 per cent in 1966; in 1967, the rate fell as low as zero and started to recover in 1968. Since 1969, growth rates have been again relatively high: between 6 and 11 per cent. One cannot be sure of the extent to which the industrial growth of Yugoslavia since 1952 has been due to the self-management organization of industry. It is a fact that the recovery of the Yugoslav economy during the immediate post-war years took place under state socialism and was as remarkable as industrial growth under self-management. Unfortunately, history does not provide stringent experimental conditions; hence, we do not know what growth rates would have been if state socialism had continued to exist in Yugoslavia. Nor do we know what rates would have been if Yugoslavia had had a capitalistic economy. One fact however, is undebatable: that Yugoslavia did show remarkable industrial growth under self-management, i.e. industrial growth and efficiency and self-management are not incompatible.

STRUCTURAL CHANGES*

When an economy expands over an extended period of time, its growth is usually accompanied by structural changes, i.e. the relative weight of the various sectors and branches of the economy changes. These structural changes are reflected in different growth rates. Every country has its particular seedbed industries, i.e. branches which started the process of industrialization. In Yugoslavia, the industrial revolution was initiated by the coal, food, tobacco, wood, textile, leather and footwear industries; these were the branches that held the dominant position in the structure of industrial production of 1952. During the last two decades, however, Yugoslavia has gone through its industrial revolution and is now on its way to industrial maturity. Old branches of industry have lost in weight; new branches have come to the forefront. Among its chief growth industries were chemical, electrical and petroleum industries. The chemical industry increased 32 times in output, the electrical industry 25 times and the petroleum industry 19 times. At the same time, the industries which propelled the economy 20 years ago have shown much slower growth: coal output rose 2.2 times and production in the tobacco industry 2.4 times. In Table 6.12 industrial branches are listed in the order of their output growth from 1952 to 1972. The average growth rate during the period was 770. The figure can be used to divide the list into two groups of industries: the slow growers and the fast growers. The fast-growing industries were, in the order of their output from 1952 to 1972, chemical industry, *other industries*, electrical industry, petroleum industry, pulp and paper industry, metal-using industries, electricity, rubber industry, non-metallic mineral industry, food industry and printing industry. The slow-growing

* Based on Nikolić (1973).

industries were, starting with the slowest-growing: coal industry, tobacco industry, wood industry, non-ferrous metallurgy, leather and footwear industry, textile industry, building materials industry, shipbuilding ferrous metallurgy and the film industry. 'The leading role in industrial development in Yugoslavia is now played by those branches which contribute most to rapid technical progress in the developed countries', says Nikolić (1973, p. 34). While increases in employment have been an important factor in the economic growth of Yugoslavia, technological progress has been the key to the development of the fastest-growing industries. This is particularly true for output in the chemical and metal-using industries which increased about 15 times: their share of total industrial production increased from 19 per cent in 1952 to 37 per cent in 1972. Consumer goods industries (wood, textile, leather and footwear, rubber, food, tobacco, film and other miscellaneous industries) recorded a much slower growth. Output in that sector grew somewhat more than 6 times, but its share of total industrial production fell from 45 per cent in 1952 to 33 per cent in 1972. Overall energy production has been relatively slow too, but this was mostly due to the slow increases in coal production, which grew only 2.2 times. The production of electricity and petroleum grew much faster. The production of electrical power increased 11 times, providing a solid basis for further industrial growth in other sectors. Simultaneously, petroleum was being imported at an increasing rate. The overall increase in energy production was 6.5 times; its share in total industrial output declined from 16 to 14 per cent.

Output of basic primary commodities and other industrial materials increased only 6.4 times. The relatively slow growth of raw materials, such as ferrous and non-ferrous metallurgy, non-metallic minerals, building materials and pulp and paper created a problem for the Yugoslav economy in that its manufacturing industries could not be adequately supplied by its extractive industries and had to rely increasingly on imports, a trend which was not fully matched by export growth. Yugoslavia's balance of trade has shown a deficit throughout that period (cf. Table 6.8). Nikolić (1973, p. 36) also thinks that,

The lag in output recorded in metallurgy and non-metallic minerals industry had a strategic significance in that it hindered the development of the most propulsive sectors of industry . . . . There are only a few signs which show that Yugoslavia has not yet developed an adequate structure of production which would correspond to the new patterns of industrial development. The attainment of this aim will require much time.   (Table 6.12)

TABLE 6.12 Industrial   branches   by   output   growth, 1952–72

	Growth indices		
	1972 1952	1962 1952	1972 1962
Chemical industry	3210	650	494
Other industries	2700	706	382
Electrical industry	2500	762	327
Petroleum industry	1890	448	422
Pulp and paper industry	1240	425	291
Metal-using industries (exclusive of shipbuilding)	1180	496	237
Electricity	1115	370	300
Rubber industry	1020	348	292
Non-metallic mineral industry	883	363	243
Food industry	850	400	212
Printing industry	800	368	218
Film industry	758	760	100
Ferrous metallurgy	720	406	177
Shipbuilding	600	184	326
Building materials industry	600	252	237
Textile industry	530	254	209
Leather and footwear industry	506	256	197
Non-ferrous metallurgy	457	237	193
Wood industry	400	200	200
Tobacco industry	236	135	175
Coal industry	225	200	113
Ratio of maximum to minimum index (max.: min.)	14.3	5.7	4.9

SOURCE
Statistički Godišnjak Jugoslavije (1971, p. 98; 1972, p. 102).

One can of course not infer from growth rates to what extent a branch of industry satisfies local demands or contributes to exports. The slow-growing industries like the wood industry which increased the physical volume of its production only about 4 times, exported large quantities of its products. On the other hand, the chemical industry which grew 32 times was unable to meet the needs of the internal market and, as a consequence, chemical products had to be imported in large quantities.

A second way of looking at structural changes in the economy is an analysis of the absolute magnitude of the social product generated by each branch of industry. This analysis changes the order somewhat at which we previously arrived. The basic pattern of structural changes remains the same; but the weight of individual branches may be different. As Table 6.13 indicates, the most important industries in terms of the value of their social product were textile industry, metal industries, wood industry, coal industry and food industry, in that order. In 1962, metal industries had moved from second to first place, switching places with the textile industry which now occupied the second rank. Third came the food industry and fourth electricity, which in 1952

TABLE 6.13 Industrial branches according to social product generated in 1972 (million dinars at 1966 prices)

	1952	1962	1972
Metal-using industries (exclusive of shipbuilding)	787	3919	9300
Chemical industry	178	1156	7700
Textile industry	1066	2711	5500
Food industry	557	2218	4740
Electricity	401	1492	4480
Electrical industry	131	996	3270
Wood industry	694	1385	2800
Non-ferrous metallurgy	507	1203	2325
Building materials industry	386	978	2320
Printing industry	232	854	1850
Ferrous metallurgy	249	1012	1800
Petroleum industry	83	371	1570
Coal industry	665	1327	1504
Shipbuilding	232	426	1390
Non-metallic minerals industry	156	570	1380
Leather and footwear industry	202	520	1020
Pulp and paper industry	80	340	990
Tobacco industry	296	402	700
Rubber industry	60	208	610
Other industries	12	85	325
Film industry	7	53	53

SOURCE
Statistički Godišnjak Jugoslavije (1971, p. 98; 1972, p. 102).

had not been among the top five at all. Wood industry had moved to the fifth place and coal had been pushed out of the top five, now occupying a more modest sixth place. In 1972, metal industries still made the biggest contribution to the social product, followed by the chemical industry, which in 1952 had ranked number 14 and in 1962 number 8. The textile industry, despite its relatively slow growth, still occupied third place, and the food industry fourth place. Electricity was in fifth place, followed by electrical industry and wood industry. Coal industry had been pushed to thirteenth place.

In terms of greatest gains in the value of the social product between 1952 to 1972 (at 1966 prices), the metal industry (exclusive of shipbuilding) produced an output in 1972 that was 8.5 billion dinars higher than in 1952; chemical industry added another 5.5 billion dinars to its 1952 output; textile industry 4.4 billion; food industry 4.2 billion; electricity 4.1 billion; and electrical industry 3.1 billion. These six branches accounted for almost two-thirds or 64 per cent of the total increase in the industrial social product during the two decades. Textile and food industries alone, which were previously listed as slow-growth industries, contributed 18 per cent of the growth of industry.

INTERNATIONAL COMPARISONS

Finally, we have to ask, how well has Yugoslavia been doing compared with other countries? In Table 6.14, Yugoslavia's growth indices of industrial production for 1955–70 are compared with those of the world, of countries with a centrally planned economy, with developed countries with a market economy and with developing countries with a market economy. The results of that comparison indicate that Yugoslavia must have done indeed its 'leap forward' during that period, its growth being well above the average growth in any of the other four groups. Socialist countries with a centrally planned economy recorded the fastest growth during the 1955–70 period, its industry growing approximately 3.8 times. In the developing countries with a market economy, production rose about 3 times, and in developed countries with a market economy, production grew 2.1 times. In the world as a whole, industrial production grew about 2.5 times. Yugoslavia topped all these groups, its

TABLE 6.14 Growth indices of industrial production in the world and Yugoslavia 1955–70 (1955–100)

	World total	Countries with a centrally planned economy	Countries with a market economy		Yugoslavia
			Developed	Developing	
Total	250	376	213	298	416
Mining	205	282	138	363	246
Coal	116	173	84	206	149
Crude oil	286	527	155	478	1240
Metalliferous ores	202	344	174	174	267
Manufacturing industries	256	380	214	269	438
Food, beverages, tobacco	203	265	178	215	373
Textile industry	186	226	168	192	292
Leather and footwear industry	186	287	151	208	410
Wood industry	212	314	170	250	370
Paper and printing industry	212	293	204	300	560
Chemical industry and refineries	373	545	335	316	950
Non-metallic minerals and building materials industry	286	497	194	310	435
Metallurgy	214	330	175	333	378
Metal products	305	573	231	433	555
Electricity	340	483	303	460	600
Max.: min.	3.21	3.33	4.00	2.75	8.30
Total exclusive of mining	2.01	2.54	2.22	2.40	3.26

SOURCE
Nikolić (1973, p. 41).

industrial production growing almost 4.2 times during that period.

During the last two decades, we have contended, Yugoslavia underwent its industrial revolution. This is reflected in the structural changes of industry, which were more similar to those in developing and in socialist countries, which on the whole are not as advanced as developed countries with a market economy. In terms of structural changes of industry, the correlation coefficient of rating was highest between Yugoslavia and developing countries (0.84), lowest between Yugoslavia and developed countries with a market economy (0.50). Its correlation coefficient with socialist countries places it—again in terms of similarities of structural changes in industry—between the two (0.70).

The range between the maximum and minimum indices of the growth of various branches of industry was by far the largest in Yugoslavia (8.30), compared with values between 2.75 and 4.00 in the three groups of countries. This wide range indicates a high intensity of structural changes in Yugoslavia—statistical expression of the fact that 'hard' changes in Yugoslavia (in terms of structure of industry) have indeed been very rapid.

To summarize the results of this chapter: The growth and development of the Yugoslavia economy in general and of its industry in particular have been exceedingly rapid. The most conservative conclusion we may safely draw from this is that self-management apparently has not been adverse to economic growth and development in Yugoslavia. This is a very remarkable result. For if there were anything truly unfeasible about self-management, this would definitely come out during the time of rapid industrialization. A mature industrial economy can 'take' almost any type of social organization of work and production, being so highly efficient—on technological grounds—that it could put up with a considerable amount of organizational waste and inefficiency. An industrializing country cannot afford this: it has to mobilize all its resources, including its human and social-organizational ones. Self-management has allowed Yugoslavia to mobilize exactly these resources.

7 The Efficiency of Self-Management

In the preceding chapter, I have shown that the Yugoslav economy has expanded very rapidly in the period during which self-management developed. No causality was claimed to exist: it was not suggested in that chapter that self-management has caused economic growth, nor that economic growth led to the rise of self-management. This question was simply left open. The only conclusion drawn was that of compatibility of growth and self-management, and, more specifically with regard to the latter part of the period under survey: that of compatibility of industrialism and self-management. This conclusion seems to represent a consensus among scholars and other observers of the Yugoslav system. Despite the enormous problems Yugoslavia has coped with, and is still struggling with, it is hard not to be impressed by its successes. As Jan Tinbergen (1970, pp. 119–20) noted: 'A rate of growth of *per capita* real income of about 6 per cent, together with a considerable degree of democracy in the everyday environment of the mass of producers, is not easily found elsewhere.' And even Albert Meister (1970, p.365), who has been most critical of self-management in Yugoslavia, admits that Yugoslavia has, 'in only 15 years, managed to bring about the basic industrialization of the country, which it took us [Frenchmen] nearly a century in our own country. And, despite some abuses, Yugoslavia attained this result in a much more human fashion.' (Transl. by Jenkins, 1973, p.113)

Burt (1972, p. 1956), in a study for The International Labour Organization's (ILO) International Institute for Labour Studies on *Workers' Participation in Management in Yugoslavia*, points out in his chapter on the impact of workers' self-management upon economic efficiency that:

> . . . bearing in mind the underdeveloped state of the Yugoslav economy before the Second World War, and the damage

suffered by the economy during the war, the growth and strengthening of the economy has been substantial. National income per capita at 1968 domestic purchasing power parity was US $600, compared with US $100 in 1939. In the period 1947–52, the average rate of growth of the social product of the economy was 2.35 per cent, and of physical volume of industrial production 6.5 per cent. The corresponding figures for 1953–64 were 8.63 and 12.85 per cent.

Adizes, another critical observer in *Industrial Democracy: Yugoslav Style* (1971, p. 222), found that, 'With all the dysfunctional behaviour . . . it should be borne in mind that self-management generally yielded amazing functional results in the long run.' He continues speculating that, 'If a hierarchical organization had existed . . . the erratic environment would have led to destructive polarization . . . '—certainly a *non sequitur*, but maybe not too far from what might actually have happened. One of the more conservative evaluations comes in fact from a Yugoslav scholar, Mitja Kamušič (1970), who asserted, on the basis of 'a coldly objective study of self-management principles', as Jenkins (1973, p. 110) put it, that self-management principles 'do not ensure the greatest economic efficiency . . . but they do not oppose it.' And Jenkins (1973, pp. 110–11), who has summarized the evaluations of self-management and of the economic performance of Yugoslavia quoted above, sums it all up by saying:

> Even if we cannot prove that the self-management system is more efficient than some other system, we can certainly make the minium claim that it does not *interfere* with satisfactory economic performance. . . .
>
> Just as kibbutz industrial management in Israel seems to lead to acceptable economic results, so companies under self-management in Yugoslavia seem to survive in a satisfactory fashion—even though neither of these peculiar ways of running companies quite fits in with traditional beliefs about the omniscience of the men at the top of the pyramid.

These evaluations are likely to be in accord with the conclusions the reader may have drawn from the data presented in the previous chapter. In this chapter, I want to go beyond these 'minimal claims' of mere compatibility between self-management and economic efficiency: Is there any evidence for a more specific evaluation of the relative efficiency of self-management?

Horvat (1971, pp. 90–1) has addressed himself indirectly to that question. He has divided post-war Yugoslav history into three phases: that of central planning from 1946 to 1952; that of decentralization from 1953 to 1960; and a third which he calls the phase of self-government from 1961 until now. Horvat's concern in that context is not self-management; he is writing about 'Growth and Cycles'. However, his three phases are almost identical with the three phases of the development of self-management which we described in Chapter 5: Paternalistic self-management, representative self-management and direct self-management.*

Table 7.1 confirms again what we found in Chapter 6: that self-management and economic growth are compatible.

TABLE 7.1 Growth of the Yugoslav economy 1946–72 during three phases (Rates of growth in % per annum)

	Central planning 1946–52	Decentralization 1953–60	Self-government 1961–72
Gross National Product	2.3[a]	9.8	6.9
Industrial output	12.9	13.4	8.5
Agricultural output	−3.1[a]	8.9	2.3
Export of commodities	−3.1[b]	11.7	7.7
Import of commodities	−3.6[b]	9.7	8.1
Employment[c]	8.3[a]	6.9	2.4

NOTES

[a] 1947–52.   [b] 1948–52.   [c] Persons employed outside private agriculture.

SOURCES
Horvat (1971, p. 91).
Statistički Godišnjak Jugoslavije (1973, p. 126).

The second analysis Horvat presents is more contentious. So far, Yugoslavia has been the only country that has lived through

---

* Horvat wrote this article in 1969. Hence, he only analyzes the time from 1960 to 1968 for the third period. We have extended the period under consideration until 1972 and recalculated the figures where necessary.

three different economic systems, he suggests—capitalism, state socialism and self-management. Hence, it may be possible to evaluate the comparative efficiency of the three systems (Horvat, 1971, p. 91). The necessary research was done by the Institute of Economic Studies in Belgrade, of which Branco Horvat is the Director.

He measured efficiency in terms of the rate of growth of output attributable to technical progress, defined as the residual after the contributions of labour and capital have been accounted for. He divided the recent history of Yugoslavia into four broad periods: First a capitalistic period from 1911 to 1932; a second capitalistic period from 1932 to 1940; a period of state socialism from 1940 to 1954; and a period of self-government from 1956 to 1967—not an ideal periodization because of limitations in the availability of data. 'The results of the analysis are extremely suggestive', he concludes (Table 7.2). 'Central planning expanded output and employment fast, and capital formation even faster, as compared with the private capitalist pre-war economy. But it also reduced overall efficiency. *Self-government accelerated the growth of output and technical progress beyond anything known before while preserving fast employment expansion.*' (Horvat, 1971, pp. 91–2; italics added)

TABLE 7.2 The use of labour and capital and technical progress in Yugoslavia under capitalism, state socialism and self-management, 1911–67

| | | Rates of growth per annum (%) | | | Rates of growth of GNP due to increased efficiency |
		GNP	Employment	Fixed assets	
Capitalism	1911–32	3.28	1.87	3.52	0.71
	1932–40	4.67	0.72	2.59	3.16
Etatism:	1940–54	5.91	4.76	9.99	−1.04
Self-government	1956–67	10.31	4.44	7.84	4.44

NOTE
The war years 1914–18 and 1941–45 are excluded. The data refer to manufacturing, mining, power generation, construction and crafts.

SOURCE
Horvat (1971, p. 92).

So far, we have presented evidence to the effect that self-management and economic growth and development are at least compatible and probably more than that: that self-management activates a considerable growth potential. Horvat (1971) has shown that self-management in fact has contributed to the efficiency of the economy as a whole. What about the efficiency of the individual enterprise? Do self-management and efficiency also go together in individual companies? The answer to this question does not follow from the finding that self-management contributes to the efficiency of the economy as a whole, nor is the reverse true. For one of the first things one learns in introductory economics is that what is good for the individual is not necessarily good for the whole, and vice versa. Or, in other words, what is true on the macroeconomic level does not necessarily apply microeconomically.

The question of the efficiency of self-management for the individual business company is closely related to the question of the efficiency of different management styles—an issue which has been investigated in depth by Rensis Likert and his Institute for Social Research of the University of Michigan. The investigation of the efficiency of Yugoslav self-managing companies has actually grown out of this school: as an additional test of the findings in American companies. The ultimate interpretation of the research in Yugoslavia has therefore to be seen in the context of the preceding investigations in the United States. The results of Likert's research in the United States have been reported in two major publications: his triple award-winning *New Patterns of Management* (1961) and his more recent *The Human Organization* (1967). On the basis of his research, Likert came up with four different management styles, Systems 1, 2, 3 and 4. Systems 1, 2 and 3 he calls 'authoritative', system 1 being 'exploitative authoritative', system 2 'benevolent authoritative', and system 3 'consultative authoritative'. System 4 he calls 'participative'. System 1, the exploitative authoritative, is very close to the traditional style of management in the United States; for brevity's sake, we will refer to it as 'autocratic'. System 4, the participative system, while far from being identical with or even very close to self-management, is at least closer to self-management than any of the three authoritative management styles. What did Likert (1967) find out about the characteristics of these management styles and how do they fare in terms of efficiency?

Let us begin with the organizational and performance characteristics of system 1 with its autocratic management style. In terms of leadership processes used, superiors have no confidence and trust in subordinates; subordinates do not feel at all free to discuss things about the job with their superiors; and superiors rarely if ever try to utilize the ideas and opinions of subordinates in solving job problems. In terms of motivational forces, fear, threats, punishment and occasional rewards are the chief manner in which motives are used; and as to the responsibilities felt by each member of the organization for achieving the goals of the organization, it is left to the upper levels of management to feel fully responsible and to the lower management levels to feel somewhat responsible while the rank and file feel little or no responsibility and often even welcome the opportunity of obstructing the goals of the organization. In terms of the character of the communication process, there is very little interaction and communication that aims at achieving the organization's objective; information flows downward; such communication is viewed by subordinates with great suspicion; upward communication via line tends to be inaccurate; and as to psychological closeness, superiors do not have any knowledge or understanding of the problems of their subordinates. In terms of the character of the interaction–influence process, there is little interaction, and whatever interaction there is occurs under fear and distrust; cooperative teamwork is absent. As to the character of the decision-making process, the formal locus of decision-making is at the top of the organization; decision-makers are often unaware or only partially aware of the problems, particularly those at lower levels in the organization; technical and professional knowledge are only used in decision-making if possessed at higher levels; subordinates are not involved in decisions related to their work; and decision-making contributes little or nothing to the motivation to implement the decision—it may actually yield the adverse motivation. In terms of the character of goal-setting or ordering, orders are issued without giving subordinates any opportunity to comment; and goals are overtly accepted but covertly resisted. Control processes are highly concentrated in top management; underneath the formal organization, as given by the organizational chart, there is an informal organization which opposes the goals of formal organization; and control data on accounting, productivity, cost etc., are used for policing and in a punitive manner.

As the reader may suspect by now, Likert found that the performance of organizations based on autocratic management practices tends to be moderate: productivity is mediocre; absence and turnover tend to be high when people are free to move; scrap loss and waste are relatively high unless workers are policed very carefully; and quality control and inspection are necessary for policing. Autocratic management is absolutely contrary to self-management; we note at this point that the autocratic management style, which is the opposite of self-management, is not very efficient (Likert, 1967, pp. 4–24).

As each management style cannot be described here in detail, let us now briefly turn to system 4, participative management, which is, of the four styles, closest to self-management.

In terms of leadership processes, participative management has complete confidence and trust in all matters; subordinates feel completely free to discuss things about the job with their superior; in problem-solving, superiors seek out the ideas and opinions of subordinates and make constructive use of them. As to the character of motivational forces, economic rewards are based on a compensation system developed through participation, and participants are further motivated by involvement in goal-setting, the improvement of various methods, the appraisal of progress towards goals etc.; at all levels personnel feel real responsibility for the organization's goals and behave in ways to implement them. In terms of the character of the communication process, there is considerable interaction and communication with both individuals and groups, aiming at the attainment of the organization's objectives; information flows freely in all directions, upward, downward and laterally; downward communications are generally accepted, but if not, openly and candidly questioned; upward communication via line tends to be accurate; and superiors tend to know and understand problems of subordinates very well. There is extensive, friendly interaction with a high degree of confidence and trust; and there is very substantial operation and teamwork throughout the organization. Decision-making is widely diffused throughout the organization, although well integrated through the linking process provided by overlapping groups; decision-makers are generally quite well aware of problems, including those at lower levels in the organization; most technical and professional knowledge that is available anywhere in the organization is in fact used;

subordinates are involved in all decisions related to their work; and participation in decision-making contributes substantially to the motivation to implement decisions. Except in emergencies, goals are usually established by means of group participation; and goals are fully accepted both overtly and covertly. The responsibility for review and control is quite widespread, with lower units at times imposing more rigorous reviews and tighter controls than top management; informal and formal organization are one and the same, and all social forces support the effort to achieve the organization's goals; control data are used for self-guidance and for coordinated problem-solving and guidance (Likert, 1967, pp. 4–24).

The performance of organizations under participative management tends to be outstanding: productivity is excellent; absence and turnover are low; the members themselves tend to use measures to keep scrap loss and waste at a minimum; and quality control and inspection tends to be useful in helping workers guiding their own efforts.

Participative management is very similar to what I have termed paternalistic self-management. And, as we have found participative management to be highly efficient, it should not surprise us if we should find paternalistic self-management equally efficient, and other forms of self-management, particularly direct self-management, even more efficient.

To illustrate his findings, Likert (1967, pp. 29–38) describes the impact of the introduction of a more participative style of management in the Weldon Company. In 1962, the Harwood Manufacturing Company, the leading pyjama manufacturer, purchased Weldon Company, the second largest in that branch of industry. Unlike Harwood Manufacturing, Weldon had been unprofitable for several years. After the merger with Harwood Manufacturing, changes were introduced in the management system of what now was the Weldon plant, and in the layout and organization of work (cf. Marrow, Bowers and Seashore, 1967):

> The major changes involved extensive engineering modifications in the organization of the work, improved maintenance of machinery and equipment, an 'earnings development' training programme for employees, training of managers and supervisors in the principles and skills required by a system of management well toward System 4, the use of this system by the

plant manager, and his encouragement of all of his subordinate managers and supervisors to do the same. All of these changes were initiated and supported by the new top management of the company. (Likert, 1967, p. 29)

The results of the changes were summarized by the chairman of the board of directors of Harwood as follows:

The improvements in cooperative relationships were noted by the technical consultants and production workers as well as by the Michigan researchers. The change in motivation and morale was reflected in the following ways:

Average earnings of piece-rate workers increased by nearly 30 per cent. At the same time total manufacturing costs decreased by about 20 per cent. Turnover dropped to half of its former level. Length of employee training was substantially reduced. Interviews by the Michigan researchers reflected vastly more friendly attitudes towards the company. The image of the company in the community changed and the organization began to show a profit. (Profit as a percentage of investment changed from − 17 per cent to 15 per cent and is still improving.)

This was attained without a single replacement in managerial or supervisory personnel at the plant. All the original members of the staff continue in their same jobs.

The basic wage structure has not been changed. The increases in earnings were a result of heightened motivation and improved managerial skills. Increases due to technological changes were adjusted within the existing rate setting structure. (Marrow, 1964, pp. 19–20. Quoted in Likert, 1967, pp. 37–8)

In this context, it is particularly interesting to note the impact of participative management on labour relations and on the problem-solving capacity of a company which Likert (1957, p. 44) studied in several additional research projects:

The evidence from these large-scale field experiments and the other studies indicates that the management system of a firm exercises an important influence on its labor relations. Typically, as they shifted their management system from system 2 to well over toward system 4, there was a marked change in union-management relationships. Real and important differences continued to exist between the union and the company, but as the shift toward system 4 progressed there was a great increase in the capacity to attain acceptable solutions to difficult problems. Effective problem solving replaced irreconcilable conflict. Differences did not become formal grievances because they were solved at the point of disagreement. New contracts were negotiated without strikes and without work stoppages. Both companies and union members have derived substantial financial benefits from the improved relationships . . . Briefly stated, labor relations appear to be best in plants whose management system falls toward the right (system 4 end) (participative management—HDS); they are poorest in plants whose management systems fall toward system 1 (autocratic management—HDS). These relationships improve when the management system shifts toward system 4; they worsen when a shift toward system 1 occurs.

Elsewhere, worker participation has been similarly successful.

For example, when Kaiser Steel Corporation announced that it would close part of its Fontana, California, plant because it could not produce steel at a competitive price, the workers together with local management asked for the chance to make changes in the machinery and work assignments. The large number of minor changes resulted in a productivity increase of 32 per cent! (*Time*, 1973; Peterson, 1973, pp. 49–50)

For Likert, the introduction of self-management in Yugoslavia provided an excellent opportunity to submit his proposition that democratically run companies do better than those under autocratic government to an additional test. The most rigorous test of the efficiency of self-management has thus derived from research on the economic efficiency of business democracy in the United States.

A group of American and Yugoslav scholars studied ten more efficient and ten less efficient Yugoslav companies. It was found that in the more efficient companies, self-management was significantly stronger and, in particular, the workers' council was perceived to be exercising more control than in the less efficient companies. It was thus concluded that self-management (or, more generally, industrial democracy) does in fact contribute to economic efficiency (Jerovšek, 1969; Mozina, Jerovšek, Tannenbaum and Likert, 1970; Jerošek and Mozina, 1970).

The overall evidence thus suggests that self-management is not only compatible with economic efficiency, it may even be superior to less democratic forms of management in terms of economic efficiency.

Yet, despite all this evidence in favour of democratic management styles in the United States, Yugoslavia and elsewhere, self-management is still viewed with great suspicion. Maybe it is because hierarchical patterns are so prevalent in our society and so deeply engrained in our mind that we are almost incapable of looking objectively at the available evidence and admit that democracy in business and in other types of organization is indeed an economically—and certainly humanely—superior structure. We simultaneously believe in democracy and practise autocracy, leaving our mind in a state of 'cognitive dissonance' (Festinger, 1957).

This discrepancy between thought and practice is perplexingly prevalent among American managers and executives, as Likert (1967, pp. 3–12) found in his studies. Likert asked several hundred managers to think of the *most* productive department, division or organization they have known well and to place them on a continuum from system 1, which I have called 'autocratic management', located on the left side of a graph, to system 4, which Likert calls 'participative management', located on the right side of a graph. He then asked them to do the same for the *least* productive department, division or organization. The result was striking. While there was some variation in the descriptions of the most productive departments, some being largely under system 4 and some largely under system 3, there was overwhelming agreement in one respect: irrespective of where the high-producing unit falls, the low-producing unit is placed to the left of the high-producing unit. 'Quite consistently, the high-producing department is seen as toward the right end of the table' (Likert, 1967, pp. 3, 11) i.e. towards the 'participative management' end. Summarizing the results of his research, Likert (1967, p. 11) found:

For the vast majority of managers, this has been the pattern for every item in the table irrespective of the field of experience of the manager—production, sales, financial, office etc.—and regardless of whether he occupies a staff or a line position. In about one case in twenty a manager will place the low-producing unit to the right of the high on one or two items. But with very few exceptions, high-producing departments are seen as using management systems more to the right (towards system 4) and low-producing units as more to the left (towards system 1).

The two major surprises of this research were the following. First, assuming that organizations and their members behave rationally, one would expect that this unusually high consensus about the most productive management style would induce managers to manage in ways consistent with their beliefs. When managers and other employees were asked, however, to describe the actual management system of their own organization, it turned out that these organizations are managed in a style 'appreciably more to the left than that which managers quite generally report is used by the highest-producing departments' (Likert, 1967, p. 11). In other words, most organizations are run in ways inconsistent with the general beliefs of managers and other employees about optimal management systems. While they agree that participatory management is more productive than autocratic management, *actual* management styles as practised by themselves in their respective companies are virtually always more towards autocratic styles. The second surprise is even more puzzling. Likert (1967, pp. 11–12) asked experienced managers:

'In your experience what happens in a company when the senior officer becomes concerned about earnings and takes steps to cut costs, increase productivity, and improve profits? Does top management usually continue to use the management system it has been employing, or does it shift its operation to a management system more toward system 1 or more toward system 4?' The surprising result of this investigation is that, 'Most managers report that, when top management seeks to reduce costs, it shifts its system more toward system 1, i.e. toward a system which they know from their own observations and experience yields poorer productivity and higher costs, on the average and over the long run, than does the existing management system of the company.'

If the available evidence is so strongly in favour of the superiority of participative styles of management over the traditional autocratic style, why is it that everybody—managers, workers, unions, scholars etc.—continues to be sceptical about participative management? How come that even those who *believe* in participative management or self-management as socially or humanely more acceptable frequently voice concern over an alleged participation–efficiency dilemma? The situation could not be more paradoxical: many managers and scholars believe in the efficiency of participative management yet voice concern over the participation–efficiency dilemma. Or, to put it very bluntly, they apparently believe simultaneously in the efficiency and inefficiency of participative management. What they seem to be saying is this: there is something to be gained from participative management; and there also is something to be gained from professional, autocratic management. But this is not all. They now go on saying that the two styles of management are mutually exclusive: you can't have it both ways. And if confronted with a choice, many tend to choose autocracy over democracy, exhibiting more trust and confidence in the former rather than the latter. Likert (1967, p. 11) presents an interesting illustration of this point, based on his own empirical findings:

Some low-producing managers, although they display the same pattern of answers as other managers, believe that a manager should move toward system 4 *after* he has achieved high levels of productivity (Miles, 1966). They feel that the way to move from low to high productivity is to use a management system well toward the left (e.g. system 1 or 2) and move toward system 4 only after high productivity is achieved. Their view is essentially that of the supervisor of a low-producing unit who said: 'This interest-in-people approach is all right, but it is a luxury. I've got to keep pressure on for producing, and when I get production up, then I can afford to take time to show an interest in my employees and their problems.' Research results show that managers who hold this view are not likely to achieve high productivity in their units. (Likert, 1961, ch. 2)

I hope that, at this point, the reader is utterly confused. After all, why should he see more clearly than all these scholars and managers where a solution to this seeming paradox could lie. Before I proceed to develop a solution, I will present some further evidence which may enable the reader to draw conclusions in the direction of a solution.

On the blueprint of a company, leadership is a very specific phenomenon, a task or function assigned to specific roles or positions. Leadership roles are located at the top of the company hierarchy, and the structure of these roles is again hierarchical, culminating in one highest and ultimate leadership role, for example that of the chairman of the board. Yet the social reality of leadership is quite different from that blueprint. In actuality, leadership is highly *diffuse* and *not* limited to any *specific* roles or positions (cf. Luhmann, 1964, pp. 206–7). Leadership functions may be carried out by any member of an organization at any time. As a matter of fact, if only those who are designated and paid for, as leaders (managers, executives) would 'lead', i.e. co-ordinate, make decisions etc., an organization would run into most serious problems.

The diffuseness of leadership has been documented by empirical studies, and the results of one may stand for all. In a study of 78 sales offices, Bowers and Seashore (1964, pp. 5–6) found:

> Our data sustain the idea that group members do engage in behavior which can be described as leadership, and that in these groups, it appears likely that the total quantity of peer leadership is at least as great as the total quantity of supervisory leadership. The groups varied greatly from one another with respect to the degree and the pattern of emphasis in peer leadership behavior. (Cited in Likert, 1967, p. 72)

Moreover, 'the analysis by Bowers and Seashore provides impressive evidence of the substantial contribution to organizational success of the leadership provided by the nonsupervisory members of an organization' (Likert, 1967, p. 73).

The reader may now at last see a way out of the paradox, but this is yet premature. For while there is 'important evidence to show that peer leadership can contribute substantially to high performance' (Likert, 1967, p. 73), there is even stronger evidence to the exact opposite: peer leadership can contribute substantially to *low* performance.

A large number of studies, starting with the famous Western Electric Hawthorne project (Roethlisberger & Dickson, 1939), have provided extensive evidence to show that 'informal organization and leadership' are present in most enterprises and, as a rule, cause costly reductions in organizational performance because of the restriction of output. Very few studies are available which demonstrate that these peer-leadership processes can result equally well in increased rather than restricted production. Three studies which do so are the Cock and French (1948) experiment, the clerical experiment (Likert, 1961, ch. 5; Morse and Reimer, 1956), and the study by Patchen (1960). (Likert, 1967, p. 73)

Does the one set of evidence invalidate the other, and is the result then a no-finding? Or is there indeed a solution to the puzzle? Likert (1967, p. 73) actually comes very close to the solution when he says:

. . . peer leadership can contribute substantially to high performance and should be used positively for this purpose rather than being permitted to restrict production through the use of system 1 or 2 management.

This is now our solution of the paradox in three postulates:

1. Postulate of the diffuseness of leadership

Most members of an organization carry out leadership functions: they co-ordinate activities and make decisions that affect themselves and others. Hence, leadership is diffuse, i.e. spread over a much wider number of members of an organization than expressed in the blueprint. Diffuse leadership is more than mere potential; it is intermittently activated by anyone in the organization irrespective of the *formal* assignment of leadership roles. There may be considerable variations between members of the organization in terms of frequency and extent to which leadership functions are carried out; but these variations are not necessarily—and definitely not fully—determined by the formal assignment of leadership functions: managers and executives do not necessarily lead 'more' than employees in nonsupervisory positions.

It is important to realize that diffuse leadership is carried out by supervisory and nonsupervisory personnel in all management systems, under conditions of autocratic management as well as under conditions of participative management. Without extensive empirical studies, there is even no way of telling whether there is more leadership carried out by nonsupervisory personnel under autocratic or participative management. The uses to which such leadership is put are of course diametrically opposed in different management systems as we will see in the following two postulates.

2. Postulate of the low productivity ('dysfunctionality') of diffuse leadership under autocratic management

In 1931, Elton Mayo and his Harvard associates studied the Bank Wiring Observation Room of the Hawthorne plant of General Electric. The result:

1. It was discovered very early that each individual in the group was restricting output in spite of the fact that the group piecework incentive plan in operation provided for a larger wage return the greater the number of units completed.

2. The working group as a whole actually determined the output of individual workers by reference to a standard predetermined but never clearly stated, that represented the group conception of a fair day's work.

3. The group output standard is only one of many social norms defined by the informal organization of the workers. Workers formed themselves into strong social groups with appropriate customs, duties, routines, even rituals. Strong social controls were constituted to command conformity to the group definitions and expectations.

4. In the contest between a management expectation and the group standards, the informal organization of the workers is most likely to prevail in determining conduct.

5. The power of the group controls is attested to by the fact that no relation was found between individual scores on dexterity or output or between intelligence test scores and output. The lowest man in output, for example, ranked first in intelligence. (Miller and Form, 1964, p. 667)

This is a classical study of what happens to output or productivity *under conditions of autocratic management: the work group utilizes its leadership potential to decrease productivity*. In 1958, Landsberger re-examined the Hawthorne studies and the numerous criticisms and comments that had been published since Mayo's *Human Problems of an Industrial Civilization, Social Problems of an Industrial Civilization*, and *Political Problems of an Industrial Civilization*, and Roethlisberger and Dickson's *Management and the Worker* (1939). His conclusion: the formation of informal groups and the restriction of output is a 'reaction of workers to threats by management' (Landsberger, 1958, p. 113), or to autocratic management.

Autocratic management does not eliminate the diffuse leadership of the workers, on the contrary, it activates it and by doing so turns it against autocratic management and the goals of the organization. High productivity as an organizational goal is thus interpreted by the workers as the goal of its 'class enemy', i.e. autocratic management—and thwarted. A situation emerges in which 'workers' management' stands against 'managers' management'—the former hidden, the latter overt; the former opting for low productivity, the latter pressing for high productivity. As workers' management turns out to be stronger than managers' management, the result of this power struggle is output restriction and lowered productivity.

Traditionally, the literature has been quick in pointing out that there is great *potential* for conflict between 'workers' management' and 'managers' management' in a self-managing economy. We have no qualms over this. But contrary to the conventional literature, we insist that this point does not prove much. There is great potential for conflict in every social relationship, and such conflict may in fact have important roles to play, as Simmel (1922) and Coser (1956) show. Against the assertion of great *potential* for conflict under self-management, we claim that there is a great *necessity* for conflict between 'workers' management' and 'managers' management' under conditions of autocratic management styles. Moreover, as we have seen in our discussion of *the postulate of the low productivity of diffuse leadership under autocratic management*, the resolutions of such conflict under self-management are likely to be in the direction of the overall organizational goals, i.e. working toward greater productivity—while such conflict under autocratic management is likely to be an integral part of the system and thus not to be solved at all, resulting in output reductions.

In short: under conditions of autocratic management, the diffuse leadership potential of workers is activated to the effect of lowering productivity. This explains why autocratic management is an inefficient method of running a company.

3. *Postulate of the high productivity ('eufunctionality') of diffuse leadership under participative management*

Participative management activates the leadership potential of two groups of organizational participants, workers and managers, to one and the same effect: high productivity. Instead of engaging in a kind of class struggle, both groups cooperate in the pursuance of the organizational goal. This postulate explains the high productivity of participative management in the United States as well as in Yugoslavia.

The suspicion towards self-management in Yugoslavia seems to be based on a misconception, namely the assumption that 'workers' management' excludes 'managers' management'. If it is then assumed in addition that only managers can lead and workers cannot, then the result of workers' management would of course be anarchism, i.e. the absence of any rule and regular decision-making, which would be chaos. But first of all, workers do have a leadership potential just as managers do; and secondly, self-management in Yugoslavia combines workers' management with managers' management. Yugoslav companies do have professional managers, with the exception maybe of very small companies that would not hire professional managers in other countries either. Emerik Blum (1970, p. 192) describes his position as general manager of *Energoinvest*, a Sarajevo-based company for the planning, designing and construction of investment projects in the field of power production and processing industries:

The director of a Yugoslav enterprise organized along the lines of workers' management is not a government-appointed employee but rather a person chosen under conditions of competition, without any interference by anyone on the outside. He may make his election or the extension of his tenure as director dependent upon a variety of elements, not all of them relating to his personal status (for instance, salary, term of office, severance pay etc.). In his work, he enjoys a sufficient degree of independence. Not only do the workers' management bodies not impede him in his work but they actually facilitate it. Naturally, the director of a Yugoslav enterprise must have the necessary knowledge and ability required under the social system in Yugoslavia. In such a case, I think *it is considerably easier for a Yugoslav director to function efficiently than it is for his colleague in the Western countries, as the workers' management bodies are not representatives of opposing interest* as are, e.g. the trade unions in the West. On the other hand, if we compare his position with that of his counterparts in the administrative systems of the East he again has the advantage as he is not subject to the assessments and will of government administration and officials, but responsible only to the internal representative bodies of the enterprise and to the collective in which he work. (Italics added)

In terms of day-to-day routine, the actual activities of professional managers in Yugoslavia may thus hardly differ from those of professional managers in the United States, as Kamušič (1970, p. 112) points out:

As to the wide range of the possibilities it offers, the pluralistic model of self-managed enterprises and the pluralistic systems of self-managing relations generally does not differ essentially from the capitalist model of enterprise and from the modern type of mixed capitalist economic systems.

The fundamental difference between the United States and Yugoslavia is of course that the means of production in the United States are *privately owned*, while they are *socially owned* in Yugoslavia. In terms of accountability, that means that American managers are responsible to the stockholders, Yugoslav managers to the workers in their enterprises. As a result of the more direct control of Yugoslav workers over management and their vested business interests in the company and the quality of management, non-professional criteria like kinship ties and many others are much less likely to be of importance in the selection of a manager in Yugoslavia than elsewhere.

An additional difference is of course that American managers may choose between participative and autocratic styles of management, while Yugoslav managers have no choice: the system only provides for participative management. This does of course not preclude the possibility that some Yugoslav managers turn out to be, or try to be, autocrats. But autocratic management is deviant behaviour in Yugoslavia and likely to be responded to by the workers accordingly.

The conclusion thus is that Yugoslavia, with its system of self-management, gets the best out of both worlds: *it utilizes the management potential of its workers and the management potential of its professional managers, combining both to the maximization of productivity*.

This may thus provide at least a partial explanation for Yugoslavia's exceptional economic growth during the past two decades. Yet a note of caution may be added here. We have to bear in mind that self-management is not activated in every company in Yugoslavia to the same extent; it is a generally accepted ideal, but its actualization has been faster in some companies than in others. As Zdenko Krstulović, general manager of Jedinstvo, pointed out to Jenkins (1973, p. 114):

You must understand that self-management is a completely new thing. Twenty years is not enough to make it perfect. We are still in the development stage and there still is a lot to be done.

Hence, differences in the degree of actualization of genuine self-management between companies may very well explain differences in productivity, perfectly in accord with the findings of Mozina, Jervošek, Tannenbaum and Likert in ten more efficient and ten less efficient Yugoslav companies (cf. pp. 128–9). There is still ample room for the further growth of self-management in Yugoslavia.

8 Equity under Self-Management: Equality or Inequality?

TO EACH ACCORDING TO HIS CONTRIBUTION

Socialism is frequently suspected of wage-equalization, a suspicion derived from the Marxist slogan 'From each according to his ability, to each according to his needs'. But this principle is very remote from socialist practice. This does not mean that socialists do not *believe* in equality. In fact, equality is the *dream* of socialists, a dream to come true in some future world under an economic system called communism. Marx (1938, p. 10) is quite explicit about the idealist and utopian character of real equality in the system of distribution:

> In a higher phase of communist society, after the enslaving subordination of individuals under division of labour, and therewith also the antithesis between mental and physical labour, has vanished; after labour, from a mere means of life, has itself become the prime necessity of life; after the productive forces have also increased with the all-round development of the individual, and all the springs of co-operative wealth flow more abundantly—only then can the narrow horizon of bourgeois right be fully left behind and society inscribe on its banners: from each according to his ability, to each according to his needs!

Equality will thus, only become possible after scarcity has been abolished. As long as scarcity is still around, inequalities seem to be needed as incentives and rewards to make the achievement slogan '*from* each according to his ability' become reality. For the Soviet Union, Stalin realized this during the second post-revolutionary decade. He then launched an attack against equality-mongering and wage equalization and began a movement of personal incentive based on differential reward (Seibel, 1976). The results of this new policy were spectacular: within little more than a decade, the Soviet Union underwent its industrial revolution.

From its inception, the new Yugoslavia accepted wage differentials as incentives to production. There were of course ideological debates over the equality–inequality issue, but at no time was there any attempt made to equalize wages *completely*. On the other hand, giving everyone, or a few, opportunities for *unlimited* incomes was similarly unacceptable. Hence, the range of personal earnings was always under some kind of control, allowing for a certain amount of income differentiation and simultaneously keeping differentiation within limits.

Shortly after the war, under state socialism, state organs determined the earnings of all employees by means of exceedingly complicated pay scales, 'differentiating them on the basis of the post they held in the hierarchy, their qualifications, the importance and difficulty of their work, and production norms set for a wide variety of jobs' (Bajec, n.d., p. 38).

The introduction of self-management in industry prepared the way for the development of self-managed inequality. Companies gained more and more control over their earnings, and the amount and significance of contributions to state-managed funds diminished gradually. The availability of company earnings for allocation to personal incomes, investments etc., provided thus the 'material base' of self-management. Within companies, decisions about the allocation of incomes to an investment fund, of profits to be redistributed among the workers and to other funds came under the authority of the workers. The basic principle that guided workers in their allocation decision was 'To each according to his contribution'.

Tito summarized the Yugoslav principle of distribution and the balancing act between too little and too much inequality in his introductory address to the Second Congress of Self-Managers:

Needless to say, as long and until individual labour remains the primary and decisive factor of social existence and progress, the product of socially organised labour shall consequently be distributed according to one's individual contribution. Economic and social inequality is therefore objectively inevitable. Any attempt to abolish the existing inequality by force would only transform people into forced labourers or turn them into drones and parasites and hence place the very existence of society in jeopardy. . . . The statistical data available indicate that personal income differentials within individual work organizations (this refers only to personal incomes deriving from the labour relationship) are not exaggerated or unjustifiedly large. . . . Moreover, an opposite tendency is increasingly noticeable, namely that income differentials in some work organizations are too small, so that experts and highly skilled personnel tend to seek employment elsewhere where personal income levels are higher—or even go abroad. Consequently, although certain acute problems exist in this sphere, they are neither of a primary or of a decisive importance. (Tito, in Starčević, 1972, p. 37)

The same principle of *income according to performance* applies also to earnings from independent work, though its enactment is of course much more difficult to control:

According to certain data published recently, for example, the share of personal income acquired outside of the labour relationship accounts for 30 per cent of total personal income in the country. This figure undoubtedly comprises a great deal of honest labour which deserves to be and indeed is remunerated properly. But it is no less certain that there are quite a few cases of profit earning without work, evasion of social control, to say nothing of various abuses. . . . Needless to say, it would be wrong to be swayed be demagogic arguments that proclaim a refrigerator, TV set, motor car etc., social evils. There is nothing intrinsically wrong with these durable consumer goods. In the final analysis, people work in order to live better, and the more affluent a society, the greater the ease with which people will acquire durable consumer goods characteristic of a high standard of living. It is a serious social evil, however, if someone attains such a standard of living at the expense of other people's labour, by the infraction of the principle of income distribution according to results of work, by virtue of one's privileged position which enable some to appropriate a larger share of total social income than is theirs by right, by curtailing the rights of other working people, by appropriating an unjustifiedly large share of total social accumulation etc. (Tito, in Starčević, 1972, pp. 38–9)

TO EACH ACCORDING TO HIS NEEDS

On principle, a company's income depends on its profits, and there is accordingly considerable variation in income between companies. Such differences between companies reflect on the personal incomes of workers. In addition, workers' incomes depend on their work contribution and on the decision of the company—specifically the workers' council—as to the amount to be distributed and the sum to be received by each. Yet it would be wrong to conclude that one's income is totally determined by the profits of one's company and by one's work within the company.

In reality, income variations are substantially reduced by the following measures:

1. Each worker is guaranteed a specific minimum personal income by each company which cannot be below the nationally determined minimum wage;
2. There is a ceiling income which must not be exceeded;
3. The law provides for consultations between companies within the same industrial sector or region and for so-called social consultations between economic chambers, trade unions, and government agencies. In these consultations, common bases are established for the apportionment of net income and for the allocation of workers' personal incomes;
4. Taxation may be imposed on the part of net incomes allocated to personal incomes which exceeds the level established in the consultations.

The principle 'To each according to his contribution' is thus being supplemented by the principle 'To each according to his needs'. 'Needs' are of course relative and depend on the level of economic development of the country. As the country develops, needs rise, and the principle 'To each according to his needs' gradually picks up weight. The more developed a country, the less important are individual contributions. As the dualism of the two principles is a firmly established part of the Yugoslav system, we may see in the future, a gradual 'withering-away' of the 'To each according to his contribution' principle.

At present, striving for more equality in income by limiting the ceiling of personal incomes is not without its problems. On 8 August 1973, I interviewed Milan Beslać, a member of the General Conference of the Socialist Alliance of Workers of Croatia, in Zagreb. He expressed concern over social differences which in his opinion were too wide:

It is now our goal to reduce them. The principle of the reduction of social differences is 'To each according to his work'. Work and its results are to be the basis of distribution. In the past many made a lot of money on account of somebody else's work; this will be eliminated.

'Will this reduction of social differences not act as a negative incentive to prospective inventors and innovators who would make a tremendous amount of money with their discoveries?' I asked.

Yes, every inventor in Yugoslavia is free to sell his invention to the US or elsewhere, and he may get rich on it. If he works for a local research institute, however, he receives a much lower share as it is assumed that the institute has directly or indirectly contributed to his invention.

It is a fact that many leave, not only inventors but also experts. In West Germany, Switzerland or Sweden, they can make a lot more money. There is a brain drain, and there is nothing Yugoslavia can, or will, do about it. This is an open country, and the brain drain is our price for this openness.

We are aware of the fact that this brain drain is a form of imperialism. For we have trained these experts, and other countries take them for free.

We can and we do try to stimulate our workers and to provide them with incentives to stay; but because of the differences in economic development we cannot pay as much as West Germany or the United States.

ATTITUDES TO EQUALITY AND PRODUCTIVITY

Yugoslav workers are very concerned about productivity, because there is a very close—and socially visible—link between their productivity and their personal income. At the same time, equality being a remote ideal, income inequalities have to stay within certain limits: there is to be no room for 'robber barons' who get rich at the expense of others. Robber barons may be easily spotted, and as all agree about their undesirability, it does not seem too difficult to prevent them from emerging. There are some groups of people about, however, for whom it is much more difficult to come up with such a simple solution. These are the innovators and inventors, the actual and the potential ones, and the latter may in fact be a great many. Innovators and inventors are important for productivity; that means they contribute to the income of all. If they are fully rewarded for their contributions as innovators and inventors, some may end up with exorbitant incomes, exceeding by far the income ceilings. The existence of such income ceilings limits of course the amount they may receive for the inventions or innovations. But suppose this has a stifling effect on these highly important people? There may thus exist an equality–productivity dilemma, which, at least theoretically, could be solved in the direction of more equality or more productivity. At present, it is difficult to estimate how concrete this dilemma is. But it has occupied the minds of Yugoslav scholars, and several survey studies have asked for popular opinions about this dilemma. One of the Yugoslav scholars who concerns himself with this dilemma is Niko Toš of the University of Ljubljana (Fakultet za sociologijo, politične vede in novinarstvo). He has done several opinion surveys in which he included questions pertaining to a supposed equality–productivity dilemma.

He starts off with the assumption that unequal rewards may be an incentive in production. That would mean that unequal rewards and rapid economic growth tend to go together, while equal rewards tend to slow down the rate of economic growth. In May and June 1969, a random sample of 2400 adult Slovenians, representative of Slovenia, confronted him with that dilemma in an opinion poll (sample I). The poll was administered by the opinion research centre of the Faculty of Sociology and Political Science at the University of Ljubljana. The question was:

What do you consider more desirable: rapid growth of productivity though this may entail increasing social differences, or more equality between individuals though this may entail lower productivity?

The proportions of the population opting for each alternative were about the same, the number of those who emphasized rapid growth with increased inequality being slightly higher (Table 8.1, column 1).

Two years later, the same question was put before a national random sample of 2500 adults, representative of the whole of Yugoslavia (sample II). The results indicate a marked preference for more equality even at the expense of sacrificing some economic growth (Table 8.1, column 7). But when broken down by republic, the data for Slovenia show only a slight change towards a preference for more equality (Table 8.1, column 7). The differences between the results of the 1969 and 1971 surveys might very well be attributed to chance. A more definite answer may be possible when the results of the 1973 survey are available.

TABLE 8.1 Attitudes to the productivity–equality dilemma in two samples, 1969 and 1971 (%)

	Higher productivity and social inequality	*More equality and lower productivity*	*Miscellaneous*	*No answer*	*Total*
Sample I (1969)					
1. Slovenia	45.5	43.4	3.2	8.0	100.1[a]
Sample II (1971)					
2. Yugoslavia	32.2	45.7	2.4	19.7	100.0
3. Bosnia and Herzegovina	28.1	46.1	0.9	24.9	100.0
4. Montenegro	23.5	40.6	0.3	35.5	99.9[a]
5. Croatia	46.1	44.8	7.7	1.5	100.1
6. Macedonia	23.2	45.9	0.8	30.1	100.0
7. Slovenia	40.6	44.4	3.2	11.8	100.0
8. Serbia	26.7	48.0	1.2	24.1	100.0
9. Vojvodina	29.7	36.3	0.9	33.1	100.0
10. Kosovo	21.1	48.0	0.3	29.7	99.1[b]

NOTES
[a] Error due to rounding.
[b] Error unexplained.

SOURCES
Toš (1969, p. 25).
Mlinar and Toš (1971, p. 43).
Toš (1971, pp. 61–1).

Confronted with the productivity–equality dilemma in relatively abstract terms as in the above question, a considerable proportion of Yugoslavs opted for increased equality. This result may very well be interpreted as an expression of a value orientation towards equality or egalitarianism. One should emphasize, as a note of caution, that the question asked for attitudes to 'more equality', not 'total equality'.

If the dilemma is put in more concrete terms, however, the equality ideal receives less support, as the answers to the following question show:

Should the innovators and actual managers receive higher wages even though this means higher inequality, or should we first attempt to decrease differences in income even though this would represent less of an incentive for managers and innovators? (Table 8.2)

TABLE 8.2 Attitudes to the productivity and equality-between-workers-and-top-personnel dilemma

	Higher productivity and social inequality	More equality and lower productivity	Miscel- laneous	No answer	Total
Sample 1 (1969)					
1. Slovenia	60.1	29.3			100
Sample II (1971)					
2. Yugoslavia	47.2	31.4	0.9	20.5	100
3. Bosnia and Herzegovina	43.1	34.0	0.5	22.3	99.9[a]
4. Montenegro	34.8	39.9	0.7	24.6	100.0
5. Croatia	59.8	26.6	1.0	12.6	100.0
6. Macedonia	29.6	43.0	0.8	26.6	100.0
7. Slovenia	55.1	31.4	2.7	10.9	100.1[a]
8. Serbia	46.3	30.7	0.9	22.2	100.1
9. Vojvodina	39.5	25.1	0.9	34.5	100.0
10. Kosovo	12.6	53.1	0.0	34.3	100.0

NOTE
[a] Error due to rounding.

SOURCES
Mlinar and Toš (1971, p. 43).
Toš (1971, pp. 62–3).

However one could also come up with a different interpretation. The answers to question 1 indicate an equality preference for the masses of the workers. The answers to question 2 show that the respondents would like to see those in top positions, the innovators and professional managers, exempt from such 'equality mongering'.

INCOME INEQUALITIES

How unequal are incomes in Yugoslavia compared with incomes in other countries? There is no simple, straightforward answer to this question, because there is no simple measurement of income inequalities. Lane (1971, pp. 72–5) examined the ratio of highest to lowest income and the ratio of highest to average income in the United States and in some socialist countries.

He found that distribution in the United States is extremely unequal, while distribution in socialist countries is less unequal. Lenski (1966, p. 27) estimates the ratio of highest to lowest income in the United States as 11,000:1 and the ratio of highest to average as 7000:1.

There are several estimates for the Soviet Union: Kostin (1960) estimates the ratio of lowest to highest income as 1:13, Bottomore (1965) estimates the income of manual workers to factory managers as 1:25 to 1:30. Lane (1971, pp. 72–4) claims that these are assertions and that 'such wide differentials have not been backed up by empirical data'. He estimates the ratio of lowest to average income as about 1:1.9. In any event, the difference between the ratio for the United States and the ratio for the Soviet Union is enormous.

Wesołowski (1966) found that the ratio of highest to lowest income in Poland has fallen from about 200:1 in pre-war Poland to 10:1 in the 1960s.

Wachtel (1973, p. 146) reports for Yugoslavia that 'the absolute level of wage differentials in the Yugoslav economy is quite narrow, when compared to other economies, especially in light of its relatively lower level of economic development which normally would herald wide wage differentials. By 1967, the highest paid skill group (white-collar workers with high school education and above) was earning only 2.5 times the lowest-paid group (unskilled blue-collar workers).'

Until 1961, wage differentials continued to increase in Yugoslavia. 'After 1961,' Wachtel (1973, pp. 145–6) found, 'wage differentials became narrower for all types of wage structures, with the exception of interindustry wage differentials.' This is in agreement with a hypothesis developed by Reynolds and Taft (1956) according to which a predominantly agriculturally oriented economy produces large wage differentials once it starts industrializing. 'The first factories . . . would have to pay relatively high wages to overcome the inertia of a rural labour force reluctant to sacrifice its familiar agricultural environment for the uncertainty of life and work in an industrial setting.' (Wachtel, 1973, p. 123.) In other words: during a country's industrial revolution, wage differentials tend to widen; subsequently, they are likely to become narrower again.

To find this tendency in Yugoslavia is remarkable in that political debate and economic policy was first, i.e. after the introduction of self-management, strongly influenced by an egalitarian wage philosophy, which led to severe restrictions in a company's freedom in wage determination until 1957 when some of the restrictions were lifted; in 1961, they were removed altogether. It is also remarkable to note the parallels to the Soviet Union where Stalin found it necessary to eliminate wage equalization—contrary to the doctrine—with the onset of the period of rapid industrialization. Just as Wachtel reports that wage differentials have subsequently diminished there are similar indications that there has been a tendency towards more equality in the Soviet Union, starting in the 1950s.

Some more precise data on Yugoslavia: inter-skill wage differentials increased between 1956 and 1961, the dispersion around the mean being 35.0 per cent in 1956 and 43.3 per cent in 1961; after 1961, it decreased. Examining the ratio of highest-wage skill group to lowest-wage skill group in individual industries, a similar pattern emerges.

In 1956, 64 percentage points separated the electric energy industry, which had the highest ratio, and the crude petroleum industry, which had the lowest ratio. In 1961 there was a difference of 127 percentage points between the industry with the greatest interskill wage differential and the industry with the lowest interskill wage differential. However, in 1966 the difference was only 52 percentage points, and in 1967, 65 percentage points. In short, not only is there a narrowing of interskill wage differentials *within* most industries in the Yugoslav economy, but over time there is also a convergence of these differentials *among* industries. (Wachtel, 1973, p. 130.)

For inter-republic wage differentials, there is a similar trend, with a 2-year time lag, however: 'Wage differentials between republics increased between 1956 and 1963 and then fell between 1963 and 1969' (Wachtel, 1973, p. 134).

Let us now look at income distribution in some companies that I have visited during the summer of 1973. In Kroj, a garment

TABLE 8.3 Income distribution in a garment company in Slovenia, 1973

Rank of position	No. of employees	Income (point value[a])
1	1	2600
2	1	2200
3	2	2000
4	1	1500
5	3	1400
6	5	1300
7	4	1250
8	9	1200
9	1	1150
10	5	1050
11	11	1000
12	4	950
13	18	900
14	8	850
15	4	800
16	4	750
17	23	700
18	20	650
19	139	620
20	4	600
Total number of employees	267	

NOTE

[a] The point value of a position is the basis on which personal incomes are calculated; the dinar amount per point is determined annually and depends primarily on expected earnings.

SOURCE
Kroj, company records.

factory in Slovenia with 267 employees, relative wages are listed on a scale ranging from 600 to 2600 points. The lowest income is that of a janitor, the highest that of the general manager. The ratio between lowest and highest income is 1:4.3, i.e. the general manager's income is 4.3 times higher than that of the janitor (Table 8.3).

Until 1961, wages were regulated by a government-established wage structure, differentiating between nine different skill and qualification groups. As companies were free to set the wage dispersion within skill or qualification groups, they had considerable freedom in wage determination—only the weighted averages had to conform to the government-regulated scale. After 1961, the government ceased to regulate wages; only a statutory minimum wage continued to be set by the government. Since then, pay scales have been determined by each company individually, following a detailed set of rules. The workers' council of a company selects a subcommittee which prepares a preliminary report on wage rates. This report is distributed among all workers of the company. At a later point in time, a meeting is frequently convened by the trade union at which the proposal of the workers' council is carefully examined. Sometimes, an additional report is then prepared by the trade union and also distributed among the workers. After a certain period, the workers' council calls a meeting to which all workers are invited to debate the proposed wage rates. Finally, the proposal is redrafted, and a general meeting of all workers in the company is convened for a final debate of the wage rates and their adoption. The final document comprises the *Pravilnici o Raspodeli Ličnih Dohodka*, the *Rules of the Distribution of Personal Income* (Wachtel, 1973, p. 104). Since 1961, the *Rules* have been binding on the company. They contain the wage rates for every occupation, which in turn may be broken down into different skill and qualification groups. Since the late 1950s, wage rates have been determined through job-evaluation techniques:

Initially, each job is evaluated in terms of a variety of criteria: skill and experience, educational requirements, responsibility, physical effort, mental effort, working conditions, materials handled on the job, and the like. For each of these criteria 'points' are assigned. At this stage, the preliminary wage structure, based upon evaluation of the job, is adjusted to take account of labor-market conditions. (Wachtel, 1973, pp. 105–6.)

The result is a point scale as presented in Table 8.3.

Personal incomes of workers in Yugoslavia consist of three components: the *fixed wage*, which the worker receives periodically for his labour input; the *variable wage*, which represents the workers' share of redistributed company profits; and various fringe benefits and allowances. The *concept* of a fixed wage and variable wage was abolished in 1961, though *in practice* the distinction continues to exist. In theory, all of the workers' income is determined by the company's profits since 1961, the fixed wage representing an *advance* payment on expected profits, which are of course calculated very conservatively, and the variable wage representing a periodical adjustment *after* profits have been calculated at the end of an accounting period, frequently quarterly. This system was codified in three provisions of the 1966 Laws on Employment Relationships:

1. A worker's income shall be fixed by the (collective) on the basis of the money available for distribution in the final (income statement);
2. In the course of a year a worker shall receive advances on his personal income, depending on the current results of work operations;
3. A worker shall be entitled to a minimum personal income, irrespective of the results of the organization's work and operations. (Institute of Comparative Law, *Laws on Employment Relationships*, Belgrade: Institute of Comparative Law, 1967, p. 36. Quoted in Wachtel, 1973, p. 100)

In Kroj, a garment factory in Slovenia, profits are computed monthly and added to each pay cheque, the base wage, which is determined through the procedure described above before each year. Because of increases in company profits, the personal incomes of the workers at Kroj went up 29 per cent in 1972. In June 1973, the average base wage was 1750 dinars net. In addition, each worker received 60 dinars as a food allowance and 10 dinars for continued service (newly-hired employees are of course excluded from this payment). Workers who were never absent received an additional 50 dinars. Profits in June 1973 added an additional 16 per cent, which brings the average personal income per worker up to approximately 2170 dinars. The income of a janitor in Kroj is about 1100 dinars, the income of the general manager is 5500 dinars. The ratio of lowest-paid to highest-paid worker is thus 1:5. The general manager in Kroj believes that there is a trend towards more equality in the company, the target ratio being about 1:3. A ratio between lowest-paid and highest-paid worker between 1:3 and 1:5 seems most widespread. In Bratsvo, a machine factory in Zagreb, the lowest wage was 1150 dinars (net), the highest 4600 dinars, the ratio being 1:4.

In Alhos, a garment factory in Sarajevo, the base wage averages approximately 1500 dinars a month, the lowest income being 1200 and the highest 5500: a ratio of 1:4.6. Profits are computed monthly and add about 5 per cent to the workers' income. In the past, workers received a vacation allowance; this was discontinued in 1973 because profits were too low. Seniority allowances may add up to 200 dinars a month to a worker's income: for each 5 years of service, a worker receives an additional 0.5 per cent of his wage, up to a maximum of 2 per cent after 20 years of service. For workers who have been with the company for more than 20 years, there may be additional payments from a so-called solidarity fund: through 'norm correction', a worker may be compensated for his loss of income due to advanced age. The company has a medical recreation programme: workers may be sent to a recreation home at the company's expense, with wage payments continuing. Meals can be purchased at the company for 6–7 dinars (40–45 cents). Workers with a monthly income of 1200 dinars receive a food allowance of 3 dinars a day, workers with an income above 1200 dinars up to 1700 dinars receive an allowance of 2.50 dinars per day.

Grmeč is a producer of bituminous and synthetic products in Belgrade. On 15 August 1973, I interviewed the general manager of the company. Also present were the president of the workers' council, the secretary of the League of Communists, and the secretary of the company. Grmeč was founded in 1926. After the Second World War it was a small company of 60 to 65 workers, with obsolete machinery. Since then, it has grown considerably. Two plants have separated and become independent. In the remaining three plants, there are about 500 workers. Grmeč is a highly productive company, the workers' incomes being about twice as high as in comparable enterprises. Slobodan Boshkovic, the general manager of Grmeč, estimates that the rates of real growth have been about 20 per cent per annum. These high growth rates and the resulting high productivity have provided the basis for the exceptionally high incomes of the workers in this company. Income payments are made monthly, and no distinction is made between a wage and a salary: both are 'personal incomes'. Everyone receives an advance on the 25th of each month, the balance being paid on the following 10th after each worker's exact performance has been calculated. Every three months, profits are computed and redistributed. In 1972, redistributed profits amounted to approximately two additional monthly incomes; for 1973, redistributed profits were estimated at about two-and-a-half monthly incomes. In 1972, the net personal income per month averaged about 2800 dinars, the lowest income being 1500 dinars and the highest 7500, the statutory maximum. The ratio between lowest and highest income was thus 1:4.8. The relatively high income allows the workers to enjoy luxuries which are still not yet very common in Yugoslavia: about every other worker at Grmeč owns a car.

Of the company's income, 58 per cent is allocated to personal incomes and 42 per cent to funds for investment, housing etc. This ratio is subject to change at any time, depending on the workers' council decision.

Grmeč provides for its workers a number of fringe benefits:

1. Seniority allowance of 10 dinars per month for each year of service completed;
2. Company canteen in which free lunch is served. The value of this service is estimated at about 200 dinars per month per worker;
3. Free transportation to and from work in company-owned buses;
4. Annual leave allowance. Until 1972, every one received 600 dinars plus additional allowances for each family member. As of 1973, allowances are differentiated by income, in a way opposite to what one would expect in other countries. Workers who earn up to 1750 dinars receive a vacation allowance of 1000 dinars; workers with higher incomes receive only 600 dinars. For each dependent, an additional

200 dinars are paid. If the wife is working, the worker does not receive a dependence allowance for her;

5. Long-term seniority award: for 10 years of service, a watch valued at about 1000 dinars is awarded. For 20 years of service, a worker receives an award of 3000 dinars;

6. Generous housing plan. After a minium of 5 years of employment with the company, workers get an apartment, or a house if they wish so. Apartments are spread all over the area, the location depending on the individual's wishes. The worker has an option between renting the apartment from the company and buying it. Most workers buy it through the company, receiving a 40-year credit at 1 per cent interest from the company. Bachelors get studio apartments, others two- or three-room apartments according to family size (approximately 75–90 square metres). The purchasing price per square metre is approximately 4500 dinars for apartments. For houses, prices are approximately 40 per cent lower, because workers put in their own labour and that of relatives, friends and colleagues—a very common practice in Yugoslavia. If a worker receives an apartment after 5 years of service, he has to stay for at least another 5 years with the company, i.e. for a total of 10 years. The company however does not enforce this rule very strictly.

7. Scholarships for workers: either for after-work training or for full-time study. If a worker does not receive the degree for which he studied, he has to return the scholarship money. If a worker receives a full-time scholarship, he has to stay with the company at least twice the length of time for which he received the scholarship.

All but one of these allowances are available to every worker regardless of income; their overall effect is thus in the direction of wage equalization. The one exception that takes income into account, the vacation allowance, favours the low incomes and thus strengthens the tendency toward equality.

Despite the existence of widespread unemployment in Yugoslavia, companies are very concerned about labour turnover; as there is a tendency for their better skilled and highly experienced workers to leave Yugoslavia for a few years and work in some other country where wages are higher, like West Germany. There are basically two ways by which companies try to attract their employees to stay on: through seniority allowances and through relatively high wages for specialists. Ognjen Prica in Zagreb, for instance, is a company which is aware of this brain drain and tries to induce its workers to a lifetime commitment to work. Ognjen Prica has recently introduced two systems of seniority allowances. The first one is a system of bonuses which are paid once every year. Starting with 5 years of service in the company, a worker receives a bonus which varies with the length of service. It is computed as a percentage of personal income, the percentage increasing from 10 per cent for five years of service by one additional percentage point for each additional year of service up to a maximum of 30 per cent after 25 years of service (Table 8.4).

TABLE 8.4 Annual seniority allowance in Ognjen Prica, Zagreb

Number of years in company	Percentage factor
5	10
6	11
7	12
8	13
—	—
24	29
25	30

SOURCE
Ognjen Prica, company records, Zagreb.

A second seniority allowance system is based on the number of working years both inside and outside the company, adding a monthly allowance to everyone's salary. The percentage factor differs for years of work in Ognjen Prica and in other companies (Table 8.5). An example: Mr Čuješ, President of the Workers' Council at Ognjen Prica, has been with the company for 23 years which entitles him, according to Table 8.5, to a monthly salary increment of 7.5 per cent. Before joining Ognjen Prica, he had worked elsewhere for 12 years, which adds another 2 per cent to his monthly pay cheque. His monthly seniority allowances thus add 9.5 per cent to his personal income.

TABLE 8.5 Monthly seniority allowances in Ognjen Prica, Zagreb

Number of working years	Percentage factor based on work		
	Outside of company	Inside of company	Total
Up to 2	0	0	0
2–5	1	1.5	2.5
5–10	1.5	3	4.5
10–15	2	4.5	6.5
15–20	2.5	6	8.5
20–25	3	7.5	10.5
25–30	3.5	9	12.5
30–35	4	10.5	14.5
Over 35	4.5	12	16.5

SOURCE
Ognjen Prica, company records, Zagreb.

Due to the system of innovation and rationalization allowances (cf. pp. 157–61), seniority allowances and piece-work rates, the wage structure in the company is very differentiated. As a consequence, the general manager, who is supposed to receive the highest income in terms of the point value of his position, in actuality, ranges only as number 40 on the income list. In 1972, this discrepancy was even more pronounced. The general manager receives a monthly salary which is calculated on the basis of a 1500 point value for his position. At a dinar value of 1.3 dinars per point, his income for 182 hours per month amounts to 3549 dinars. In addition, he receives a bonus of 500 to 700 dinars as an incentive based on monthly production results, and his share of redistributed profits. Thus, his total monthly income is approximately 5000 dinars. In 1972, however, there were several typesetters in the company who earned between 5000 and 8000 dinars. The very top earnings had been cut off in 1973. In reaction to a new law which set a ceiling income of 7500 dinars for all of Yugoslavia, the industrial branch to which Ognjen Prica belongs agreed to limit monthly incomes to a maximum of 7120 dinars.

Fringe benefits ('non-wage incomes') add considerably to wage incomes though, with increasing wages, the overall trend has been to pay an increasing proportion of the total income in wages.

The proportion of wages as a percentage of total income in the social sector, which employed about 98 per cent of all workers outside of agriculture in 1967, was 64.5 per cent in 1956 and 72.7 per cent in 1967 (Table 8.6).

TABLE 8.6 The composition of personal incomes in the
social sector in 1956, 1964, 1966 and 1967 (%)

	1956	*1964*	*1966*	*1967*
Wage income	64.5	69.1	71.0	72.7
Non-wage income	35.5	30.9	29.0	27.1
Travel and vacation allowances	4.3	6.9	4.4	4.5
Pensions and disability compensation	6.7	7.8	9.8	10.0
Children's allowances	9.6	4.4	3.6	2.7
Health allowances	10.6	7.0	6.4	6.2
Miscellaneous	4.3	4.8	4.8	3.7

SOURCE

Nevenka Janković, Lični Dohoci kao Faktor Podizanja Živ-
otnog Standarda (Personal Income as a Factor in Raising
Living Standards), Obračun i Respodela Osobnih Dohodaka
u Radnim Oranizacijama. Opatija: Visoka Privredna Škola
Sveučilišta u Zagrebu, 1968, p. 159, cited in Wachtel (1973, p.
127).

INCENTIVES FOR INNOVATIONS AND RATIONALIZATIONS

For every company, innovations and rationalizations are important sources of productivity. Many Yugoslav companies have
incentive plans in order to stimulate workers to come up with
inventions, innovations and suggestions for rationalizations.
Some examples were reported in Chapter 4. In TOZ, for
instance—a highly productive company where wages average
2380 dinars per month and worker (net) and the annual growth
rate is approximately 31 per cent—there is an annual innovation
and rationalization competition: the worker who makes the
biggest contribution in terms of innovations or rationalizations
receives a car, a Fiat 750. The award is actually given for a
composite achievement, encompassing the biggest saving,
orginality, its lasting value and technological innovativeness. In
1972, 34 suggestions for innovations and rationalizations were
submitted and accepted. They saved the company approximately
1,770,000 dinars, and about 100,000 dinars were paid in
incentives.

I asked if such incentives are a cause of envy to those who receive nothing. 'To the contrary,' stated Ivan Švifter, general manager of TOZ, 'everyone realises that these innovations are for the benefit of all. Besides,' he added, 'we fight hard against the egalitarian system.'

From 1965 to 1972, innovations and rationalizations saved the company an estimated amount of 3,110,930 dinars; 166,822 dinars were paid in incentives to 76 workers (Table 8.7).

TABLE 8.7 Innovations and rationalizations in TOZ, Zagreb, from 1965 to 1972

Year	Amount saved (000 dinars)	Number of innovators	Total amount of incentives (000 dinars[d])
1965	78	3	3
1966	276	4	15
1967	327	6	6
1968	198	7	11
1969	97	5	10[a]
1970	240	6	20
1971	133	11	15
1972	1770	34	87
Total	3111[b]	76	167[c]

NOTES

[a] In 1969, the number of innovations decreased because the plant was reconstructed and moved to a different site. The move kept the potential innovators apparently too busy.

[b] Exact amount: 3,110,930.38 dinars.

[c] Exact amount: 166, 821.70 dinars.

[d] Incentives are based on the amount saved, which is calculated for a one-year period, regardless of whether or not an innovation gives long-term results, which is usually the case. This policy is based on the company's *Rules and Regulations*.

SOURCE
Company records.

Another example is Ognjen Prica, a printing company in Zagreb, which I visited on 8 August 1973. In 1956, the workers' council of Ognjen Prica regulated the system of incentives for innovations and rationalizations in a publication, *Pravilnik Normi i Premija*. Originally, incentive amounts ranging from 1500 dinars to 5000 dinars were set out for various innovations and rationalizations. It was soon realized that the maximum limit might have a stifling effect on the workers' innovativeness. A second incentive system was added, therefore, for extraordinary innovations and rationalizations which offered incentives up to a maximum proportion of 15 per cent of the amount saved or 15,000 dinars, whichever was smaller. Today, the company induces its workers to be innovative through an incentive system which is unlimited in the amount a worker may receive; the percentage a worker receives from the amount saved varies, however, with the amount saved (Table 8.8).

TABLE 8.8 Innovations and rationalizations in Ognjen Prica, Zagreb

Amount saved in (dinars)	Incentives as (% of amount saved)
Up to 1000	30
1000–5000	25
5000–10000	20
10000–50000	15
Above 50000	10

SOURCE
Ognjen Prica, Company Records, Zagreb.

TABLE 8.9 Innovations and rationalizations in Ognjen Prica, Zagreb, 1950, 1960, and 1970

Year	Number of innovators	Amount of incentives (dinars)
1950	1	400
	1	150
	3	100
	5	50
1960	1	1500
	2	750
	1	500
1970	1	2500
	2	1200
	1	1000
	2	600

SOURCE
Ognjen Prica, company records, Zagreb.

To give an example: In 1972, a worker proposed a new binding technique which saved the company 40,000 dinars. The worker received a bonus of 15 per cent, i.e. 6000 dinars.

Ognjen Prica provided data on innovations and rationalizations for 1950, 1960, and 1970. In 1950, there were ten innovations for which a total of 700 dinars were paid in incentives. In 1960, there were four innovations which were rewarded with 2750 dinars. In 1970, there were six innovations for which the innovators received 5300 dinars (Table 8.9).

There is no linear trend in the amounts of incentives. Relative to the highest and lowest incomes in the company, the most sizeable payments for innovations were made in 1960; in 1970, they were lower than in 1950 and in 1960 (Table 8.10).

TABLE 8.10 Rationalizations and innovations relative to incomes in Ognjen Prica, Zagreb, in 1950, 1960 and 1970

	1950	*1960*	*1970*
Highest personal income in dinars	170	700	4200
Lowest personal income in dinars	63	150	1100
Average amount of incentives per innovator			
in dinars	70	690	880
as a multiple of highest income	0.4	1.0	0.2
as a multiple of lowest income	1.1	4.6	0.8
Total amount of incentives			
in dinars	700	2750	5300
as a multiple of highest income	4.1	3.9	1.3
as a multiple of lowest income	11.1	18.3	4.8

SOURCE
Ognjen Prica, company records, Zagreb.

There is an interesting coincidence between the data in Table 8.9 and Wachtel's (1973) findings on wage differentials. Wachtel found 1961 to be the turning point: differentials increased until 1961 and decreased afterwards. In a similar fashion, our data from Ognjen Prica reveal that comparing incentives for innovations and rationalizations in 1950, 1960 and 1970, by far the largest payments—relative to incomes at that time in the company—were made in 1960. Similarly, the ratio between lowest and highest income in the company was highest in 1960, namely 1:4.7; in 1950 it was 1:2.7; in 1970 1:3.8 (Table 8.8).

It may in fact be that during the time we have characterized as Yugoslavia's industrial revolution, incentives for innovations and high productivity were most needed and produced, therefore, the highest income differentials.

9 Industrial Relations under Self-Management

THE ROLE OF TRADE UNIONS

'Under capitalism, trade unions are supposed to protect the workers against the capital owners and the executives of capital owners, i.e. management. Under bureaucratic socialism, as found in the Soviet Union and most other countries of Eastern Europe, one could see the role of trade unions in the protection of the workers against the state and the state bureaucracy with its various organs. But what is the role of trade unions in Yugoslavia, where companies are run by workers? Do they protect the workers against themselves?' I asked Ivan Kuković, President of the Slovenian Trade Union Federation in an interview on 6 August 1973, in Ljubljana. Mr Kuković knew of thirteen reasons for the continued existence of trade unions under self-management:

1. One of the goals of trade unions in Yugoslavia is an *increase in*, not total, equality. They are trying to diminish social differences. The maximum ratio between the lowest and the highest income in Slovenian industry is about 1:7.5. About 5 per cent of the companies fall into that category. The trade unions are presently trying to decrease this ratio to 1:6. One has to take into consideration, however, that very few workers receive the lowest or highest wage. For the majority, the ratio is something like 1:3.5.
2. Closely related to the first goal is the trade unions' role in the determination of minimum and maximum incomes. The legal minimum basic net wage is 900 dinars, the maximum 6000 dinars. The absolute maximum, which includes redistributed profits and various allowances, is 7500 dinars. This is the maximum for any position in

Yugoslavia. The minimum wage of 900 dinars is normally higher because of various allowances and of redistributed profits, i.e. between 1000 and 1100 dinars. The trade union federation is presently fighting for a legal minimum wage of 1200 dinars.

3. Trade unions take an influence on the social services offered by a company: food allowances, vacation allowances, training allowances etc. As a consequence of the new autonomy granted to companies, social services varied at first considerably between companies. As a result of the activities of trade unions, some basic rules about minimum and maximum services have been generally accepted.

4. An example of trade union influence on company policies concerning social services is the provision of subsidized basic foods, prices of which are highly inflationary in Yugoslavia. Many companies now offer staple food like potatoes to their workers at subsidized prices.

5. Housing is a serious problem in Yugoslavia. The trade union federation has pressed companies to provide housing for their workers. The advantage would not necessarily be a lower rent (approximately 240 to 280 dinars, that is less than US $20 for an apartment of 60 square meters, which is a one- or two-bedroom apartment) but rather the availability of apartments. There is presently a tremendous housing shortage, and enormous 'broker fees' are paid on a black housing market.

6. While attendance at workers' universities is free, training at other institutions is not. The trade union federation therefore tries to increase the availability of scholarships for workers' advanced training.

7. Trade unions take part in the elaboration of self-management agreements within branches of industry. Through the trade union federation as an intermediary, the companies within a branch of industry agree on common rules of the division of profits into personal incomes and investment.

8. Trade unions organize the elections for workers' councils. They set up the lists of nominees in collaboration with the workers. If workers and trade unions disagree on a nomination, workers have the last word, according to Mr Kuković; against the will of the workers, the trade unions

can neither remove a nominee from a list nor can they insist on a nomination.

9. The trade unions are instrumental in the choice of a general manager. Mr Kuković stated that the trade union has a kind of veto right and that the workers accept such a veto 'under normal circumstances'. If the workers insist on a candidate, however, the candidate may be chosen by the workers despite the trade union's dissent.

10. As anywhere else, trade unions protect workers in a most general sense. For example, the trade union federation offers legal services to workers and to company unions.

    In this context, unions consider it as one of their obligations to detect moot points in company regulations and practices concerning workers.

11. Trade unions also have a broader political function, i.e. they create links between workers' self-management and the political system. A concrete example is that the allocation of gross profits to societal funds and to funds for personal income on the one hand, and for investment on the other hand, are regulated by general statutes. The trade unions engaged in political discussions about these statutes and the allocation of funds, and gradually undermined these statutes. Eventually, they co-ordinated the workers' discussions of these statutes and of their constitutional basis and assisted in the redrafting of a new constitution.

12. The new constitution, which was adopted in 1974, was discussed on all levels throughout 1974. The trade unions played a major role in organizing the discussions. The trade unions probably played no small role in the shaping of the new constitution, according to which workers are now represented on all levels of the political system.

13. A final and most basic goal of the trade unions is the future development of self-management. Mr Kuković considers the new constitution of 1974 as an example of the success of trade union activism.

I had another interview with Neca Jovanov, Secretary of the Trade Union Federation in Belgrade. Neca Jovanov is very actively engaged in the theory and practice of Yugoslav trade unionism. He sees trade unions in Yugoslavia rooted in the political economy on the one hand and in workers' self-management on the other—and consequently changing with the one and the other. I interviewed him on 14 August 1973, in Belgrade. The following is a summary of his views.

Under state socialism, unions transmit and carry out the decisions of the party. According to Lenin, trade unions should protect their workers against their bureaucracy, the state. Stalin introduced a different policy: trade unions were but the mouthpiece of the party and the state.

There are two dangers for any newly created socialist society, including Yugoslavia: one from the bourgeoisie and another from the bureaucracy and party. As to the former, there is presently no chance in Yugoslavia for its re-emergence. Former members of the bourgeoisie may still exist in small numbers, but they are without any power, capital etc. The threat from the bureaucracy and party, however, is much more imminent. Instead of reigning on behalf of the working class, Lenin suggested that the state may reign *over* it. Hence, there may be a conflict between the working class and its own bureaucracy. Examples for this are easily found in Hungary, Poland and Czechoslovakia. It is this conflict which presents a basis for strikes in Yugoslavia.

Under capitalism, there is a conflict between the capitalist's profits and the workers' wages; under state socialism, the conflict lies between the state's profits and the workers' wages. The state tends to take an unduly large share at the expense of the workers.

The state has relinquished much of its economic power in Yugoslavia. Yet, this has not entirely been to the benefit of the working class. While we are witnessing a process of rapid weakening of the state, there has been a simultaneous increase in the power of the banks as the new centres of economic power. This is incompatible with the ideal of self-management. Our present task is thus to check the power of the financial centres, i.e. the banks: loan terms are too short and interest rates too high. The beneficiaries are the banks and their employees. Those who produce should decide over the allocation of the results of their production: this is what trade unions are pushing in the present debate of the draft for a new constitution.

Trade unions are a mass organization of the workers. The

Communist Party, unlike in the past, no longer reigns over the trade unions. The trade unions' main task is now to organize the working class so as to make their struggle most efficient and to transform the 'power on behalf of the working class' into the 'power of the working class'. As Marx said: The liberation of the working class is to be performed by the working class itself.

So far, changes in Yugoslavia have been introduced by the party from above. The party had the leading political role. But it is not the task of the workers to carry out the decisions of the Communist Party as a party, but it is the role of the Communist Party to be the vanguard of the working class in its struggle. Without self-management, there is no true liberation. The most important goal of trade unions is the rapid economic development of Yugoslavia. This implies that the trade unions have to inform the workers that only highly developed economies can have real self-management. Even now self-management is only embryonic. Equality is not equality in poverty but in wealth.

The educational function of trade unions is based on the recognition of the importance of individual consciousness. About half our workers are still unskilled or semi-skilled without a full elementary school education. Their ability for self-management is far too low. That is why trade unions co-operate with workers' universities. They offer courses in three branches: elementary education; technical training; self-management training. It is the trade unions which are mainly responsible for the introduction of workers' universities. They also take a major share in their financial support.

Within the trade unions, additional opportunities for further education are offered, in cooperation with the workers' universities, for instance through self-managers' clubs, which are organized by the trade unions and attached to workers' universities. There is also a federal association of these clubs.

Further on, they have a protective role: according to Lenin against their own state, an ever-present danger.

Trade unions are presently in a state of transition: they are partly under the domination of the party, partly independent.

Concerning cadres, the party nominated the functionaries of trade unions in the past. Today, trade unions have emancipated themselves from the domination of the party: since about 1968 they have elected their own functionaries.

In the past, functionaries of trade unions in companies and in the federation of trade unions were party-introduced, not formally, but in actuality.

Ninety-five per cent of the workers are members of trade unions; the remaining 5 per cent are mainly seasonal workers. Yet membership is not compulsory or automatic.

A fee of 6 per cent of the monthly income is directly deducted from the worker's income. Membership does not bring any direct material privileges; it is mainly a matter of protection.

The difference to the Socialist Alliance of Workers where membership is also almost universal is that the Socialist Alliance is a territorial organization; trade unions are not.

The withering away of trade unions will only come in communist society. To the extent that self-management becomes a reality, the role of trade unions will gradually decrease.

Self-management is the chief objective of trade unions. Trade unions are a political means for the workers to carry out their policy towards self-management.

Self-management is the objective; trade unions are a means. Trade unions are the means of the workers in their struggle for self-management. Unlike Stalin, we believe that power rests in the working class, not in the party.

STRIKES

Self-management has not done away with industrial conflict. While it may have decreased the intensity of such conflicts, it has not eliminated their occurrence. Who participates in strikes? Why do workers strike under self-management? Against whom are strikes directed? And what effect do strikes have?

Below are reported the results of a study on strikes in Yugoslavia by Neca Jovanov (1972), based on three empirical studies done in 1965, 1968 and 1969. The first strike occurred on 13, 14 and 15 January 1958. It was a strike of about 4000 employees in the mines of Trbovlje and Hrastnik. There was total participation: all 3726 miners, 157 technicians and foremen, 17 engineers and 141 administrators, functionaries included, were involved. Why did they strike? Personal incomes in the mining industry were drastically lower than in other branches of economic activity. Prices for coal and for investment goods were centrally determined, and while it was in the interest of state organs to fix low prices for coal and high prices for investment goods needed in the mining industry, workers had of course conflicting interests. The workers went on strike after all other means had been exhausted. In 1958, strikes were illegal, and the miners' strike consequently received no official publicity. In the grapevine, the strike made headlines. On the day after the strike, 1200 miners in Zagorje ob Savi entered into a sympathy strike. The strike was partially successful: the miners *did* receive higher wages; however, they continued to be below the wages in most other branches of industry. The year 1958 witnessed a total of 28 strikes, and in subsequent years the number of strikes went up to a high of 271 reported strikes in 1964 and then fell off to between 118 and 182 strikes per year between 1966 to 1969.

During the 4 years and 8 months Jovanov covered in his study, he found information on 869 strikes and 77,597 participants, the actual figures being somewhat higher because of strikes that remained unreported. On average, about 90 people participated in a strike.

The first strikes occurred in Slovenia, the most highly industrialized part of Yugoslavia. Croatia and Serbia followed, Bosnia and Herzegovina were third and Macedonia and Montenegro were last. It took 10 years until the first strike occurred in Kosovo, the least developed area of Yugoslavia. An interesting pattern emerges here: the more highly developed a region, the earlier did workers in that area start going on strike. On the whole, more strikes occurred in the developed areas than in the underdeveloped areas of Yugoslavia.

The total number of strikes took place in 351 work organizations. In 265 organizations there was one strike, and in 86 organizations there were two or more strikes.

Most of the strikes were in manufacturing industry (71.2 per cent), followed by construction (7.3 per cent) and mining (5.5 per cent); the first of these sectors employs 47.9 per cent of the workers, the second 9.2 per cent and the third 37.8 per cent. In industry, most of the strikes took place in the metal industry, wood industry and textile industry. These are also the three industries with the highest proportions of strike participants. The fact that these three industries rank very low in wage level compared with other industries suggests that income is the main cause of strikes in these industries.

Yugoslav strikes seem to be somewhat different from labour

struggles elsewhere. They appear to be more of symbolic importance, rather than the expression of serious conflicts. This at least is the interpretation one may come up with when examining the duration of strikes; one-third of them lasted only up to three hours, and of all strikes about four-fifths lasted one day or less. A cartoon in *Jez*, a Belgrade paper: 'Well, is this supposed to be a work stoppage? Or just a coffee break?' (Adizes, 1971, p. 179.)

There is a wide range in the number of participants per strike. Two strikes (0.4 per cent of all strikes) involved 5300 workers (8 per cent of all workers); there were another 191 strikes (40.5 per cent of all strikes) which involved the same total number of participants as these two strikes.

In most cases (80 per cent), only production workers went on strike. In all other strikes both production workers and white-collar employees went on strike—the latter virtually never go on strike by themselves. Jovanov interprets this phenomenon as a contradiction between ideology and reality, or between ideal and actual structures. Ideally, all power is in the hands of the workers. In reality, management has considerable influence in the company, exceeding by far the power formally vested in their hands. On the whole, this situation may be accepted by the workers because such influence may be justified by managerial expertise—it may in fact be in the workers' best material interest. There may, of course, emerge situations in which management usurps an influence which is not in the best interest of the workers, however, or at least not viewed by the workers as being in their best interest.

Most strikes do not appear to be strikes of workers against their own self-management organs, for in 85 per cent of the strikes the members of the organs of self-management joined in the strike. In 15 per cent of the strikes, members of self-managerial organs did not join. 54,095 (92.9 per cent) of the workers participated in strikes in which members of organs of self-management were involved; only 4132 workers (7.1 per cent) participated in strikes in which the members of self-management bodies kept out. Jovanov suggests that this indicates worker dissatisfaction with the actual influence structure in the company: workers have formal power but little actual influence. If workers cannot reach their goals through the various organs of self-management, they go on strike. And as the members of self-management bodies who have fought unsuccessfully for the workers' interest are possibly even more frustrated than other workers, they are of course likely to be the first to join, if not to instigate, a strike. In the large majority of cases, the occasion for the strike was stated as income-related. Digging somewhat deeper, one finds that the actual causes within the work organization are somewhat different. The mode of income distribution turns out to be the most important cause, followed by dissatisfaction with the absolute amount of income. Dissatisfaction with an insufficiently developed self-management system within the company ranks third.

Behind these reasons may be found deeper-seated dissatisfactions which go beyond the work organization. The frustrations of the workers may not always derive from internal problems in the company. Of those who answered this question, 91 per cent stated that the strikes may have been caused by the unsatisfactory performance of the company on the market, which may or may not be the company's fault; this, however, may reflect more the opinion of those who filled in Jovanov's questionnaires than the opinions of the workers. It is interesting to note that the first question (about the occasion of the strike) was answered by 98 per cent of those who returned a questionnaire; the second question (about the actual causes within the organization) by 88 per cent— a good return but somewhat lower than the first percentage—the third question (about extra-organizational causes) was answered by a significantly lower number: only 44 per cent replied.

If one factor is to be singled out as a chief cause of strikes, it is the low level of evaluation and rewarding of productive work from within and from without the company. The jobs of production workers are less prestigious and less well paid, and production workers have less influence in the system of self-management than white-collar workers, management and workers in other branches of the economy.

In a majority of answers (72.2 per cent), the respondents felt that workers did not exhaust all available means before going on strike, while 27.7 per cent thought that the strike was used as a last resort after all other efforts had failed. The failure of workers to exhaust first all available means underlines the symbolic nature of strikes as pointed out earlier. The strike is a public outcry of the workers pointing to injustices in the evaluation and rewarding of their work, to a serious discrepancy between the formal power vested in workers and their actual influence.

Yet these are, in the eyes of the workers, not necessarily 'social strikes': 85.4 per cent of the respondents indicated that the workers on strike expressed dissatisfaction only against the work organization; 10.2 per cent expressed dissatisfaction only against extra-organizational forces and 4.4 per cent against both. For most strikes have to receive their immediate justification from intra-organizational events and relationships, which may however in reality stand for deeper frustrations related to extra-organizational matters. It is thus not too much of a surprise to find that the demands of the workers were satisfied only in a little over half the cases.

In most cases (70.1 per cent), the strike was directed against management. In more than a quarter of the cases, however, the workers did go on strike against their own organs of self-management, an indication that the dangers of bureaucratization many 'leftist' Yugoslav writers have been decrying are in fact present and even threatening the very structure of self-management.

A major result of Jovanov's investigation of strikes pertains to the relationship between workers and their unions. Most of the strikes were wildcat strikes, and one may assume that in a certain number of cases these strikes may even indirectly aim at the workers' own unions. For only in 11.3 per cent of the strikes and for only 7.7 per cent of the strike participants was the strike supported by the union. In almost half the cases (44.5 per cent) the union sympathized with the demands of the workers but condemned the strike as a means. In more than one-fifth of the strikes the unions neither supported the demands nor the strike as a means and in an additional one-fifth of the strikes the union stayed out of the conflict altogether.

This lends additional support to the suspicion that unions may be a tool of the party or the state and not of the workers. In this light it is understandable why so many Yugoslavs say that self-management is far from perfect and that they still have a long way to go. Finally, Jovanov reports attitudes to the role of unions: Which role should unions play concerning strikes? About two-thirds suggest a preventive role for the unions: they should cure the ills before they have to be operated on. Only about one-quarter supports a union involvement in strikes as an ultimate means.

We may now be able to understand the puzzle of workers'

strikes under workers' self-management. Wachtel (1973, p. 77) summarizes the paradox:

> The role of trade unions in a socialist society has always been a perplexing one. The basic contradiction lies in having an institution that represents workers' interests when the whole society is supposedly controlled by the workers. This contradiction is particularly acute for Yugoslav society, organized on the principles of workers' management in which the enterprise is run by, and presumably for, the workers. Why have another organization to represent the workers?

The result of Jovanov's (1972, pp. 66–8) study is: strikes are organized outside the organs of self-management, the League of Communists, the unions and the youth organizations. Technically, all strikes are thus *wildcat strikes*. While none of these institutions formally organizes strikes, the participants of strikes usually belong to at least some of these institutions. Membership of the League of Communists, of the workers' council etc., does not seem to prevent many from striking. Who are the two parties in Yugoslav industrial conflicts? On the one side, there are those who have a decisive influence in the decision-making process. On the other side, there are those who formally have power but actually little influence: the production workers. The first group derives its income from its function, its position in the work process; the second group from the results of its work, work input and monetary rewards being directly related. The workers on strike are in fundamental respects different from those against whom they strike: the workers have less social influence, their income is significantly lower and within the general social structure they form the lower stratum. Hence, *a strike results from class conflict*, concludes Jovanov. The ideal system of self-management is one which has eliminated classes, and consequently operates without strikes. The actual system of self-management as it exists in Yugoslavia today has failed to completely eliminate classes, and strikes, therefore, continue to exist. From the actual to the ideal system of self-management— and industrial relations—is still a long way. But as Yugoslavs have been marching steadily for the past 30 years on the road towards self-management, there is a fair chance that they may continue coming slowly closer to it.

10 Beyond Industrial Self-Management

SELF-MANAGEMENT IN SOCIAL SERVICE ORGANIZATIONS

Self-management was first introduced in industry. From there it started to spread and to enter other organizations. Some incipient forms of self-management began to appear in hospitals, schools and similar organizations around 1957. The beginnings of self-management in these institutions were slow, however, because one major attraction of self-management was missing: self-managed income distribution. Around 1957, self-management had no 'material base'. Change came in sight in 1961 when it was proposed to decide on the allocation of funds from federal, republican or communal budgets to social service institutions through self-managerial methods. This remained a proposal at first; but based on the Constitution of 1963, a law was passed which accorded self-managerial status to all forms of associated labour regardless of the type of activity performed. Under the provisions of this law, all institutions had the right and duty to choose their organs of management and to decide on their activity, income distribution, conditions of work, remuneration and future development through self-management.

Subsequent to this law, self-management grew quickly in social service organizations. They may not lend themselves as easily to self-management as industrial organizations, at least not in the eyes of Yugoslavs, who believe that there must be a 'material base' to self-management, i.e. organizations under self-management must be able to run their own business affairs, offer their services on the market, work for a profit and then distribute profits self-managerially among the employees. Non-Yugoslavs may hold quite different opinions. Some may consider the introduction of self-management in social service institutions much less risky than in business; these are the people who distrust workers' self-management. Others may regard the material base as irrelevant—people with overconfidence in workers' self-management. But be that as it may, in Yugoslavia the material base is believed to be a crucial component of the system of self-management, at least at present, and for all practical purposes they may be quite right with that assumption.

Among the various types of social service organizations, self-management developed first in public health institutions, i.e. in hospitals, clinics, out-patient clinics, health centres etc. For in this sphere, self-management found a material base. Public health institutions concluded contracts with social insurance agencies and had their own independent income.

In other spheres, as in schools, for instance, self-management was more difficult to introduce because of an insufficient material base. Yet self-management was formally introduced. On the one hand, this may have meant relatively little; yet, once introduced. the dynamics of growth and development of self-management started to set in and to work towards the creation of that base which is considered crucial for meaningful self-management.

The new solution combines two principles: the principle that the direct producers (the workers) shall decide on the use of the income they have created; and the principle that all workers, including those who are not involved in production, shall run their affairs through self-management. The solution is the *interest community*. In a given area, a public health community of interest comprises three groups of people; delegates of the workers in business organizations, delegates of the community and delegates of the public health institutions in that area. As an interest community, they decide on the funds to be allocated to public health, and it is then up to the members of the organs of self-management in these public health organizations to decide on how to manage with these funds. The same principle applies to schools and other social service institutions. Today, self-management is ubiquitous in social service organizations. There seems to be a lag in their development, however, compared with self-management in the business sector. In business, self-management has entered the phase of *direct self-management*. In the social service sector, most organizations seem to be under representative self-management, if not still under paternalistic self-management.

There were close to 9000 councils in social service organizations in 1972 and about half that many managing boards.

More than 200,000 individuals were council members, and an additional 35,000 individuals were managing board members (Table 10.1).

TABLE 10.1 Self-management in social service organizations, 1972

Organization	Councils	Council members	Managing boards	Managing board members
Primary and secondary schools	4718	128 871	2899	18 810
Institutions of higher education	232	6719	190	3711
Scientific institutions	309	6091	194	1374
Cultural-educational and artistic-entertainment institutions	1428	21 726	334	2441
Public health institutions	980	20 845	795	6310
Social welfare institutions	974	18 591	362	2500

SOURCE
Statistički Godišnjak Jugoslavije (1973, p. 79).

SELF-MANAGED MEDICAL SERVICES

What has self-management meant to public health and to medical doctors in particular? How is it for a doctor to practise medicine not only under self-management but also under conditions of socialized medicine?

Below I will report the results of an interview with Dr Marjdjn Balog and with Danko Venos, a hospital administrator, at Klinička Bolnica 'Dr Mladen Stojanovic', a teaching hospital in Zagreb, where I saw Mr Venos and Dr Balog on 10 August 1973.

'Dr Mladen Stojanović', named after a doctor who was killed during the war, is a teaching hospital in Zegreb with about 1250 beds. It employs about 1400 people: 150 doctors, 450 nurses and 800 in various other categories. It comprises 23 different departments, each one a 'basic organization of associated labour' (OOUR) as of January 1973.

Self-management was introduced to this hospital in 1953. But, as a social rather than a productive organization, the hospital did not have the same problems factories had, and has, therefore, been quite slow and gradual in introducing self-management: 'We are still in the process of introducing it', Dr Balog explained.

Each department has its own council, which is the decision-making organ. The Ear, Nose and Throat department, for instance, of which Dr Balog is the head, has 83 employees. Seven of them are members of the department's council: three are doctors, three are nurses and one is an auxiliary. The composition of the council is such that all major groups of employees are represented. During election, there are at least two nominees for each slot. The head of the department may attend the meetings of the council but he has no voting power.

The hospital is just about ready to enter a new organizational phase. As of 1 January 1973, the hospital comprises 23 OOURs, presently known as departments. Each is to be run by a council of from five to seven members. Each council is to send a delegate to the hospital's council, which will then have 23 members.

There is to be a professional collegium of 24 members: 23 heads of departments and the director of the hospital.

The transition to the system of OOURs had been prepared by the economic reform of 1965 when departments became economically independent and started to calculate all hospital services. Until 1961, the hospital was organized on a budget principle, with a lump sum being allotted to it. As of 1961, the hospital started to calculate its services and to have some moderate influence on its 'earnings'. In 1965 it started the system of internal calculations in which departments 'pay' one another for their services, as for example, the Medical ward is charged by the X-ray department for X-rays taken. Regardless of whether hospital services are calculated or not, the amount of money available to the hospital is always within the limits of 5 per cent of the gross national product which is allocated to health services. There is thus a chronic shortage of funds which chiefly results in very low salaries. Whether this will change when the new constitution is introduced and hospital employees, industrial workers and other members of the commune form an 'interest community' which decides on the availability of funds remains to be seen.

What exactly happens at the council meetings? Is this just a ritual where doctors continue to have all the power? Or do nurses and other members have any real say, too?

Dr Balog cites as an example the agenda of the last council meeting in the Ear, Nose and Throat department:

1. A woman doctor applied for a five-day leave of absence and for 1700 dinars to attend a medical congress in France. All travel expenses were to be paid by herself; the 1700 dinars were for the congress fee. The application was approved even though the 1700 dinars exceeded the amount left in the hospital fund; the balance was advanced from the fund for 1974.
2. A nurse asked for her resignation in order to work in Switzerland. The resignation was granted.
3. The problem of filling the beds in the ward was discussed. To break even, 96 per cent of the beds have to be filled. As the ward has to be prepared for epidemics, the percentage of beds filled is below 96 and the ward is thus running a deficit.

At the beginning of the existence of a new council, nurses tend to be shy and submissive, still impressed by the medical authority of doctors. This lasts for approximately 3 months. After that, they have adjusted to the new power situation and speak up freely. As a matter of fact, they become quite protective of their rights and watch carefully over the granting of privileges to doctors, i.e. over the allocation of funds for dissertations, attendance of congresses and further training.

The actual influence of nurses versus doctors depends very much on the issue. Professional issues are largely determined by doctors. With regard to investments, doctors tend to have a major influence. In personnel and organizational matters, nurses and doctors tend to have an equal influence.

Has self-management made any real difference to the hospital? Before the introduction of self-management, nobody had to think. Now the nurse knows the relationship between her work and the outcome. Hospital problems now become personal problems, not only of doctors but also of nurses and other employees. Before, everyone was just responsible to the head of department; now everyone is responsible to everyone else. The work of the individual has become more responsible, and possibly more efficient. But, most of all, the system of self-management has made a difference in human relations.

The ratio between the lowest and the highest income in the

hospital is approximately 1:5, the lowest income being approximately 1200 dinars, the highest 5600 dinars. The starting salary for a nurse is 1700 dinars. Because of the shortage of money, a specialist is paid only about 3500 dinars. He augments this income somewhat through night-shifts and by moonlighting in small clinics around Zagreb that cannot afford a fulltime specialist. But even with all this additional income he rarely makes more than 6000 dinars a month.

There are very few private practices in Yugoslavia, and those that do exist are mainly run by retired doctors, or by those who cannot find a job in a hospital.

Dr Balog does not think that socialized medicine reduces the quality of medical services in Yugoslavia. On the contrary, the patient gets better services because he is taken care of by several specialists, depending on need. It may be psychologically more gratifying to receive the personal attention of one doctor in a private practice, but a private doctor tends to do things by himself that in a system of socialized medicine would be referred to another specialist.

Nor does Dr Balog think that the low salaries have an impact on the quality of professional services. 'Doctors are like actors and prostitutes', he adds. 'They always try to do things as well as possible—and better than their colleagues. We who have grown up in the system accept salaries as they are though we may not be satisfied with them. For those who once had a high salary and later had to accept a lower one, this may be more problematical. But there are very few of those in Yugoslavia. There have been ten bad years during and after the war; and instead of complaining we may as well be appreciative that things are getting better. After the war, we developed a new attitude: the attitude of building a new socialist society.'

There is a brain drain, Dr Balog explains.

Many leave for West Germany and for other countries, and some stay abroad for good. Others go to Africa or Asia within our technical assistance programmes. It is usually the young doctors who leave; consequently we do not know if it is the best who leave or not: they haven't proven their quality yet.

As to the quality of medical services, this is difficult for us to judge. We think it is high, and it seems that many foreigners agree with us. Medical services in Yugoslavia are cheap and good. Sofia Loren had her baby here, and the Queen of Morocco and her children have come here for operations. Many Americans come here, too.

On the whole, people in Yugoslavia are satisfied with the quality of medical services. They only complain about the red tape. You first go to a general practitioner who sends you to a specialist who sends you to the hospital which puts you on a waiting list.

'Then there is the problem of discipline: you give patients a date when there will be a bed available, and then they do not turn up. Weeks later they appear as emergencies when you don't have a bed, and then you have to put them up.'

Do party bosses, general managers and university professors receive better services than workers or clerks?

'We are not a perfect society. There is a difference; but the difference does not lie in the quality of services but rather in human relations: the director's wife receives more personal attention.'

SELF-MANAGED EDUCATION

Self-management was late in coming to schools and other educational institutions. Most schools have apparently not gone far in introducing self-management. For while the Statistical Yearbook (1973, p. 302) lists 13,907 primary schools for 1972, only 4718 self-management councils are listed for primary *and* secondary schools together (Table10.1). Most schools do not even appear yet in statistics on self-management, and in those which have introduced it self-management seems to be still quite remote from full realization.

Lojze Malovrh, Vice-President of Škofja Loka and director of its high school (see Chapter 4), explained that schools are social organizations and that self-managed education is therefore different from self-managed business. Every resident of a community can participate in self-management at the schools of the community. Or as Mr Malovrh put it: 'Everyone who has time to spare may get involved.'

Škofja Loka's high school has 290 students, 14 teachers, a

director and some additional personnel. Its highest decision-making body is a school council of nine members: five teachers, two students, one parent, and one other community member delegated by the community as its representative. The director may be present during council meetings but has no voting rights.

The fourteen teachers, under the presidency of the director, form the managing board. The managing board is in charge of the daily routine of education and for periodical conferences in which all teachers and a representative of each grade participate. At these conferences, anything pertaining to the school and to education may be discussed, including teaching methods, the performance of students and the performance of teachers. The director is hired for periods of 4 years. After each term of office the position is publicly advertised by the community. A search committee is appointed by the community council, and the director is selected by the community council from among the candidates suggested by the search committee.

EDUCATION FOR SELF-MANAGEMENT

Of special importance to self-management is the education and training of self-managers, especially workers. Training for self-management has two components: improvement of the general education of the workers and instruction in special self-management skills.

After the war, the general educational level of workers was very low in Yugoslavia. As late as 1953, almost half the population over ten years of age were illiterate. By 1967, this situation had improved tremendously: only 11.4 per cent of the labour force had no schooling at all or had not completed more than three years of elementary school. The improvement of worker education was a key factor in the development of self-management. As self-management grew, institutions developed which aimed at training workers for their new functions. Of these institutions, the so-called workers' universities are most important.

There was a mushroom growth of workers' universities all over Yugoslavia, and by 1967/68 there were 236 workers' universities and, in addition, 230 people's universities, offering seminars and lectures to 311,000 and 111,000 students respectively. In 1967/68, over 2 million people attended public lectures at workers' universities and 900,000 at people's universities. More recently, this type of education has been more and more replaced by regular forms of education: at technical schools, technical universities etc., where scholarships from companies, state institutions and other sources are increasingly available. Workers' and people's universities seem to have filled a void when the growth of regular training institutions could not keep pace with the mounting demand (Burt, 1972, pp. 152–3).

The number of people's and workers' universities has, therefore, stopped growing. In 1970–2, there were 217 workers' universities, offering 10,707 courses and seminars to almost 400,000 people; while 210 people's universities offered 4219 courses and seminars to 116,000 individuals. There seems to be a

TABLE 10. 2 Workers' and people's universities in 1970–2

	Univer-sities	Seminars and courses		Public lectures	
		No.	Audience (000s)	No.	Attendance (000s)
PEOPLE'S UNIVERSITIES	210	4219	116	5238	396
Bosnia & Herzegovina	60	516	19	1419	96
Montenegro	5	14	1	19	2
Croatia	82	2140	51	1413	125
Macedonia	4	26	1	186	14
Serbia	59	1523	44	2201	159
Autonomous provinces	43	1243	35	1860	124
Vojvodina	15	251	8	341	35
Kosovo	1	29	1	—	—
WORKERS' UNIVERSITIES	217	10 707	398	15 489	806
Bosnia–Herzegovina	38	1121	44	5498	173
Montenegro	7	183	3	19	4
Croatia	16	1357	33	636	45
Macedonia	24	703	22	699	74
Slovenia	47	2920	126	5919	287
Serbia	85	4423	170	3218	223
Autonomous provinces	53	2141	83	1229	104
Vojvodina	27	2148	82	1976	115
Kosovo	5	138	5	13	4

SOURCE
Statistical Pocket Book of Yugoslavia (1973, p. 111).

trend away from casual lectures to regular courses and seminars, just as there is a trend away from workers' and people's universities to regular institutions of higher learning. For while the number of people taking seminars and lectures at people's universities and at workers' universities has gone up between 1967/8 and 1970–2, the number of people attending single lectures has gone down (Table 10.2).

There is a workers' university in Skofja Loka, which I visited on 3 August 1973. Mr Malovrh explained:

The workers' university is that institution which offers every worker the opportunity to learn a new trade, improve his skill or advance his general education. The large majority of workers take advantage of this opportunity. In Škofja Loka, three to four thousand workers register annually; that is about a quarter of the gainfully employed population. The workers' university of Škofja Loka has three branches:

1. Through technical courses, a worker may become a skilled worker, journeyman, artisan or technician. As a technician, he may then enroll at a regular university. He may also take courses in business and administration with degrees up to a level which qualifies for admission to a regular university. The workers' universities offer only the courses; they do not take the examinations. Examinations are centrally administered by the technical or commercial schools in Ljubljana, which also award the final degree.
2. Special seminars, courses or lectures may be offered upon the suggestion of a company. This is custom-made training without official certification. Its main function is improvement of specific skills at the work-place.
3. In a third branch, workers receive a social-political education which prepares them specifically for the task of self-management.

'For the worker is not only a producer but also a self-manager', explained Mr Malorvh. Offerings depend on the needs of those registered. They may concentrate on the legal aspects of self-management, on the history of workers' councils, their economic functions etc.

In addition, courses are offered in several foreign languages.

SELF-MANAGED COMMUNITIES

The basic social–political territorial unit in Yugoslavia is the community. Several communities form a so-called commune. The number of communes has been considerably reduced, thus strengthening the relative power of the individual commune. In 1956, there were 1479 communes; today there are only 500.

The development of self-management in the business world did not leave the political–administrative sphere unaffected. Within the general course of reducing state-bureaucratic control, many functions of the state were transferred to local bodies. The holder of most territorial power was originally the district; in 1956 there were 107 of these. When the local government bureaucracy was gradually dismantled, districts were abolished and communes were territorially enlarged and economically strengthened. This found a direct expression in the numerical change mentioned above.

At the beginning of communal self-management under paternalistic self-management, the functions of local government were carried out by a people's committee, a single representative body composed of deputies elected by all citizens of voting age on the territory of a commune. 'In practice', Bajec (n.d., p. 48) said, 'it was the president of the commune and his apparatus who held the real power in their hands.' Next, the people's committees were transformed into two-chamber assemblies, comprising a communal council, elected by all citizens of voting age in the commune, and a council of producers, elected only by those employed in the economy. Finally, the second chamber, as the council of working communities is called now, came to be elected by persons employed in the economy and in other branches of activity, i.e. in public health, education, culture, public administration etc. This basic model of the multi-chamber assembly is today found on all levels of government: federal, republican and provincial. There is, however, one difference: the assemblies on the federal, republican and provincial level have five chambers: the social and political chamber, the economic chamber, the educational–cultural chamber, the health and social welfare chamber and the general representative chamber. In the federal assembly, this last chamber is called the Chamber of Nationalities, comprising delegates from the six republics and the two autonomous provinces. Bajec (n.d., pp. 48–9) suggests that,

This breakthrough—the inclusion of separately elected representatives of the economy and other public activities in all these assemblies—was of great significance in the further development of worker management, since these representatives, as deputies of chambers which enjoyed equality with the political chambers, played an important role in the further elaboration of the self-management system and the complete transformation of the traditional state into a unique self-managing community.

Yugoslav citizens may thus exert their self-management rights through two channels: through territorial self-management in communities and communes and through self-management in work organizations. In both types of setting, direct participation manifests itself in referenda, general rallies, electoral meetings and of course membership in the various bodies of self-management. In 1972, there were 8999 local communities in Yugoslavia. Each of them was run by a community council. In those 7610 communities which submitted a report to the Bureau of Statistics, there were 93,818 council members; 3.05 per cent of the council members were women. In addition, there were 6696 councils of conciliation with a total of 25,170 council members, of which 3.6 per cent were women (Table 10.3). As usual, women are drastically under-represented. As before, an important determinant of women's representation in organs of self-management is the level of economic development of a republic. In Slovenia, the most highly developed republic, women make up 6.75 per cent of the council members and 12.4 per cent of the members of councils of conciliation. In Kosovo, the most underdeveloped area of Yugoslavia, women make up only 1.05 per cent of the council members and 0.85 per cent of the members of councils of conciliation. In both areas, women are severely under-represented, but less so in the developed areas than in the underdeveloped areas.

During the period of 1969 to 1974, there were 500 communes and communal assemblies in Yugoslavia, with a total of 40,791 councillors. Women were under-represented, representing only 6.9 per cent of the councillors, but less so than in local communities. About half the councillors served in communal chambers and half in chambers of working communities (Table 10.4).

TABLE 10.3 Self-management in local communities in 1972 by republic

	Yugoslavia	Bosnia–Herzegovina	Montenegro	Croatia	Macedonia	Slovenia	Serbia proper	Vojvodina	Kosovo
Local communities	8999	784	74	2739	869	1032	2818	498	185
Councils[a]	7610	784	74	1925	817	883	2489	493	145
Council members	93818	11424	1054	23718	7492	11022	29424	7979	1705
Women	2863	320	31	738	69	743	619	325	18
Youth	7769	1096	80	1708	723	639	2682	639	202
Councils of conciliation	6696	1255	117	1092	823	592	2123	419	275
Council members	25170	4996	465	3772	2733	2669	7687	1674	1174
Women	904	146	4	149	18	327	161	89	10
Youth	1037	328	19	80	126	24	319	52	89

NOTE

[a] Refers only to local communities who submitted a report to the Bureau of Statistics.

SOURCE

Statistički Godišnjak Jugoslavije (1973, p. 76).

TABLE 10.4 Self-management in communes, 1969–74

	Yugoslavia	Bosnia–Herzegovina	Montenegro	Croatia	Macedonia	Slovenia	Serbia
Communal assemblies	500	106	20	105	30	60	179
Councillors	40 791	7636	1379	9015[a]	2612[b]	3591	16 558
Women	2821	460	48	638	111	254	1310
Youth	3443	724	69	681	139	225	1605
Councillors of communal chambers	20 283	3791	684	4488	1284	1797	8239
Councillors of chambers of working communities	20 508	3845	695	4527	1328	1794	8319

NOTES
[a] No data for re-elections of 63 councillors.
[b] No data for re-elections of 148 councillors.

SOURCE
Statistički Godišnjak Jugoslavije (1973, p. 76).

THE ROLE OF BANKS IN SELF-MANAGEMENT

Banks are under self-management. The organs of self-management are assemblies, workers' councils and executive boards. Table 10.5 presents the statistics on the number of organs of self-management and of members in these bodies in the national banks and in the various other banks.

TABLE 10.5 Self-management in banks, 1972

Self-management body	National bank	Banks
Assemblies	—	42
Assembly members	—	6745
Workers' councils	8	43
Council members	134	818
Executive boards	—	42
Board members	—	780

SOURCE
Statistički Godišnjak Jugoslavije (1973, p. 79).

On 17 August 1973, I visited the main branch of a large bank in Sarajevo, *Privredna Banka*. The bank was founded 1 July 1971 by fusing five smaller banks. Privredna Banka has 20 branches, with their headquarters in Sarajevo. Privredna Banka comprises 21 OOURs—20 branch banks and the headquarters. The smallest branch has 20 employees, the biggest about 650. Each OOUR has its workers' council, with 12–30 members, depending on the size of the OOUR.

An OOUR has to have more than 20 members in order to form a workers' council; if it has 20 or fewer employees, the workers' collective is the decision-making body.

Each OOUR and the organization as a whole has six commissions: a commission for statutes and by-laws; a personnel commission; a personal income commission; an awards and recognitions commission; a living standards and recreation commission; and a commission for assistance and contributions to other organizations.

The central workers' council has 21 members: one from each OOUR.

Each OOUR has its own workers' control committee.

Unlike other organizations, banks have a dual structure: a self-management structure as described above and an administrative structure.

The highest administrative body of the bank is the assembly, *skupština banke*, with about 170 members. The number of votes per member is variable and depends on the amount of money deposited in the bank by the organization of which the assembly member is a delegate. Each member has one vote for each one million dinars (US $65,000) deposited.

The executive committee, with 27 members, is elected by the bank's assembly.

There are two committees which are of particular economic importance: a committee for long-term credits and a committee for short-term credits. Each of these committees has between 7 and 11 members; 51 per cent of the members must be representatives of industry.

The average net personal income in Privredna Banka is about 2500 dinars; the minimum is 1000 and the maximum 6500. Profits are computed and distributed quarterly.

Employees receive seniority allowances of 0.5 per cent of their basic personal income for each year of work with the bank or elsewhere, up to a maximum of 1500 dinars per month.

The amount of vacation allowance varies from year to year. In 1972, every employee received 750 dinars. The decision for 1973 is still pending. It is expected that the workers' council will decide to give each employee one average income, i.e. the same amount for everyone—except for those in the lower income brackets who will receive somewhat more.

Any amount exceeding 150 dinars per month for transportation is paid by the bank.

When salaries are not frozen, employees receive between one half and one full extra monthly income at the end of the year.

No information was available on the amounts of profit that were distributed: the only company in Yugoslavia of those I visited which declined to reveal their profits. This would be hardly surprising if this happened in another country; in Yugoslavia however it is unusual.

My three informants noted that the role of banks is presently controversial. So far, banks have managed all financial matters of the economy; they have become *the* centre of economic power. Delegates of industry are represented in all decision-making bodies of banks: in the executive board, which comprises representatives of industry only, and in the credit committee which consists of both representatives of industry and of bank personnel. When the new constitution (of 1974) goes into effect, decision-making bodies in banks will consist completely of representatives of industry. Banks will then only be an executive and service organ of industry.

Presently, the general manager of the bank is *ex officio* head of all boards and committees and of the bank as an organization. After October 1973, the general manager will continue to preside over the bank as an organization, but he will no longer preside over committees and boards.

'Is it correct that banks watched their own business instead of being a service institution to the economy? Did they indeed tend to invest their money in hotels at the Adria?' I asked.

'In our view, it is in order for a bank to invest in local industries', was the enigmatic reply.

'What are the banks' reactions to the new development initiated by the new constitution?'

'There is some resistance from banks; but the general trend is understood and accepted. The new Constitution is expected to have a very positive effect on the economy. Productive organizations and social funds will decide on the use of money, not the banks.' Investment credit interest rates are presently up to 8 per cent. It is expected that they will go down to 3–4 per cent.

This would of course be greatly welcomed by industry, and it is a concession that banks certainly did not make voluntarily. Slobodan Boshkovic, general manager of Grmeč, a very well-to-do producer of bituminous and synthetic products near Belgrade, voiced some bitterness over the past role of banks and optimism over the future when I interviewed him on 15 August 1973:

> So far, the enterprises could not solve any major investment problem without the banks. Banks held a very powerful influence over companies and their development. They charged high interest rates and gave short-term loans when you asked them for long-term loans. Banks did exceedingly well that way, accumulating large amounts of capital for themselves which they invested for their own profit.
>
> We had to give up our own development plans because of the terms offered by the banks. Next year, after the new Consti-

tution goes into effect, we expect that interest rates will go down and loan terms will be more favourable.

Banks are already anticipating this change and have already started to change the terms of their loans. Two years ago, for example, our loan application did not come through even though the general manager of Grmeć is a member of the executive board of the bank. This, by the way, indicates how much, or rather how little, it actually meant to have industry represented on the executive boards of banks. We have been approached, meanwhile, by the bank and are just about to come to terms with them: we will get a longer loan period, namely 5 or 10 years instead of 3; we will get a lower interest rate, approximately 5–6 per cent instead of 7; and we will obtain a foreign currency credit by another company: everything we wanted.

At last, banks will become service institutions to the economy. In future, enterprises will share in the profits of the banks. While banks used to invest their money in hotels at the Adria and in other tertiary activities, investments will now start to flow into industry.

Until 1951 banks had served as mere cashiers and book-keepers of state finances. After this date, banks began to grant credits to the economy and to invest their own profits. In 1963, banks started to act as agents for central and other investment credits. Under the law of 1965, banks became independent economic institutions providing services for enterprises. Within a short time, the economic power of banks grew immensely and they soon began to do business on their own account. The power of the banks grew at the expense of other companies and at the expense of the system of self-managemant, undermining the profitability of business enterprises, i.e. the 'material base' of self-management. In his introductory speech to the Second Congress of Self-managers in 1972, Tito then found it necessary to say:

> . . . the role of the banks, foreign and home trade must be adjusted to self-managerial relations. Needless to say, no one denies their important place in the economic system: but their alienation from production or imposition of their interests on production cannot be tolerated, as this entails an unfair transfer of income at the expense of the direct producers. (Starčević, pp. 23–4)

Statistics on the investment structure show that the allegations against banks were not based on imagined fears. Between 1955 and 1969, the proportion of investments financed from within the political—administrative sphere fell from 55.2 per cent to 15.8 per cent. The intention behind the state's pulling out of economics was to strengthen the economy and particularly to create a genuine 'material base' for self-management. This goal was not only not achieved, the economic power of business even went down: their percentage share in investment financing fell from 44.0 in 1955 to 34.9 in 1969. The beneficiaries were the banks. Their share went from about zero (0.8 per cent) to one-half of all investments (49.4 per cent) (Table 10.6).

TABLE 10.6 Sources of investment funding, 1955–69 (%)

Year	Business enterprises	Banks	Political— administrative bodies	Total
1955	44.0	0.8	55.2	100
1960	37.4	1.0	61.6	100
1965	36.8	31.7	31.5	100
1969	34.8	49.4	15.8	100

SOURCE
Jovanov (1972, p.48).

Banks thus became the new centres of finance. The 'withering-away' of the economic function of the state strengthened the banks instead of invigorating self-management. Banks not only accumulated the capital created through productive labour, they also invested on their own account and to their own advantage.

An interesting side aspect of the new strength of banks has been observed by Jovanov (1972, p. 49). There have been no strikes in banks, for their social position has been above that of production workers who—as we claimed—went on strike precisely because of their inferior position *vis-à-vis* those placed in 'better' positions, among them all employees in banks.

11 A Model Constitution of Self-Management

On 30 and 31 January 1974, a new Constitution of the Socialist Federal Republic of Yugoslavia was adopted by the Chambers of the Federal Assembly, and promulgated by the Chamber of Nationalities on 21 February 1974. The 1974 Constitution is a unique document in that it results from a quarter century of experience with self-management; in no other country has self-management ever survived that long on a nation-wide scale. Neither this Constitution nor the actual practice of self-management is perfect yet, and the Yugoslavs are the first to emphasize this. Even in his motion to adopt the 1974 Constitution, Mijalko Todorović pointed to the preliminary character of the document:

> By carrying into effect the new social relations, which are also pregnant with new social contradictions, our society will necessarily be faced with new problems which it will have to solve. Because of this, it is indispensable to follow the development of society in a comprehensive, scholarly and scientific way, constantly and critically to re-examine our own practice, to detect new laws emerging from the soil of new relationships, and to determine conditions for the solution of these problems. (The Constitution of the Socialist Federal Republic of Yugoslavia, 1974, p. 48)

At the same time, Yugoslavia has become very self-confident with her system of self-management, realizing that it has not failed to arouse considerable interest among those who have become aware of its existence, and suggesting it may serve as a kind of model to the world:

> The character of contradictions in the so-called 'welfare societies' shows that one of the fundamental questions is that of

how to reconcile the powerful development of productive forces and increasing material demands with the humanization of society, emancipation of labour, social justice and the abolition of all forms of political domination. The question of self-management, the relations and forms through which the working people will manage production and distribution, and in general the question of real democratic management of social affairs, are today the central themes of modern society.

The tendencies in the development of relations among nations in the international community, and the deepening gap that separates the developed and the developing countries, and finally the present ever sharper and deeper crisis of international economic relations, also show that relations among nations can no longer be resolved through imperialistic domination and hegemony.

Under these conditions of our society's development towards socialism, the ideas of integral socialist self-management and of the new type of federation, as defined in the proposed Constitution, have aroused great interest among the progressive forces of the world. They are seen as a unique experience of the working class for the solution of problems of the contemporary world. Because of its complex structure, the Yugoslav multinational community is in a way a world in miniature. By resolving its own problems, it contributes to the practice of the international workers' movement in its struggle for the resolution of the fundamental contradictions of contemporary society on a progressively democratic and humanistic and socialist basis. (Mijalko Todorović, *Report on the Final Draft of the SFRY Constitution*, The Constitution of the Socialist Federal Republic of Yugoslavia, 1974, pp. 45–6)

Too many constitutional laws and amendments have been called a Magna Carta of self-management during Yugoslavia's recent history to attach this term to the 1974 Constitution. But it is certain that no previous document—one can probably add: in any country—gave such far-reaching rights to workers. In the English translation, the Constitution comprises 258 pages, and most of these deal with self-management in one way or the other. Constitutionally, Yugoslavia is a self-managing society, with its economic and political relations based on the tenets of participatory, direct democracy.

In the preamble to the Constitution, 'socialist social relations based on self-management by working people and the protection of the socialist self-management system' are defined as the foremost objective of the nations of Yugoslavia. 'The socialist social system of the Socialist Federal Republic of Yugoslavia is based on the power of the working class and all working people and on relations among people as free and equal producers and creators whose labour serves exclusively for the satisfaction of their personal and common needs.' The bases of this system are stated as: 'social ownership of the means of production'; 'the emancipation of labour as a means of transcending the historically conditioned socio-economic inequalities and dependence of people in labour'; 'the right to self-management'; 'the right of the working man to enjoy the fruits of his labour and of the economic progress of the social community in keeping with the principle: "From each according to his abilities—to each according to his labour" '; 'solidarity and reciprocity by everyone towards all and by all towards everyone'; and of course 'democratic political relations', 'equality of rights' etc.

Economic decision-making power is decentralized and vested in the workers who organize themselves in basic organizations of associated labour:

Man's labour shall be the only basis for the appropriation of the product of social labour and for the management of social resources. The distribution of income between the part which serves for the expansion of the economic foundations of social labour and the part which serves for the satisfaction of the personal and common needs of working people in conformity with the principle of distribution according to work performed, shall be decided upon by the working people who generate this income. . . . The basic organizations of associated labour, which are the fundamental form of associated labour in which workers exercise their inalienable right by working with social resources to manage their own labour and conditions of labour and to decide on the results of their labour, shall be the basis of all forms of pooling of labour and resources and of self-management integration.

While decision-making in the economic sphere is highly decentralized, strong elements of centralization have been retained in the political domain, namely through the party. In the preamble to the Constitution, the party's role is interpreted as that of the vanguard of the working class. But while this may theoretically very well be the role of the party, it provides politicians at the same time with a structure which enables them to centralize control and strengthen their own position. The preamble states:

> The League of Communists of Yugoslavia, as the initiator and organizer of the National Liberation War and Socialist Revolution, and as the conscious champion of the aspirations and interests of the working class, has become, by the laws of historical development, the leading organized ideological and political force of the working class and of all working people in the creation of socialism and in the realization of solidarity among the working people and of brotherhood and unity among the nations and nationalities of Yugoslavia.
>
> Under conditions of socialist democracy and social self-management, the League of Communists of Yugoslavia, with its guiding ideological and political action, shall be the prime mover and exponent of political activity aimed at safeguarding and further developing the socialist revolution and socialist social relations of self-management, and especially at the strengthening of socialist social and democratic consciousness, and shall be responsible therefore.
>
> The Socialist Alliance of the Working People of Yugoslavia, created during the National Liberation War and Socialist Revolution as a voluntary and democratic front of the working people and citizens and all organized socialist forces, headed by the Communist Party, and further developed under conditions of a socialist society based on self-management, shall be the broadest base for socio-political activity in the socialist system of self-management.

The all-encompassing Socialist Alliance of the Working People of Yugoslavia is assigned the task to:

— discuss social questions and take political initiative in all fields of social life, adjust views, lay down political stands regarding the solution of these questions, etc.;
— draw up joint programmes for social activity and lay down

common criteria for the election of delegations in the basic
organizations of associated labour, local communities and other
self-managing organizations and communities, and for the
election of delegates to the assemblies of the socio-political
communities; ensure democratic proposition and determination of candidates for members of delegations in self-
managing organizations and communities and candidates for
delegates to the assemblies of the socio-political communities . . . ; consider general issues of cadre policy and the
formation of cadres, and lay down criteria for the selection of
cadres;
— review the work of the organs of power and of the managing
bodies of self-managing organizations and communities and of
the holders of self-management, public and other social
functions, express their opinions and pass judgements and
exercise social supervision over the criticism of their work,
especially with regard to ensuring the publicity of and responsibility for their work;
— create conditions for the all-round participation of young
people and their organizations in social and political life;
— make sure that the working people and citizens are kept
informed, and ensure their influence on the social system of
information and the realization of the role of the press and
other media of public information and communication;
— fight for humane relationships among people, for the
development of socialist democratic consciousness and norms
of socialist life, and to prevent practices which check the
development of socialist self-management democratic social
relations or are in any way harmful to them.

The party is thus the watchdog of the nation, and the age-old
question arises: Who shall guard the guardians? The new
Constitution entails thus a very basic contradiction: that between
extreme decentralization in the economic sphere and, at least
potentially, centralization in the political sphere through the
party. Those who wrote the Constitution seem to have been very
much aware of this contradiction, or at least of the danger that
economic decentralization and political centralization may
become a fundamental contradiction. For at the end of the
preamble, the 'bodies of self-management, state agencies, self-
management organizations and communities, socio-political and

other organizations, working people and citizens directly—are called upon through the entirety of their activities' among other things 'to expand and develop all forms of self-management and socialist self-management democracy, especially in those fields where the functions of political power predominate; to curb coercion and create conditions for its elimination; and to build up relations among people based on an awareness of common interests, on the socialist code of ethics, and man's free creative endeavour.'

Below we will reproduce those articles of the Constitution which spell out the details of the self-managerial structure of the Yugoslav socio-economic system.

LABOUR AND SELF-MANAGEMENT

Article 10   The socialist socio-economic system of the Socialist Federal Republic of Yugoslavia shall be based on freely associated labour and socially-owned means of production, and on self-management by the working people in production and in the distribution of the social product in basic and other organizations of associated labour and in social reproduction as a whole.

Article 11   Man's economic and social status shall be determined by labour and the results of labour, on the basis of equal rights and responsibilities . . .

Article 14   . . . all workers in associated labour working with socially-owned resources, shall be guaranteed the right . . . to manage the work and business of the organization of associated labour and the affairs and resources in the totality of relations of social reproduction, to regulate mutual relations in labour, to decide on income realized through various forms of pooling of labour and resources, and to earn personal income.

Basic organizations of associated labour are the basic forms of associated labour in which the workers directly and on terms of equality realize their socio-economic and other self-management rights . . .

Article 16   Workers in organizations of associated labour active in the fields of education, science, culture, social welfare and other social activities shall earn income through a free exchange of their labour for the labour of the working people whose needs and interest they serve, or through their organizations of associated labour and self-managing communities of interest. . . .* The principles of free exchange of labour shall also apply to the earning of income by workers in organizations of associated labour in other activites in which the action of market laws cannot be a basis for the adjustment of work and needs, nor a basis for assessing the value of labour.

INCOME DISTRIBUTION

Article 17 . . . Basic organizations of associated labour shall distribute among themselves the entire income jointly realized. . . .

Article 19 Workers in basic organizations of associated labour shall allocate income to personal and collective consumption, the expansion of the economic foundations of associated labour, and the reserve fund.

SELF-MANAGEMENT AND FOREIGN INVESTMENTS

Article 27 . . . Workers in organizations of associated labour which make use of resources invested by foreign persons shall have the same socio-economic and other self-management rights as workers in the organizations of associated labour which in their operations use resources of other domestic organizations of associated labour.

A foreign person who has invested resources in an organization of associated labour in the Socialist Federal Republic of Yugoslavia may share in the income of this organization only within the limits and under conditions prescribed for mutual relations among domestic organizations of associated labour.

COMPENSATION FOR INVESTMENTS

Article 28 In order to expand the economic foundations of labour, organizations of associated labour may collect financial resources from citizens and ensure them, in addition to the repayment of these resources, compensation for investment in the form of interest or other benefits determined by statute.

---

* Such communities of interest, which link the producers with those who offer special public services, exist in education, science, health, welfare, housing construction, power production, water management, transportation etc.

WORK COMMUNITIES

Article 29 Workers who in an organization of associated labour perform administrative–professional, auxiliary and similar activities of common interest to several organizations operating within it, and workers who perform such activities in an agricultural or other kind of cooperative, and also workers in an organization of a business association, bank or insurance community, shall form a work community. Workers in such a work community may organize themselves into an organization of associated labour under conditions specified by statute. . . .

Article 31 Working people who with their personal labour independently perform, as their occupation, an artistic or other cultural activity or a legal or other professional activity shall, in principle, have the same socio-economic status and basically the same rights and obligations as workers in organizations of associated labour.

Working people performing some of these activites may pool their labour and form temporary or lasting work communities, which shall basically have the same status as organizations of associated labour . . .

RECIPROCITY AND SOLIDARITY AMONG ORGANIZATIONS AND WORKERS

Article 32 . . . Organizations of associated labour and socio-political communities shall be bound, in conformity with the principles of reciprocity and solidarity, to provide economic and other kinds of assistance to organizations which have run into exceptional economic difficulties, and to take measures for their financial rehabilitation, if this is in the common interest of the organizations of associated labour, or in the social interest.

An organization of associated labour, alone or in agreement with other organizations of associated labour, shall, in keeping with the principles of reciprocity and solidarity, ensure resources for the employment, retraining and the realization of the acquired rights of workers, if their work is no longer needed in their organization of associated labour, or if an organization operating within it has ceased to operate.

Until he has been ensured an appropriate job which corresponds to his abilities and qualifications, no worker may lose the status of worker in a basic organization of associated labour if, due to technological or other kinds of innovation which contribute to the rise in labour productivity or to a greater success of the organization, his work is no longer needed in this organization. . . .

TAXATION

Article 33   Workers in associated labour shall contribute to the satisfaction of constitutionally determined general social needs in the socio-political communities by paying taxes and other dues to these communities on the income of their basic organizations of associated labour and on their personal incomes. . . .

THE FOUNDING OF WORK ORGANIZATIONS

Article 35   . . . A work organization may be founded by organizations of associated labour, self-managing communities of interest, local communities, socio-political communities and other social artificial persons.

A work organization may, under conditions and in the way specified by statute, be founded by working people with a view to realizing their right to work or to satisfying their needs with the products and services of the organization they are founding.

A work organization may, in conformity with statute, also be founded by civil artificial persons.

Working people or civil artificial persons who have invested their resources in an organization of associated labour which they have founded, may in respect of this organization have, on account of these resources, only those rights which are vested in citizens from whom organizations of associated labour collect resources to expand the economic foundations of their labour . . . .

Work organizations shall have the same status and workers in them the same socio-economic rights and responsibilities, regardless of who has founded the work organization concerned.

Article 37   Workers in basic organizations of associated labour shall have the right to have their basic organization split away from the work organization of which it is a part . . .(unless it) lead to a major hindrance or prevention of work in other basic organizations . . . .

BANKING AND INSURANCE

Article 39   Organizations of associated labour, self-managing communities of interest and other social artificial persons may by self-management agreements found a bank as a special organization in charge of the conduct of credit and other bank activities. . . . The income realized by the bank . . . shall be distributed among these artificial persons . . . . No socio-political community may found a bank nor manage the affairs of one . . . .

Article 41   Organizations of associated labour, self-managing communities of interest and other social artificial persons shall, in organizations of associated labour which, besides other activities engage in banking and similar business, in principle, have the same rights in respect of this business as social artificial persons have in a bank which operates with their resources . . . .

Article 42   Organizations of associated labour, self-managing communities of interest, socio-political communities and other social artificial persons may by self-management agreement found a community of life and property insurance . . . insurees shall participate in the management of their respective insurance communities or risk communities . . . .

PRODUCTION AND SALES ORGANIZATIONS

Article 43   Relations between organizations of associated labour engaged in the sale of goods and services and productive and other organizations with which they do business shall be based on the principles of cooperation and self-management pooling of labour and resources within the framework of this cooperation. These organizations shall, on a basis of equality, exercise a mutual influence on business and development policies, bear joint risks and joint responsibility for the expansion of the economic foundations of labour and the rise in labour productivity in production and trade, and shall share in the income earned through this cooperation according to their contribution to the realization of this income . . . .

INVESTMENTS ABROAD

Article 44   Organizations of associated labour may carry out their activities and invest the means of social reproduction abroad, under conditions and within the limits laid down by federal statute.

Rights and resources acquired abroad on any ground by an organization of associated labour shall become a component part of the social resources managed by the workers of this organization.

Workers in an organization of associated labour operating abroad shall have the same rights, obligations and reponsibilities as the workers of this organization working in Yugoslavia.

DISPUTE SETTLEMENT

Article 47   If a dispute arises in an organization of associated labour between workers in individual units of the organization, or between the workers and bodies of the organization, or the workers of the organization and an agency of a socio-political community, which it has not been possible to settle by regular proceedings, the workers shall have the right and the duty to present their demands, stemming from the dispute through their trade union organization . . . to institute proceedings for the settlement of the dispute . . . .

BUSINESS ASSOCIATIONS

Article 50   Organizations of associated labour which carry out economic activities and their business associations shall associate in chambers of economy or other general associations with a view jointly to promoting work and business, adjusting special, common and general social interests, reaching agreement on working and development plans and programmes and on the self-management regulation of socio-economic policy, and with a view to considering and resolving other questions of common concern . . . .

COMMUNITIES OF INTEREST

Article 51   Self-managing communities of interest shall be formed by working people, directly or through their self-managing organizations and communities, to satisfy their personal and common needs and interests . . . working people shall pay contributions to these communitites from their personal incomes and from the income of basic organizations of associated labour, in line with the purpose or aims for which these resources are to be used.

Article 52   Workers and other working people who in the fields of education, science, culture, health and social welfare realize, on the principles of reciprocity and solidarity, their personal and common needs and interests, and workers in organizations of associated labour which carry out activities in these fields, shall form self-managing communities of interest . . . .

Mutual relations in such self-managing communities of interest shall be regulated so as to secure the rights of the workers and other working people who have pooled resources in them to decide on these resources, and also the rights of the workers in organizations of associated labour which perform activities in the field for which a particular community of interest has been formed to realize through free exchange of labour the same socio-economic status as workers in other organizations of associated labour.

Article 53   In order to ensure their social security, working people shall form self-managing communitites of interest in the fields of pension and disability insurance and other forms of social security. . . .

Article 57   Self-managing communities of interests and basic communities and units making part of them, and also associations of self-managing communities of interest, shall be artificial persons with the rights, obligations and responsibilities vested in them under the constitution, statute, self-management agreement on the formation of the community of interest and/or association of communities of interest, and under their by-laws.

SELF-MANAGEMENT IN AGRICULTURE

Article 61   Farmers and members of their household engaged in farming . . . shall, in principle, have the same status and basically the same rights as workers in associated labour working with social resources . . . .

Article 62   Farmers may pool their labour and resources in agricultural cooperatives and in other forms of farmers' association, or pool them with organizations of associated labour. Agricultural cooperatives shall, in principle, have the same status, rights, obligations and responsibilities as organizations of associated labour. . . .

MANAGEMENT AND SELF-MANAGEMENT WITH PRIVATELY OWNED MEANS OF PRODUCTION

Article 64   The freedom of independent personal labour with means of labour in citizens' ownership shall be guaranteed, provided the performance of activities with personal labour corresponds to the mode, the economic basis and possibilities of personal labour, and provided it is not contrary to the principle of income earning according to work performed or to other foundations of the socialist social system . . . .

Article 67   A working man who independently performs activities with his personal labour using resources in citizens' ownership may, on a self-management basis, pool his labour and means of labour with the labour of other persons, within the framework of an organization of associated labour founded under contract.

. . . [he] shall have the right to conduct, as manager, the business of the contractual organization and, together with other workers, decide on its operation and development.

The manager and workers in a contractual organization of associated labour shall, on the basis of their labour, be entitled to resources for the satisfaction of their personal and common needs; the manager shall, on account of the resources which he has pooled, also be entitled to part of the income accruing to him in conformity with the principles applying to the pooling of labour and social resources in organizations of associated labour.

The part of income realized in a contractual organization of associated labour which is left after the allocation of resources for the satisfaction of the personal and common needs of the manager and workers and of the part of income accruing to the manager on account of the resource he has pooled in the organization, shall become social property. The workers, together with the manager, shall on the basis of their labour manage this part of income as social resources . . . .

The manager of a contractual organization of associated labour shall retain the right of ownership over, and other contractual rights regarding, the resources he has pooled in this organization. With the withdrawal or repayment of these resources, the rights the manager enjoys in the contractual organization in his capacity of manager shall be extinguished.

DECISION-MAKING UNDER SELF-MANAGEMENT

Article 89   Working people shall exercise power and management of other social affairs through decision-making at assemblies, through referenda and other forms of personal expression of views in basic organizations of associated labour and local communities, self-managing communities of interest and other self-managing organizations and communities, through delegates in managing bodies of these organizations and communities, through self-management agreements and social compacts* through delegations and delegates to the assemblies of the socio-political communities, and by guiding and supervising the work of bodies responsible to the assemblies.

Article 98   A worker in a basic or other organization of associated labour shall realize self-management, on terms of equality and mutual responsibility with other workers in the organization, through decision-making at workers' assemblies, through referenda and other forms of personal expression of views, through delegates in workers' councils elected and recalled by him together with other workers in the organization, and through supervision of the execution of decisions and the performance of work of the bodies and services of this organization . . . .

WORKERS' COUNCILS

Article 99   Basic and other organizations of associated labour shall set up workers' councils to take charge of the management of the work and business of these organizations, or managing bodies which in status and function correspond to a workers' council.

* Social compacts are self-management enactments concluded on an equal basis by organizations of associated labour, chambers of economy, government agencies and socio-political organizations under which the parties thereto ensure the regulation of socio-economic and other relations of a broad interest. Their purpose is to replace the state's role in the resolution of social contradictions and the realization of cooperation and solidarity in the economic and other spheres of life. Social compacts have the character of law. (The Constitution of the Socialist Federal Republic of Yugoslavia, 1974, p. 305)

Basic organizations of associated labour with a small number of workers shall not set up workers' councils.

Specific executive functions in basic and other organizations of associated labour may be entrusted to the executive bodies of the workers' councils. . . .

Article 100   In exercising the functions of management of work and business of an organization of associated labour, the workers' council shall draw up draft by-laws and pass other enactments, formulate business policy, enact working and development plans and programmes, take measures for the implementation of business policy and working and development plans and programmes, elect, nominate and relieve of office executive bodies, individual business executives and business boards or their members, ensure that the workers are kept informed, and shall conduct other affairs as specified by self-management agreements, by-laws and other self-management enactments of their respective organizations. . . .

Article 101   The workers' council of an organization of associated labour shall consist of delegates of workers in all phases of the labour process . . . elected directly and in the way and by a procedure specified by the self-management agreement on association. . . .

Article 102   . . . Members of a workers' council or executive body may not be elected for a term of more than two years.

No one may be elected to the same workers' council or executive body for more than two consecutive terms.

A worker who as an individual business executive or member of the business board is responsible to the workers' council may not be elected to it, nor may a worker who independently performs other managerial functions specified by the by-laws and statute.

BUSINESS BOARDS AND BUSINESS EXECUTIVES

Article 103   In every organization of associated labour there shall be a business board and/or an individual business executive in charge of the business of the organization of associated labour, the organization and adjustment of the labour process, and the execution of decisions of the workers' council and its executive body.

Every organization of associated labour shall be represented by an individual business executive or by the chairman of the business board, unless otherwise specified by the by-laws or other enactments of this organization.

The business board and the individual business executive shall be independent in their work and shall be responsible to the workers and the workers' council of their organization of associated labour.

The individual business executive and/or the chairman of the business board shall also be responsible to the social community for the legality of work and the fulfilment of the statutorily-established obligations of their organization of associated labour. . . .

Article 104 The individual business executive and members of the business board in an organization of associated labour shall be nominated and relieved of office by the workers' council.

Individual business executives shall be nominated on the basis of public competition, on the proposal of a competition commission. In basic organizations of associated labour specified by statute and in other organizations of associated labour the competition commission shall be composed of a statutorily-specified number of representatives of the organizations of associated labour and the trade unions concerned, and of representatives of the social community nominated or elected in conformity with statute. . . .

The tenure of an individual business executive and of members of a business board shall not last longer than four years. After the expiration of their tenure they may be renominated to the same function by the same procedure. . . .

BY-LAWS

Article 106 All organizations of associated labour shall have by-laws.

The by-laws of a basic organization of associated labour . . . [,] of a work organization or a composite organization of associated labour shall be passed, on the proposal of its workers' council, by a majority vote of all workers in each of these organizations. . . .

WORKERS' SUPERVISION OF SELF-MANAGEMENT

Article 107 To achieve and safeguard their self-management rights, workers in basic and other organizations of associated labour shall have the right and duty to exercise self-management workers' supervision directly, through their organization's managing bodies, and through special bodies of self-management workers' supervision. . . .

PERSONAL RESPONSIBILITY UNDER SELF-MANAGEMENT

Article 108   Every worker shall be personally responsible for the conscientious exercise of his self-management functions. Delegates in the workers' council of a work organization or a composite organization of associated labour shall be responsible to the workers and the workers' council of the basic organization which has elected them as delegates.

Members of a collective executive body, individual business executives and members of a business board shall be responsible for their work to the workers' council which has elected or nominated them, and to the workers of the organization of associated labour in which they perform their functions. They shall be personally responsible for their decisions and for the execution of decisions of the workers' council and of the workers, and also for keeping the workers' council and workers truthfully, timely and fully informed. They shall also bear material responsibility for any harm caused by the execution of decisions taken on the basis of their proposals, if in making these proposals they concealed facts or consciously gave untruthful information to the workers' council or the workers. . . .

The responsibility of members of collective executive bodies, individual business executives and members of business boards shall be determined according to their influence on the making and implementation of decisions. . . .

COMMUNITIES OF INTEREST, LOCAL COMMUNITIES, AND COMMUNES

Article 110   A self-management agreement on the formation of a self-managing community of interest and its bye-laws shall regulate affairs of common concern to the members of the community. . . .

Article 111   Affairs of a self-managing community of interest shall be managed by its assembly. The assembly shall be made up of delegates elected and recalled by the working people and organizations of associated labour and other self-managing organizations and communities, as members of this community of interest. . . .

Article 114   It shall be the right and duty of the working people in a settlement, part of a settlement or several interconnected settlements to organize themselves into a local community with a view to realizing specific common interests and needs. . . .

Article 116   The Commune is a self-managing community and the basic socio-political community based on the power of and self-management by the working class and all working people. . . .

Article 118   In order to satisfy common needs in the Commune, workers in basic organizations of associated labour and other working people and citizens in local communities, self-managing communities of interest and other self-managing organizations and communities, and in the Commune as a whole, shall by referenda and other forms of personal expression of views and by self-management agreements and social compacts decide on the pooling of resources and their utilization. . . .

SELF-MANAGEMENT AGREEMENTS

Article 120   By means of self-management agreements and social compacts workers and other working people shall, on a self-management basis, regulate their mutual relationships, adjust interests and regulated relations of broader social significance. . . .

Article 122   Trade unions shall have the right to initiate and propose the conclusion of self-management agreements and may institute proceedings for the revision of a self-management agreement already concluded. . . .

PROTECTION OF SELF-MANAGEMENT RIGHTS

Article 129   The self-management rights of the working people and social property shall enjoy special social protection . . . [and]

shall be ensured by the assemblies of the socio-political communities and agencies responsible to them, by courts of law, constitutional courts, public prosecutors and social attorneys of self-management. . . .

Article 130   If in an organization of associated labour or another self-managing organization or community, self-management relations have become essentially disrupted, or if serious harm has been caused to social interests, or if an organization or community does not fulfil its statutorily-established obligations, the assembly of the socio-political community shall have the right, under conditions and by a procedure specified by statute, to dissolve the workers' council or another corresponding managing body of the organization. . . .

Article 131   Social attorneys of self-management, as independent agents of the social community, shall take measures and use legal means and exercise other statutorily defined rights and duties to ensure social protection of the self-management rights of working people and of social property. . . .

ASSEMBLIES

Article 132   The assembly is a body of social self-management and the supreme organ of power within the framework of the rights and duties of its socio-political community. . . .

Article 133   Working people in basic self-managing organizations and communities and in socio-political organizations shall form delegations for the purpose of direct exercise of their rights, duties and responsibilities and of organized participation in the performance of the functions of the assemblies of the socio-political communities. . . .

Article 134   Members of delegations shall be elected by the working people in basic self-managing organizations and communities from among members of these organizations and communities by direct and secret ballot. . . .

The composition of delegations must be such as to ensure adequate representation of workers in all phases of the labour process and to correspond to the social composition of the basic self-managing organization or community concerned.

Members of delegations shall be elected for a term of four years. . . .

No one may be elected member of a delegation of the same self-managing organization or community for more than two consecutive terms.

Article 135   Candidates for members of delegations of basic self-managing organizations and communities shall be proposed and determined by the working people in these organizations and communities in the Socialist Alliance of the Working People, notably in its organizations, or in trade union organizations.

The procedure for the nomination of candidates shall be conducted by the Socialist Alliance of the Working People or trade union organizations. . . .

Article 137   . . . the delegations shall formulate basic stands for the delegates to follow in the work of the assemblies and in their participation in decision-making.

Delegations shall be bound to keep the basic self-managing organizations or communities informed of their own work and the work of the delegates in the assemblies, and shall be responsible to these organizations or communities for their work. . . .

Article 141   In taking stands on questions being decided in the assembly, the delegates shall act in conformity with the guidelines received from their self-managing organizations and communities and with the basic stands of the delegations or of sociopolitical organizations which have delegated them, and in conformity with the common and general social interests and needs; they shall be independent in their options and voting.

Delegates shall be bound to keep the delegations and basic self-managing organizations and communities or socio-political organizations which have elected them informed on the work of the assemblies and on their own work, and shall be responsible to them for their work.

Article 142   Delegations and each of their members, and individual delegates to the assemblies may be recalled . . . in the way and by the procedure applicable to the election of delegations and delegates. . . .

Article 146 The assembly of a socio-political community may call a referendum to enable working people to express their views in advance on individual questions falling within the assembly's competence, or to endorse statutes, regulations and other enactments. Decisions taken through referenda shall be binding.

12 Social-Economic Bases for Self-Management in the Developing World: the Cooperative Network

What basis is there for the introduction of self-management in the developing world? Is it an alien concept to be introduced from the outside, or is there an indigenous basis for it?

In this chapter, it will be shown that self-management has been an integral part of the social-economic life of a great many societies in the premodern era. The particular organizational form in which self-management is found is that of cooperative societies which are extremely widespread all over the world in both modern and premodern times. Indeed, it may be hard to find more than a dozen agricultural societies without some cooperative structure in premodern times. In Asia and Latin America, in Africa and Oceania, there are literally thousands of peoples that have cooperative societies of one kind or the other. Here we are not talking of the existence of cooperation in some broad sense but of formal cooperative societies in the narrow sense of the definition. Following the conventions in most modern cooperative laws, we define a cooperative as a voluntary, open and permanent association of equalitarian structure in which the members secure for themselves certain economic interests through communal self-help. We consider it open when it is not limited to kinship groups. It is permanent when it is not formed *ad hoc* but operates for some months or years. Equalitarian property structure implies that the members have the same rights to the results of cooperative efforts according to their inputs; while equalitarian social structure implies that all members are, on principle, equal and that everyone has the same chance of becoming a leader or any other office holder and holds the same voting rights with regard to the election to office and the enactment of rules and by-laws. Cooperatives generally have a formal structure. If one of the elements defined as constitutive for a cooperative is missing, namely voluntariness, openness, permanency, equalitarian property structure, economic purpose, or communal self-help, it will be subsequently referred to as a group rather than a cooperative. We found that there exists, among most peoples, usually a rather sharp distinction between cooperatives in the sense of the definition and other groups of economic cooperation, both linguistically and institutionally.

In fact, there may be no purer type of practiced self-management than that found in a traditional cooperative society. It should be quite clear that we are referring here not to modern cooperative societies. They do incorporate the idea of self-management (at least as far as primary cooperatives are concerned); but as they usually have been introduced into the Third World during and through colonialism, we do not want to include them here, though they may have become an important part of the respective national economies. Instead, it is our intention to point to the existence of cooperative societies as an institutional base for self-management before the impact of colonialism was felt.

Such premodern cooperatives have usually been ignored in development policies, regardless of the political affiliation of their originators. At the same time, there are very few thorough studies. Descriptions of varying quality are usually found in ethnographies which are trying to give a picture of a whole society. For West Africa, we have examined the ethnographic literature for evidence of such cooperatives (Seibel and Koll, 1968). While we found many references to cooperative societies, including craft guilds, and even some excellent descriptions, the overall evidence turned out to be very unsystematic and of very uneven quality. Instead of trying to put together the scattered evidence from societies all over the world, we decided to present one country which we studied in depth, namely Liberia*. Liberia was chosen because the various societies have been left rather unaffected in their traditional culture until recently. Also, the size of Liberia makes it possible to include all tribes, sixteen in

* This study was carried out in 1968–69. It was supported by the German Research Council.

number, omitting none. The details would of course have been quite different had we chosen New Guinea or Nigeria; but the basic notion of the existence of vigorous cooperative societies would have been the same. The following description will now be limited to Liberia.

The basic principle of African cooperatives is that, at regular or irregular intervals, goods, money or labour services are pooled for the benefit of one member at a time in a rotating system.

According to what is pooled, goods or money on the one hand or labour on the other hand, there are two classes of cooperatives: saving cooperatives and work cooperatives. According to the activities for which labour is pooled there are different types of work cooperatives, and according to what is saved and with what secondary purposes saving is combined, there are different types of saving cooperatives. The same applies to those groups where one or more of the elements specified in the definition to be constitutive for a cooperative are absent. The following typology will present the basic patterns of cooperatives and of other groups of economic cooperation.

WORK COOPERATIVES

A work cooperative comprises a group of farmers who work in turn on each member's farm. Distribution of labour services rendered and received is based on strict reciprocity. Work cooperatives were universally found in all tribes both in traditional and in modern culture. This makes them the most widespread, and with regard to traditional culture for many tribes even the only type of cooperative. With regard to economic relevance two zones may be distinguished: a western and an eastern one. Among the more centralized western tribes (Mano, Kpelle, Gbandi, Loma, Kissi, Mende, Gola and Vai) they are of highest relevance, the bulk of agricultural work on rice farms being done cooperatively. Among the segmentary eastern tribes (Kru, Sapo, Kran) they are of moderate relevance. Among the Bassa, who are located between both groups although belonging linguistically and culturally to the eastern tribes, their relevance lies in between. Among the De, who are located west of the Bassa and who also belong to the same ethno-linguistic group as the eastern tribes, the relevance of work cooperatives is close to that of the western tribes; this may be so because the De have been strongly influenced by the neighbouring tribes for centuries. Among the Belle, who also belong ethno-linguistically to the eastern tribes but are located in the west, work cooperatives are about as relevant as among western tribes. The Dan, who are the most eastern of the western tribes, take an intermediate position.

The two main reasons given overtly in all tribes for forming work cooperatives are that work is (1) done faster and (2) more enjoyable. Both may be summarized in one manifest economic function: increase in labour productivity.

'Friendship among members' is occasionally stated as one of the reasons for joining a work cooperative. Socially, work cooperatives appear to have two integrative functions: a horizontal one and a vertical one. The following overall relationship was found to exist between social structure and cooperative structure: The more segmentary the social structure of a society, the weaker work cooperatives, and the more centralized and hierarchical a society, the stronger work cooperatives. This may be taken as a corroboration of the hypothesis that work cooperatives fulfil primarily a vertical-integrative function and only secondarily a horizontal-integrative function.

In Liberia work cooperatives are predominantly found on rice farms, since rice farming is the most important type of agricultural production and at the same time very labour-intensive. Cooperatives may also be formed, however, for work on other farms, for example on cassava farms, and more recently on coffee, cocoa, or sugar-cane farms. The basic principle of work cooperatives, that is, pooling labour for the benefit of one member at a time in turn, is also applicable to other activities, as for example building, spinning, transportation, marketing, rum production, or palm-oil production. Work cooperatives formed for work on rice farms may also help their members in house-building, thus functioning as an informal work group whose membership happens to coincide with the work cooperative.

There are four activities which are invariably found to be part of the cooperative work programme in all tribes: clearing the underbrush, felling trees, sowing and harvesting. In most, though not all tribes, the following activities may also be done cooperatively: burning the dried underbrush and trees, cleaning the farm of the unburned remainders and weeding. In a very few tribes hauling rice, building a fence around the rice farm and building a rice barn may also be done cooperatively.

Cooperatives exist mostly in pairs, one for men and one for women. The number of cooperatives, or such pairs, depends upon the size of the village and also upon the habitual size of cooperatives. Some tribes tend to form one or two large cooperatives in every village, others prefer several small ones.

The theoretical minimum size of a cooperative is two members, and there are in fact cases where a cooperative consists of two members. For practical reasons an upper limit is set by the number of work-days in a period during which a certain agricultural activity has to be done; if one day is spent on each farm the maximum number of members equals the number of work-days. Among the western tribes work cooperatives tend to be large in size, numbering between 10 and 30; for certain activities figures of up to 50 have been reported. In the east, cooperatives are small comprising only some 2 to 6 and up to 10 members.

Most work cooperatives are formed for one agricultural cycle, that is, in most cases for about half a year, since the activities performed by men fall in one half and those of women in another half of the year. Cooperatives may also be formed for one agricultural season, that is, for one type of activity, or for several years, or for an unlimited period. In the large majority of cases in traditional society and quite often still today, cooperatives are legally limited by their members to a duration of one year. Sociologically, however, cooperatives may be considered to be established for an unlimited period, since the same cooperative with about the same members is re-established every year.

On principle, membership is open to everyone though women and men in eastern Liberia of different age grades may form their own groups. For technical reasons membership is closed once work has started because otherwise the principle of strict mutuality would be broken. New members may, however, be admitted between two round turns.

Work cooperatives are organized along the lines of the system of sexual labour division in each tribe. The heavy work, that is, clearing underbrush, felling trees, burning, cleaning farms, building a rice barn and constructing a fence, is invariably done, at least traditionally, by men. Weeding is done in all cases but one by women. The pattern of which sex does the harvesting varies greatly from tribe to tribe: it may be done by men, by women, by mixed groups or alternatively by any combination of these.

Anybody may found a work cooperative. The founder is often a respected person in the community whose appeal to form a cooperative has a good chance of being effective. He gathers the prospective members and organizes a first gathering.

At this first gathering the cooperative is formally established as such. Among the tribes of eastern Liberia the organizational meeting is of limited relevance since work cooperatives are not as highly formalized as among the western tribes. The three main tasks of the organizational meeting are to delineate membership, to determine the rules and bye-laws of the cooperative and to elect the officers. The rules and bye-laws pertain to the purpose of the cooperative; the activities which will be done cooperatively; the number of days to be spent on each farm; and the length of time for which the cooperative will be in existence. Special laws are enacted to regulate the behaviour of members. Fines are determined with regard to arriving late, absence from work and breaking other rules. It is also agreed upon whether or not the cooperative is to be hired out, and if so, what the compensation should be.

Only cooperatives in eastern Liberia (among the Kru, Sapo, Kran) may or may not have a leader. In all other tribes cooperatives are headed by at least one leader.

The structure of offices is presently becoming increasingly complex. Offices are in principle open to everyone. The allocation of an office is based on achieved criteria, not on ascription. In small villages there is a tendency for cooperative leadership to coincide with community leadership, but this is not made a rule. Criteria for leadership were stated to be general leadership abilities, ability to settle disputes, being well-known, sociability, honesty and trustworthiness, industriousness, strength, being a fast worker and agricultural skill. Main duties of the leader are to organize, control and supervise the work, and to judge matters in dispute. The leader joins work without enjoying any privileges. The only compensation he gets for his office is in terms of prestige. Traditionally there was only one leader, who was represented by an acting leader during his absence. Very large groups may have been divided into subgroups which were headed by sub-leaders. During recent years a mushroom growth of offices has started to take place as is found in most voluntary associations in Africa.

This development has gone farthest among the Mano where practically every member of the cooperative may be at the same time an office-holder. Many of these offices have no real function. Standard offices with real functions are those of the treasurer, collector, secretary and/or clerk, messenger, law-enforcement officer and policeman. Offices are usually modelled along the lines of the political structure of the central government. Hence cooperatives may be said to fulfil a function of political socialization.

In some tribes large groups were divided into subgroups. In about half the tribes, namely among the Kpelle, Gbandi, Loma, Kissi, Grebo, Mende, Gola, and Bassa, work performance is organized on a competitive basis. A farm is divided up into portions which are assigned to groups or individuals of the cooperative. These compete with each other, the winning party or individual gaining prestige. Competition increases work speed considerably.

In work cooperatives drumming and singing accompanying the work plays an essential part. Not only does music contribute to the enjoyment of the members, but it also supplies a rhythm for the work movements which are performed much faster than those in individual or family work.

Since work performance is based on reciprocity no compensation is given. Food may be either provided by each farmer individually or by the farmer on whose farm work is being done; in the latter case all farmers provide reciprocally an equal amount of food an equal number of times.

Fines are set up as sanctions in case somebody breaks the rules on the cooperative. Such fines are in kind (rice, chicken, commodities) or, as a recent innovation, in money; people may also be assigned extra work, or they may be ordered to provide the food for x number of days. Attendance is strictly enforced by traditional and modern legal means. A person may get a leave of absence by: (1) asking for permission stating special reasons; (2) sending a substitute; (3) paying a compensation to the owner of the farm where he misses a session; (4) agreeing that the farmer on whose farm he is supposed to work will miss a work session reciprocally. Normal social pressure is usually strong enough to make a person choose one of these alternatives. If somebody misses a session without permission and excuse he is fined, the fines being in most cases between 50 cents and US $1; in some cooperatives, however, these are considerably higher. If the fine is not paid, the matter may be referred to the court.

Due to the strong position of secret societies, information about religious beliefs pertaining to cooperative work is difficult to get. Only among the Mano and some groups of the Dan was it found that an elaborate set of religious ceremonies was practised by the cooperative, including the use of masks. In the other tribes it appeared that the application of ceremonies and medicines was a private rather than a cooperative matter. In a few tribes it was observed that members behave as animals during work.

Though still functioning largely according to the traditional pattern work cooperatives have undergone some major adaptations to the new economy: (1) While they were fully integrated into subsistence agriculture in traditional society they may nowadays be instrumental in producing rice for sale. (2) The pattern of cooperative work has been applied to newly introduced cash crops like coffee, cocoa or sugarcane, and also to new activities like rum production. (3) In a gradually increasing number of instances the traditional system of sexual labour division is being changed or given up to increase agricultural production. (4) Only in the traditional culture of the Gola, not among the other tribes, was it possible to hire work groups. However it was generally found that cooperatives may be hired by non-members against the payment of money. It appears that in most cases the price for cooperative labour is higher than the price for individual wage labour. This may be justified by the higher labour productivity of work cooperatives and/or by the higher prestige which accrues to somebody who hires a cooperative and displays his wealth by providing a rich meal and drinks.

The principle of cooperative work may be applied to a number of activities other than farm work, for example to building, palm-nut harvesting, spinning, transportation, palm-oil or rum production. All these may be considered sub-types of the cooperative for farm work. They are all of minor importance found only in one or two tribes each, and even there only in a few instances. Their structure is usually much less elaborate than the one of work cooperatives proper.

Building cooperatives as found among the Kpelle and Belle may be formed for constructing or thatching the houses of all members in turn. In most cases, however, such work is done by informal work groups.

Among the Loma and Belle palm-nut harvesting cooperatives may be formed either attached to existing farm work cooperatives or independently. They consist of men among the Loma and of both men and women among the Belle.

Spinning cooperatives were only found in traditional Kpelle culture. They consist of about 6 to 10 women and are headed by a leader. Once a week one member brings a certain amount of cotton to be spun cooperatively; the yarn is returned to that person. This is done in turn until every member has once used the cooperative's services for one day.

In response to the money and market economy cooperatives have been formed among the Kpelle for the transportation of agricultural products to the market. Each member's product is transported in turn.

Palm-oil may be produced cooperatively in traditional Kpelle and Bassa culture. Such cooperatives are still in existence. The harvesting of palm-nuts may be done cooperatively or individually. The palm-oil produced is given to one person at a time in turn. Today the palm-oil may also be marketed cooperatively, the proceeds being turned over to one member at a time in turn. Among the Kpelle and the Gbandi it was found that the proceeds were kept by the group for community purposes. It appears that cooperative production of palm-oil is slightly increasing in spread and importance.

The local distilling of rum is of recent origin and is now being practised widely among Liberian tribes, since it is not inhibited by any laws. A few groups have been found among the Gola who purchased and run a rum distillery cooperatively.

Two or more of these cooperatives, or other cooperatives (for example, saving cooperatives), or groups may be combined into one.

Among the Kru, fishing groups are formed to man fishing boats. Since no reciprocity of services is involved they are not considered as cooperatives. The owner of the boat sells one part of the catch and distributes another as a compensation among his helpers.

Community work groups are universally formed by all tribes for the clearing and maintenance of paths, for the building of bridges, formerly for the construction of fortifications, and for other community projects. Since membership is compulsory, comprising all men or all young men of a community, they are not considered cooperatives in the sense of the definition. Community and work group leadership usually coincide. Work performance is often organized on a competitive basis. Neighbouring villages mostly co-ordinate work in such a way that road-clearing groups meet half way between two villages.

In some areas among the Kru community work is done by small informal groups of young men who are gathered *ad hoc*. Membership is voluntary.

Among the Kru semi-cooperative farming is occasionally practised. A cooperative is formed for the surveying of a very large farm, the clearing of the underbrush, the felling of trees, the burning and the cleaning of the farm. Then the land is divided among the members of the cooperative and each individual is responsible for the further cultivation of the land. Each member is free to join a work cooperative of his choice which is institutionally not identical with the one which first surveyed and cleared the land.

Community farming, locally referred to as government farming and sometimes as communion farm, was found among the Mano, Kpelle, Gbandi, Kissi, Mende and Gola, that is, among most of the western tribes. It is of recent origin. It has sprung up in response to requisitioning demands of government officials and agents. A whole village cultivates one farm communally and keeps the produce for government visitors. Since membership is compulsory it is not considered a cooperative; the terms used in the tribal languages differ from those used for cooperative. Community and work-group leadership coincide. In most cases the farm is a rice farm. In some cases palm-oil may be produced communally for the same purpose. More recently, there seems to be a tendency towards selling some surplus production and keeping the proceeds for the payment of community taxes and local levies, and most recently to use the money to build up a loan fund for community members and for financing community projects.

Only in a very few instances was it found among the Kpelle that chiefs requested community members to work on their farms without compensation, abusing the power vested in them by the central government. The subject of compulsory group work for persons higher in the political hierarchy than chiefs cannot be discussed here.

Non-reciprocal work groups represent the most important

form of economic cooperation among the eastern tribes. This organizational pattern is not found among the western tribes, with the exception of the Dan who are located between Kran and Mano; they seem to have been strongly influenced by the cooperative culture of both tribes. Non-reciprocal work groups are absent among the Bassa although they belong to the eastern tribes. Among the De and Belle they appear to be somewhat less important than among the Kru, Kran and Sapo. The basic pattern is that a large group is called together to work on one farm for one or two days. Only the wealthy can afford to hire such a group since the group has to be compensated by a large meal for which goats and/or cows have to be slaughtered and by drinks. Today a payment which is between US $5 and US $40 has to be added. Besides its economic function of providing farm labour the institution of organizing large non-reciprocal work groups has also a socio-political function. While in centralized societies political power usually leads to economic power, segmentary societies (without chiefs or kings) tend to reverse this order: wealth leads to political power via the social prestige gained by displaying (and distributing) the wealth. Thus hiring large-scale work groups enables the rich man to display his wealth, to win thereby social prestige and hence pave his way to political power. At the same time, it provides a mechanism for redistributing wealth, thus limiting the continuous accumulation of wealth. Without such a mechanism the unrestricted accumulation of wealth might eventually lead to the transformation of a segmentary system into a centralized one. Non-reciprocal work groups are organized in irregular intervals. They tend to be very large, comprising usually about 40 to 50 and occasionally more than 100 members. Traditionally membership was usually drawn from age grades. Such groups are not organized for minor agricultural tasks. With regard to the frequency at which groups are formed, clearing the underbrush ranks highest, followed by felling trees, harvesting and sowing, in that order; clearing the farm appears to rank lowest in frequency. The pattern of sexual labour division follows largely the one found in work cooperatives among these tribes, the only exception being a stronger engagement of men in mixed groups for harvesting. The number of men's groups seems to exceed the number of women's groups considerably. A farmer who wants a group to work on his farm applies to somebody he considers able to organize and supervise a group. This person receives a token payment or present. It is mostly him who will be the leader of the group. Considerable prestige accrues to a man who has proved to be an able leader of a non-reciprocal work group. Work is accompanied by drumming and singing. Quite often elaborate religious ceremonies are practised. Semi-professional groups of dancers and drummers may be hired by the leader of the work group to accompany the work and the concluding feast. Among the Kru, Kran and Sapo non-reciprocal work groups are institutionally of two kinds: small-scale and large-scale. They are perceived as two different types.

Small-scale non-reciprocal work groups may have between 2 and 15 members, mostly, however, between 5 and 10. They are less prestigious than large-scale groups and are hired by farmers who cannot afford the large ones. In some areas, especially among the Sapo, they have become more frequent in recent times since most farmers cannot afford the rising price of large-scale groups. Among the Kran large-scale groups are still prevalent. Such small groups may also be employed by a farmer who has previously hired a large group; it is not common for one farmer to hire two groups in one year. The basic pattern of small-scale and large-scale groups is about the same, the only exception being that drumming is not usual during work. In some Sapo sub-tribes small-scale groups have no leader.

Large-scale non-reciprocal work groups are supposed to have more than 10, preferably more than 20 members. Large-scale groups of 15 members are distinguished from small-scale groups of the same size by (a) different terms; (b) different amounts of compensation; and (c) different prestige accruing to the person who employs the group. Work is always concluded by a large, often village-wide, eating, drinking and dancing party.

Permanent non-reciprocal work groups are of very recent origin. They were found among the Kru and Kran and Sapo where they are of minor importance and among the Dan where they represent today the most important type of economic cooperation. Non-reciprocal work groups of the traditional type are only established *ad hoc*, even though in practice membership may quite often be largely identical in subsequent sessions; however, according to the organizational pattern they are considered non-permanent. With the coming of the cash economy and the increasing importance for wage labour more and more non-reciprocal groups are being formed on a permanent basis to be hired by wealthy farmers. They are a commercialized version of the old prestigious work group. Leadership is permanent, too. Among the Kran and Sapo such groups tend to keep the money they receive for their services and build up a loan fund (see below). Since membership is permanent and voluntary and such groups also have a formal structure they are to be considered as co-operatives. They deviate from the usual pattern of allocating all goods or services to one member at a time in turn; however, since the proceeds accrue to all members equally and since they are earned by communal efforts all criteria of the definition of a co-operative are met.

Informal work groups are universally found in all tribes. Their economic relevance varies from tribe to tribe. Groups of neighbours, relatives and friends may be called from the same or from different villages for any type of work. The groups are not permanent nor do they have a formal structure. No strict reciprocity of services is involved. An economic activity in which informal work groups are essential in most tribes is house-building. A short-term compensation for the work done lies in a meal provided. The mode of compensation differs from that in non-reciprocal small-scale or large-scale work groups in that now goats or cows are slaughtered; when meat is provided it is usually chicken.

There may be other voluntary or non-voluntary associations which fulfil cooperative functions, such as age grades, secret societies, burial societies, entertainment societies. Quite often it has been observed that the economic function of such groups has proved to be the strongest of all: many groups lost all functions but the economic one, thus retaining existence as a pure co-operative.

In comparison with countries like Nigeria or Tanzania, very little effort has been made to build up a cooperative movement in Liberia although the Liberian Code of Laws provides for it. The few efforts made seem to show (a) that large cooperative enterprises may be successful if strictly supervised; however they are only nominally cooperatives; and (b) that small-scale projects may be successful with a minimum of supervision if based on traditional cooperatives.

SAVING COOPERATIVES

Rice-saving cooperatives are of traditional origin among the Mano, Kpelle and Dan. They are predominantly formed by women during or after rice harvesting. About 4 to 30 members may join and contribute every week a stipulated equal amount of rice. The total is given to one member at a time in turn. Members may also pay a multiple of the basic unit, thus being entitled to a multiple number of turns. The rice is used to acquire some large object. Rice-saving cooperatives have largely disappeared, being substituted by money-saving cooperatives and saving and loan cooperatives. During a transitional phase which may still be found to be in existence in some areas such saving groups acted as marketing cooperatives selling the rice and distributing the money to the members or keeping the money in a common fund, that is for loans.

Among the Loma, cooperative saving was traditionally done in primitive money, specifically in long twisted iron bars of 10–20 inches length. The habit has spread from there into Kpelle territory. In a few instances such cooperatives are still found today among the Loma.

Another object of saving in kind is palm-oil as found among the Kpelle and, when connected with the production of palm-oil, among the Bassa and Gbandi. While it is found traditionally as well as presently among the Kpelle and Bassa it is of recent origin among the Gbandi.

The principle of saving rice or palm-oil is also applicable to a number of other commodities, such as coffee.

Money-saving cooperatives are a modernized version of rice-saving cooperatives, the main difference being that money is being substituted for rice. They developed around 1930 when Firestone started its operations and for the first time cash became available to the hinterland population. Those tribes without traditional saving-in-kind cooperatives said they learned the pattern from other tribes at the Firestone plantations. Contributions may be weekly or monthly. Groups may range from very small ones to very large ones. The amounts contributed may vary between 5 cents and US $50 and more. Groups may be mixed or consist of either men or women. They may be found in the capital, in towns in the interior as well as in remote villages. The range of variability is very wide, except for the basic pattern that the total amount collected at each meeting is handed over to one member at a time. In the absence of banks saving cooperatives and related organizations derived from them provide the only saving institutions. They are found in most though not all tribes. Small groups have no leader; large groups are headed by a so-called president and sometimes by other officers. Saving cooperatives may also fulfill an insurance function: In case of necessity a member may receive the total in advance.

A modification of saving cooperatives was found among the Belle and Kru where regular contributions are made for a period of one year, after which they are redistributed. No further use is made of the money during the saving period.

In traditional Kru society cooperatives used to be established in which members contributed chicken, goats, cattle, rice or any other commodity. This was used to build up a fund from which members could take loans. No interest was paid. Among the Sapo, cooperatives were formed around 1930 on the basis of former age grades; they built up a fund of cattle and commodities which were later on exchanged for money. Members could borrow cash or kind to finance a burial, to pay taxes or court fines, etc. The money could also be used to finance a feast. Today these groups have been largely transformed into saving and loan cooperatives.

The most important indigenous development from saving cooperatives are saving and loan cooperatives. They were found in most tribes though of varying importance. Among the Mano the majority of the population belong to saving and loan cooperatives. Although less than 30 years old in their origins they are already very widespread and are continuing to gain in number and importance. The basic principle is that the money contributed weekly or monthly by the members is kept in a fund from which members and non-members may get loans. Sometimes loans are interest-free for members; more often members pay around 25 per cent and non-members between 30 and 50 per cent; interest rates are not calculated for certain time periods though loans are actually limited to periods between 1 week and 3 months, occasionally up to 6 months. In some areas saving and loan cooperatives are more popular among the literate population, in others more among illiterates. The degree of elaborateness of book-keeping and accountancy varies greatly depending upon the skill of the 'secretary'. Saving and loan cooperatives are usually highly formalized. There is nearly always a written constitution and a code of bye-laws. Groups are headed by committees consisting of several officers, the most important ones usually being a president, a vice-president, a treasurer, a collector and a secretary. Saving and loan cooperatives are usually established for one year, after which the money is distributed among the members. Among the Sapo saving and loan co-operatives are either identical with former saving and loan in kind cooperatives or have been established recently; the former cattle fund is partly or fully converted into a monetary fund, or monthly contributions between 10 cents and US $1.50 are made. Contributions in kind may still be substituted for contributions in cash if otherwise members could not pay.

Among the Mano and Loma a few saving and loan cooperatives were found which had added an investment function. Instead of distributing the fund after one year among the members the total was given to one person (according to the pattern of saving cooperatives) to be invested in a bus or taxi. This procedure was repeated each year until every member had had the total once. Such groups are usually small, and they are formed by wealthy traders or other relatively rich persons.

Among the Kissi, Mende, Sapo and Kran the principles of cooperative work, saving and loaning may be combined. Work groups are established, to be hired by farmers against payment of a fee. The money is used to build up a loan fund. Among the Kru it is a frequent practice for a person to hire his lineage or a lineage to which he does not belong. Once a lineage head has agreed to supply a work group, participation is compulsory for the lineage members. The money paid for the work may be used to build up a lineage fund for loans, run the same way as other saving and loan funds. Since membership is compulsory the term cooperative is not applicable to such groups.

Among the De and Bassa saving and consuming groups of traditional origin were found. Various kinds of foods are contributed by the community members and used for a big feast. Such groups are usually very large.

In traditional Belle society, groups used to be formed on a community basis for the collection of strips of 'country cloth'. These were used for garments to be given as presents to official visitors. Since such community-wide organizations usually compell all villages to join the group they are referred to as a group rather than a cooperative.

A total of three community saving and building groups were found among the Gola and De. Among the former, two villages save money to construct one new house for every four villagers every year. Among the latter, money is saved for the construction of a church and a school.

Community saving and loan groups with additional purposes were found among the Gola, Loma, Kpelle, Mende, Kru, Kran and Sapo. In a number of tribes they are of considerable economic importance. They are usually established for an indefinite period of time. Most of those found in existence originated between 1940 and 1960. They may be established on a lineage or community basis, or they may comprise several villages up to a sub-tribe. Small groups may have 10 to 60 members, large ones several hundred. It is common that in an area over which such a group extends every adult male and unmarried adult female is a member. Such community groups serve two broad purposes: they extend loans to individuals and they finance community projects. There are three principal ways of building up a fund: either by communal rice-farming, the rice being sold and the proceeds being put into the fund; by contributions in kind (rice, chicken, goats, cattle) which are either immediately sold or in case of animals bred for a number of months or years and sold then; or by monetary contributions. The latter are usually on a monthly basis. The amounts paid in by each member are mostly small: between US $10 and US $2. Individual loans are only granted for narrowly defined and socially recognized purposes, as for example burial, sickness, court fines, dowry, house-building, purchase of land and investments in a bus, taxi, or trade. Loan periods are in some tribes up to one month, in others up to three months. While non-members always pay interest there is some variation for members: they may pay no interest, or rates may be, according to tribe, 5–10 per cent, around 25 per cent or between 25 and 40 per cent. Community purposes for which the fund may be used are: construction and/or maintenance of motor roads, district taxes, community projects like a church or a school or a community feast. Such community groups are usually headed by an elaborate committee consisting of a president, vice-president, treasurer, secretary, collector, judge, messenger and often many other officers. Local chiefs may serve as witnesses at all transactions. There is a rather tight control system to avoid fraud. Wherever fraud occurs on a large scale or repeatedly, it may decrease considerably the propensity of the population to form such groups. On the whole, however, there is a strong tendency for community groups, based on communal saving, loaning and financing community projects, to increase in number, size, amounts collected and projects undertaken.

Other groups like age grades, burial societies, entertainment societies, soccer clubs etc., may adopt the functions of cooperative saving and loaning. It is probably the majority of voluntary associations in West Africa which provides some material help when members are in need.

OTHER COOPERATIVES

Cooperatives of clearly traditional origin are also found among plantation and industrial workers and in the cities. Among plantation and mine workers, particularly, saving cooperatives seem to be widespread.

In a mining enterprise (Bong Mining Company, located on Kpelle territory) 36 per cent of a probability sample of 383 workers stated to be members of a saving cooperative. In two rubber plantations 43 per cent of a probability sample of 539 workers were stated to be members of a saving cooperative, the proportion in LAC (located on Bassa territory) being 49 per cent ($N = 338$) and in COCOPA (located on Mano territory) 33 per cent ($N = 199$).

The mean contribution per month of 163 workers at LAC who indicated membership in a saving cooperative was US $11.60. Education does not appear to be a factor influencing membership in a co-operative. In the two plantations an equal proportion of 43 per cent among both literates and illiterates stated membership in a saving cooperative. The higher pay literate workers receive enables them to make slightly larger contributions: literates contribute US $12.52 per month, illiterates US $11.09. Since work at the plantation ends usually between 12 noon and 2 p.m., enough time is left for the workers to engage in agricultural work on their own. The majority seem to have their own farms nearby. Thirty-two per cent stated that they were members in a work cooperative; at LAC the proportion was 37 per cent, at COCOPA 25 per cent. Of the illiterate workers 37 per cent stated membership in a work cooperative, of the literate workers 24 per cent.

Saving and loan cooperatives are not common among workers.

Although no systematic study of cooperatives in Monrovia was included, it appears that saving cooperatives are extremely widespread. The number of members is from two onwards. Small groups seem to be more common than large ones. There is hardly anybody who has not, at some time or another during his life in Monrovia, been a member of a saving cooperative. Even the fact that fraud may occur any time has hardly discouraged the formation of saving cooperatives.

Saving and loan cooperatives are also common. They are considerably larger than saving cooperatives, the average ranging from about 30 to 60 members. Contributions tend to be around US $5 per month. They are either organized for a period of one year after which the total amount is redistributed, or for an unlimited period. They are usually highly formalized, being governed by an elaborate constitution and by bye-laws, copies of which are often distributed among the members in mimeographed form. They all have elected officers. The money is usually deposited in a bank, and many precautions are taken to avoid the possibility of fraud.

RECEPTIVITY TO CHANGE

While traditional cooperatives have been reported to be on the decline in many parts of the world, the overall situation of traditional cooperatives is one of change and adaptation, but not of weakening. It is true that many actual cooperative organizations have vanished; but at the same time, the growth of new types of cooperatives has been astonishing, pointing to an enormous receptivity to change. The main points should be summarized briefly:

1. During a period of changing economic, social, and political conditions most traditional institutions of economic cooperation have continued to exist. They still play a very important economic role;
2. During the process of adaptation to changing economic conditions traditional institutions of economic cooperation underwent a number of structural and functional changes.

Functionally work cooperatives have changed in that (a) they produce rice now or other cash crops for a market while traditionally they operated in a subsistence economy; (b) they may be hired for money by outsiders—an entirely new function; (c) they may process agricultural products, e.g. palm-oil and sugar-cane for the market. Structurally they have changed in that (a) the pattern of sexual labour division is not as strictly observed as before in order to increase agricultural production; (b) in many cases an elaborate committee has been elected which controls the cooperative business; (c) non-reciprocal work cooperatives formed *ad hoc* among the eastern tribes have been converted in many instances into permanent work cooperatives to be hired by outsiders; (d) the social control mechanisms of cooperatives have taken advantage of the modern legal apparatus. Functionally saving cooperatives have changed in that (a) saving in kind where still in existence now often includes marketing; (b) money has been substituted for kind; (c) the loan business has been added as an entirely new function; (d) saving and loan cooperatives have spread from the original three tribes to all other tribes and have become extremely popular in all sections of the population. Structurally they have changed in that they have adopted (a) a complex body of officers; (b) a constitution and bye-laws regulating the conduct of the members and the business of the cooperative; (c) mechanisms and procedures to control the saving and loan business of the cooperative;

3. As a result of the application of traditional patterns of co-operation to modern economic conditions new institutions of economic cooperation have been generated. A combination of the basic patterns of work cooperatives and community work groups has led to the new institution of community farming. Many work groups have been transformed into groups to be hired or have adopted hiring as a new function. Saving in kind cooperatives have been most prolific in generating new types: short-term and long-term saving cooperatives; saving and loan in kind cooperatives; saving and loan cooperatives; saving, loan and investment cooperatives; saving and consuming cooperatives; community saving and building groups; and community multi-purpose groups. Combining the patterns of cooperative

work and saving, work, saving and loan cooperatives have come into existence;

4. Cooperatives proper (in the sense of the definition) of all forms of economic cooperation appear to be most receptive to change. On the whole, indigenous cooperatives have increased rather than decreased in number, variety and economic importance;

5. Two major trends have been observed: (a) With the transformation of the subsistence economy into a market economy work cooperatives proper become somewhat less frequent. At the same time hired work cooperatives which have come into existence in response to the introduction of the market economy become more frequent. (b) Saving cooperatives which started to develop around 1930 and saving and loan cooperatives which started to develop about 1950 are spreading very fast and are becoming increasingly important. In future, saving and loan cooperatives are to be expected to develop more rapidly than saving cooperatives and both more rapidly than work cooperatives. A most recent innovation are community multi-purpose cooperatives which are based on communal saving and loaning and which finance community projects. They may compromise one or several communities (comparable to cooperative unions and federations). They are rapidly growing with regard to number, size, funds raised and projects undertaken;

6. Most institutions of economic cooperation, and among these particularly cooperatives, could be considerably improved by technical aid (much less so by capital aid). Such aid could have two major aims: (a) to improve the operation of already existing functions of cooperatives (e.g. to improve the functioning of saving and saving and loan cooperatives by training accountants, forming cooperative unions and federations etc.); (b) to add new functions to already existing ones (e.g. to add the function of cooperative marketing to already existing work cooperatives) hence using existing cooperatives as a channel for the introduction of a modern economy. Adding new functions to cooperatives may also counteract the process of weakening in case of work cooperatives (for a detailed case study cf. Seibel and Massing, 1974).

Whether or not traditional cooperatives can or should be saved and used as channels for modernization is not the issue here. What we have demonstrated is that cooperative societies represent the original form of self-management, or worker participation, and that they are exceedingly widespread in traditional cultures. Instead of eliminating the indigenous institutions of self-management by introducing so-called modern forms of alienated work, it is suggested that the existing self-managing potential be reinstated. What is possible in Yugoslavia should also be possible in the Third World.

13 Political Bases for Self-Management in the Developing World: Participation in Open Societies

Self-management is a system designed to utilize fully the potential of every individual participating in an organization. Its success is then of course contingent upon the extent to which the various individuals possess a potential that could be utilized. We do not intend to dig into that question as a philosophical issue. Suffice it to say that most people have many more useful talents and abilities than managers in industry and administration are aware of. The crucial question is then whether or not the respective cultures permit the members of society to activate their talents and to participate directly in all affairs or whether they relegate the individuals to some very limited function like cogs in a machine.

PARTICIPATION IN PREMODERN SOCIETIES

It is frequently assumed that the traditional cultures in developing countries are of the latter type. In fact, there are many societies to which this assumption applies. If for generations the message has been only to obey orders and never to move of one's own accord, then the introduction of self-management may indeed be problematic for a long learning period. However, even in those societies, there are usually spheres of activities in which some principles of self-management are practised, namely in cooperative societies. In our preceding study of cooperatives in Liberia, it was shown that traditional cooperatives are particularly strong in the more centralized societies. If we add to that the evidence from the various kingdoms in traditional West Africa, then we can also point to the widespread existence of cooperative organizations in crafts, usually referred to as guilds. These present a vivid example of a combination of hierarchical structure with cooperative or self-management principles. Hence, even to hierarchically organized, centralized societies, the idea of self-management may not be totally alien.

There exist, however, a great many traditional societies in which the principles of self-management and participation are built right into the political and economic structure. We may refer to them as open societies. Politically, they are open in the sense that every adult (or at least every adult male, as there seem to exist only very few perfect open societies) participates in all political decisions. Economically and socially, they are open in the sense that all positions are on principle available to everyone, that there is free competition, that only individual achievement counts and that individual achievement and success must not lead to class privilege. Politically, such societies may be called grassroots democracies; economically, they may be called achieving societies. Not in all societies are the political and economic spheres matched in such a way that they can be truly called open. Some may be more open in the political and more closed in the economic order, or vice versa; but there is a general tendency, at least in premodern societies, for the two orders to correlate.

Before presenting some descriptions of premodern open societies, we have to deal briefly with the more theoretical question of why some societies are more open while others are more closed. As we will see at the end of this chapter, this is not of purely theoretical interest, for it will tie in with the political dimension of self-management.

OPEN AND CLOSED SOCIETIES

With reference to the system of social stratification, we may rephrase our question: What are the conditions under which political, economic and social roles are allocated by achieved criteria, and what are the conditions for role allocation by ascription?

For an example, let us first take an everyday setting as it widely occurs in every society. Decisions have to be made all the time in which the result of a choice between several alternatives or of a decision is irrelevant as long as the choice or decision is made.

For example, it does not matter whether lunch is served at twelve or one o'clock. All that matters is that those concerned know the time when lunch is served. The role of decision-maker (a particular type of work role) in this situation cannot be allocated on the basis of achieved criteria because everyone could make the decision and no one is particularly suited for the role. Or, in terms of a more precise definition of achieved roles, criteria of role allocation in that situation cannot be germane to the performance instructions of the role of decision-maker. The same applies to other types of roles. In many premodern societies, farming is unproblematic. Differences in performance are largely irrelevant; if all farmers attempted to maximize their output, they would produce a surplus they could not consume. As every extended family is a subsistence unit and surpluses cannot be sold, the farmer's goal is, in the terminology of decision theory, satisficing rather than optimizing.

In normal social life it has to be clear to everyone in most situations who takes up certain roles, lest there be strife or chaos. The system of role allocation most suitable to that situation is based on ascribed criteria like age, sex, or family or lineage affiliation. Its effectiveness lies in the elimination of uncertainty about role incumbents; it is predictable by every member of society who will then assume a certain role. Thus, individuals can be trained for these roles, from early childhood onwards. Anthropologist Ralph Linton (1936, p. 129) has even suggested that it is the normal state of a society in which the uncertainty arising out of the perennial search for the best man for a given role has been removed by placing the system of role allocation on a predictable ascriptive base:

> Social systems have to be built upon the potentialities of the average individual, the person who has no special gifts or disabilities. Such individuals can be trained to occupy almost any status and to perform the associated role adequately if not brilliantly. The social ascription of a particular status, with the intensive training that such ascription makes possible, is a guarantee that the role will be performed even if the performance is mediocre.

The underlying theorem can be summarized as follows: *In settings where the performance of work roles is unproblematic in the sense that differences in the quality of performance or in the degree of optimality of solutions to work problems are non-existent or irrelevant, work roles are allocated on the basis of ascribed, or non-achieved, criteria.*

Let us now consider a setting in which decisions and work activities are problematic, where conditions of uncertainty prevail. There are situations in which the fate of a group, sometimes even its survival, depends on the maximization of work-role performance or on the optimality of decisions; where it is of vital importance that certain roles are occupied by those who are most competent. Examples of such roles may be war leaders, heart surgeons or aircraft pilots. In such a setting, work roles are typically allocated on the basis of achieved criteria. Thus, our first proposition is complemented by a second: In settings where the performance of work roles in problematic in the sense that high quality of performance in work roles or optimality of solutions to work problems are both possible and important, work roles are allocated on the basis of achieved criteria.

The two propositions may now be applied to societies: *Societies characterized by a predominance of unproblematic settings tend to allocate work roles on the basis of ascribed criteria. Societies characterized by a predominance of problematic settings tend to allocate roles on the basis of achievement. The former may be called closed, the latter open societies.*

Once this theorem is accepted, one may infer from an emphasis on achieved roles that a society is characterized by a predominance of problematic settings; an emphasis on non-achieved roles leads us to conclude that a society is characterized by a predominance of non-problematic settings.

From the above static theorem, a dynamic theorem can be derived: *Any change in the predominance of unproblematic versus problematic settings in a society may lead to a subsequent shift in the emphasis on ascribed versus achieved roles, and accordingly to the emergence of a closed versus an open society.*

A major source of such change may be seen in technological innovations from within or without.

In a historical dimension, change may thus take place in two different phases that can be expressed in the form of two sub-theorems: *As a predominance of unproblematic settings in a society changes to a predominance of problematic settings, the emphasis on ascribed roles may shift to an emphasis on achieved roles,* i.e. a closed society may turn into an open society.

Similar thoughts had been expressed by Linton (1936, pp. 129–30):

> As soon as changes within the culture or in the external environment produce maladjustments, it has to recognize and utilize these gifts (i.e. special skills and talents germane to the performance of certain roles) . . . For this reason, societies living under new or changing conditions are usually characterized by a wealth of achievable statuses and by very broad delimitations of the competition for them.

As a predominance of problematic settings in a society changes to a predominance of unproblematic settings, the emphasis on achieved roles shifts to an emphasis on ascribed roles, i.e. an open society turns into a closed society.

Again, Linton (1936, p. 130) described that process in some detail:

> As social systems achieve adjustment to their settings, the social value of individual thought and initiative decreases. Thorough training of the component individuals becomes more necessary to the survival and successful functioning of society than the free expression of their individual abilities. To ensure successful training, more and more statuses are transferred from the achieved to the ascribed group, and the competition for those which remain is more and more limited. To put the same thing in different terms, individual opportunities decrease. Well-adjusted societies are, in general, characterized by a high preponderance of ascribed over achieved statuses, and increasing rigidity of the social system.*

AFRICAN SOCIETIES

We will now look at the evidence from premodern, and particularly from pre-literate societies. From its beginning, there has

---

* For a systematic presentation cf. Seibel (1974a; 1975).

been a long-standing tradition in sociology to speculate cursorily about 'primitive peoples', rather than study them seriously. As the transition from medieval estate society was seen as a change from a closed to an open society, it was concluded by inference that all premodern societies must be closed systems. No advice came from anthropologists who concentrated mainly on kinship structures. When politically interested, they managed to detect absolute rulers in all societies. When the colonial policy of 'indirect rule' was based on the assumption of universal absolutism, some tribes started to revolt (e.g. the Ibo of Eastern Nigeria in the Aba riots of 1929), for they had never before recognized any central authority. After some initial confusion among government anthropologists, it was eventually discovered that many if not most pre-industrial societies were 'tribes without rulers' (Middleton and Tait, 1958), i.e. segmentary rather than centralized political systems.

Inspired by the Middleton–Tait discovery, a few political scientists shifted their interest from 'states' to 'political systems' which allowed them to include segmentary, or stateless, societies among their objects of study (Almond and Coleman, 1960). As segmentary societies are not characterized by hereditary positions in a hierarchical order, the question now arose: how do they allocate roles?

In our studies of premodern societies, we found that many, particularly the less-developed ones, place a major emphasis on achievement in their system of role allocation. Several examples will be presented for illustrative purposes, some from Africa and some from Oceania, although any other part of the Third World might have been chosen as well.

The Kran are a society in Eastern Liberia with a very simple technology. For their subsistence, they depend first on agriculture and second on hunting and gathering. Individual achievement is strongly emphasized, and important roles are filled by a person only as long as he is found to be the most competent. Thus, the Kran may be called an achieving society. As no society ever allocates all roles by achievement, however, the complexity of the Kran system of role allocation has to be examined in more detail.

In everyday Kran life, decisions have to be made all the time in which the outcome is irrelevant: any alternative will do equally well. For instance, it does not make any difference whether a family works today on one farm and tomorrow on another or *vice versa*, as long as the family members know when to work on which farm. According to our first theoretical proposition, the role of decision-maker in this situation cannot be allocated on the basis of achieved criteria because everyone could make the decision and no one is particularly suited for the role. The non-achieved criteria chosen by the Kran, and many similar societies, are kinship, age and sex. They define unmistakenly who is in charge of unproblematic decisions. The oldest person of the smallest social unit (such units are usually kinship units) that is directly concerned makes the decision. Decisions that concern both sexes are made by men. Women make decisions according to seniority when the decisions pertain to women only.

The Kran arrive thus at a simple, formal authority system for unproblematic decisions. The largest unit subject to the authority of its eldest is the tribe (*bloa*). However, as the tribe emerges as a social reality only in the form of war alliance between lineages, i.e. in a problematic situation, the role of the tribal eldest (*bloa dioi*) is purely ritual. The largest permanent social unit is the lineage (*tshe*), presided over by the lineage eldest (*bo klaa*). If a lineage is a residential unit inhabiting a village (*vulo*) its eldest is at the same time the village head (*vulo ba*). If a lineage is spread out, its segments (*unu*) are residential units under its eldest (*unu dioi*); they typically occupy a village section (*lü*). In village affairs, the segments are under the authority of the eldest of the oldest, or founder, lineage *(vulo ba)*. This role is of only ritual importance as there are hardly any unproblematic decisions on that level; most unproblematic decisions in a village are made by lineage, or lineage segment heads and by heads of smaller social units. A segment consists of several extended families (*buli*) each of which lives in its own compound. Every extended family is headed by its oldest male (*nyo klaa de buli*).

Unlike in centralized, hierarchical societies, decision-making power in segmentary societies is strongest in the smaller, and weakest in the larger social units. This finds its logical conclusion in the fact that the Kran do not recognize the role of eldest within the very largest unit, the alliance of tribes (*bloa dru*) which is only formed in major wars. On that level, no unproblematic decisions exist; the authority of an eldest would thus be zero.

Our first proposition applies equally to other work roles among the Kran. In so far as hunting, gathering, farming, basket- or mat-weaving and other activities are unproblematic, they are assigned without reference to differences in competence. As anyone can perform these roles, and as differences in the quality of performance are considered irrelevant, they are open to everyone. Criteria of role allocation are non-achieved, as everyone, or everyone of a certain sex, may assume these roles, permanently or intermittently.

A second sub-system of role allocation is structured along the dimension of problematic decisions and activities. There are settings, in which it is of crucial importance that certain roles are occupied by the most competent members. As traditional Kran society is under constant danger of attack, the most problematic setting is the military. Hence, the prevalence of achieved criteria in the allocation of roles is most pronounced in war and war-related activities, as suggested by our second proposition. The Kran consider the role of war leader (*bio*) as the one that is most important in their role system. This role is entirely problem-oriented. Its functionality is emphasized by the fact that in peace the *bio* may be a respected person but no special authority accrues to him. Rank and importance of the *bio* vary with the kind of social unit that is involved in warfare, e.g. a village or a tribe. In minor wars, the *bio* may participate in combat; in major wars, he is a strategist only. Accordingly, different weights may be assigned to his strategic abilities on the one hand and to his strength and fighting skills on the other. In any event, all criteria of selection are achieved, i.e. directly germane to the role. Age is irrelevant. What ultimately matters is a person's ability to win wars. More specific criteria are strategic skills, self-control, bravery, strength, endurance, reconciliatory talents and expertise in the production of medicines, charms and arrow poisons. Someone is *bio* only as long as he is considered the most capable. His role is only activated during war. (With the pacification of the Kran by the Monrovia government early this century, the role of *bio* has ceased to be activated.)

In major wars, the *bio* is aided by head warriors (*taa nyo*) whose roles are also achieved. Main criteria are courage, bravery, strength and endurance.

In the economic sphere, the Kran consider as crucial two roles in which optimality or high quality of performance can be reached: the role of the 'richest man' (*pa nyo*) and the role of the 'gentleman' (*gaa nyo*). Both are allocated on the basis of achieved criteria. As land is plentiful and the amount of capital negligible, wealth is largely proportionate to the amount of labour someone has at his disposal. Through hard work, the richest man has been able to afford the bride-wealth for several women. As he has many wives and children, he can afford to hire large work groups (*pã*) to extend his farm. As a compensation to the work group, he has to give a big party, the affluence of which indicates the amount of his wealth. Thus, the party is at the same time a major mechanism of redistribution: the prevention of excessive wealth is built right into the process of accumulating wealth. The richest man can only retain his role as long as he constantly proves his affluence through work parties. As in the case of the *bio*, past achievements are irrelevant; the role has to be earned anew all the time. For those farmers who decide to compete for the role of 'richest man', farming becomes a problematic setting in which high quality of performance matters. Unlike the average farmer, they try to maximize their production. For them, farming becomes an achieved role as they strive for the higher status they may gain through hard work, skill in work organization and other criteria germane to the role of a 'high status farmer'. Hence, a dual role of farmer emerges: the role of the average farmer within subsistence agriculture, based on non-achieved criteria; and the role of the rich farmer, for surplus production, based on achieved criteria. The incumbents of the latter role compete for the role of 'richest man'.

The term 'gentleman' refers to the most generous man in the village. While the richest man uses redistribution in a calculated manner to increase his wealth, the gentleman considers redistribution, generosity and helpfulness as ends in themselves. He is ready to work with and for anyone who needs help; he readily offers visitors accommodation and food and he may help a young man pay his bride-wealth without asking for special privileges.

Further avenues to respected roles are found in a variety of associations (e.g, cooperatives), in which leaders are largely chosen on the basis of individual merit and ability.

Analytically, settings may be divided into problematic and unproblematic ones. Social reality, however, is frequently mixed. Accordingly, the actual system of role allocation among the Kran is very flexible. Depending on the extent to which settings are problematic or unproblematic, criteria of role allocation may include both achieved and ascribed roles. In such a mixed setting, a person may be chosen on the basis of both achieved and ascribed criteria, or persons chosen from different sub-systems of role allocation may contribute to the outcome. For instance, in a moderately problematic setting, the eldest may participate nominally while the *bio*'s contribution may carry more weight; the converse may be true in moderately unproblematic situations.

Social, economic and political affairs among the Kran are characterized by two types of settings: problematic and unproblematic ones. Accordingly, the Kran allocate roles on the basis of achievement or ascription, respectively. As no society is ever completely achievement-oriented, it is justified to call the Kran an achieving, or open, society (for detailed ethnographic data cf. Schröder and Seibel, 1974).

The extent of problematic settings varies considerably between societies. A comparison of three pre-industrial societies in Nigeria shows that the importance of achievement in their systems of role allocation varies accordingly. It should be again noted that these descriptions pertain to the premodern, not to the present situation.

The Ibo are an agricultural society in Eastern Nigeria with a simple technology. While they are, economically speaking, slightly more advanced than the Kran of Liberia in that they do not rely on hunting and gathering, their economy is rather unsophisticated compared to the economy of many other Nigerian societies, particularly those which are kingdoms. There are no towns, and villages are split into hamlets which consist of dispersed homesteads. There are only small local markets, and very few specialized craftsmen. Craft technology is very crude. Before the advent of the British, the Ibo had no common name, nor a common tradition of origin. The socio-political structure is segmentary, the largest political unit being the village group. There is no central political authority, and authority is, in principle, never vested in one individual. In each community, political functions are served by a council of elders whose decisions have to be ratified by the community. With the exception of the cult slaves (*osu*), there are no hereditary positions or strata into which a person is born: everyone is born equal.

Living in very small communities, with a simple technology, and under constant danger of attack, survival is precarious for the Ibo. Their life is characterized by a preponderance of problematic settings. Hence, their system of role allocation is strongly based on achieved criteria, as suggested by our theory. On principle, all economic and political roles labelled important are achieved, involving a person's competence, aptitude, capability etc. Personal efforts and the use of one's abilities lead to a rise in status. War leadership goes to the one who proves to be most efficient. Matters in dispute can be judged by a number of persons or councils; there is no office of judge. One chooses whom one considers best in judging and to whom both parties agree. Thus, there is considerable social mobility, every position being, in principle, open to everyone. A person has alternative choices between various ways of gaining prestige and between various occupations. The opportunity for upward or downward mobility is almost unlimited. Mobility is not confined to the political, economic, or occupational sphere; a person may also improve his position by high performance in athletics, arts and more recently in literature and science.

Thus, Ibo society may be characterized as an open society where roles may be attained on the basis of occupational skill, enterprise and initiative, individual achievement being one of the highest values.

However, as the Ibo are technologically slightly more advanced and survival is somewhat less precarious than among the Kran, the prevalence of problematic situations is not quite as pronounced as among the Kran. Both societies allocate important roles on the basis of achievement. But while the Kran are very rigorous in that such role incumbency is always transient, a role being awarded to the most competent at any given time, the Ibo have introduced an element of stability through their so-called title societies which allow the translation of achieved economic wealth into permanent political status. Every free-born male member of society may buy his way into the title society and then, through additional payments, up the ranks of titles within the association. But while the way into and up the association is earned, the status and prestige that accrue to a title do not have to be constantly renewed through permanent efforts.

The Yoruba comprise a number of closely related kingdoms which, under the Oyo empire, dominated a large part of the West African coast. They are technologically very advanced, their economy being based on agriculture, highly developed crafts organized in guilds and extensive trading. The Yoruba have the highest rate of traditional urbanization in Africa, cities and hinterland being connected through considerable economic exchange and through a net of administrative channels. Politically and economically, the Yoruba have reached a high degree of political and economic control over their environment, i.e. their existence is characterized by a predominance of unproblematic settings. This implies that economic and political processes and their outcomes are largely predictable. This predictability is rooted in their system of status allocation which is primarily based on ascription. People are born into positions and can thus be trained for them from birth onwards. The achievement principle according to which the most competent is assigned to any given role would introduce an amount of uncertainty that would be incompatible with the stability of the economic and political system. Conforming to our theory, Yoruba society is thus highly stratified, with a layer of royal families at the top of the hierarchy, a stratum of hereditary chiefs and representatives of major territorial and associational groups beneath, commoners without hereditary claims to titles below them, subdivided into two main layers of craftsmen and farmers, and slaves at the bottom. During the last 250 years, however, there has been a sharp increase of problematic settings among the Yoruba. After a series of wars against the kingdom of Dahomey in the eighteenth century, civil war led to internal disintegration during the nineteenth century. This enabled the Hausa–Fulani in the north to penetrate into Yoruba territory and to islamize its northern part. The Yoruba emerged from this divided into largely independent kingdoms. The introduction of problematic settings added a strong element of achievement to an otherwise ascriptive system of role allocation. As a consequence, there is some interstratum mobility. A wealthy man, for example, may be appointed to council membership and even receive a chieftaincy title which involves the crossing of strata boundaries. Moreover, there is considerable intra-stratum mobility, each stratum being a differentiated system of substrata. Mobility within strata is largely dependent on individual achievement, with the Ogboni society, similar to the Ibo title society, allowing the transformation of achieved roles into permanent positions. Especially during the wars of the nineteenth century, a number of other avenues were open to men of ambition: in the army, in crafts which produced weapons and other supplies for the armies, and in agriculture which had a permanent market among full-time craftsmen as well as in the armies. In each of these fields, a man could strive for roles on the basis of his competence and improve his status through personal efforts. Even in the selection of a king from among several royal families, personal competence and merits matter. Thus, the life of every Yoruba is characterized by the presence of both problematic and unproblematic settings and accordingly affected by achieved as well as ascribed criteria of role allocation.

Technologically and organizationally, the Hausa are one of the most advanced societies of pre-industrial Africa. Since the thirteenth century, when the islamic faith was adopted, the Hausa have had a highly developed system of government with a centralized bureaucracy, a well-organized tax system and a highly qualified judiciary. Each of the eight Hausa states is administered from its capital, which is the seat of the emir, an absolute ruler. The degree of differentiation of occupational roles is most remarkable; there is an elaborate marketing structure that connects not only every village with the capital but also the empires across the Sahara with the North African coast. Crafts are very advanced, both technologically and organizationally. The nomadic Fulani who had been immigrating peacefully into Hausaland from around the year 1500 onwards, led a holy war (*jihad*) against the Hausa aristocracy in 1802, overthrew them and set up a feudal government under Fulani emirs.

As the Hausa have exercised, for centuries, perfect control over their environment, social, political and economic life has been rather unproblematic for them. Interaction processes have become a routine, with all inputs and outputs predetermined and thus predictable: a near-perfect state of equilibrium. Complying with our theory, achievement as a criterion of role allocation is non-existent:

> The Hausa system of occupational status is almost . . . wholly ascriptive in its orientation, since its units are closed descent groups between which all movements is disapproved. . . . The occupational status model . . . incorporates such ascriptive factors as descent and ethnicity. (M.G. Smith, 1959, p. 251)

The system of ascribed roles that are organized into a multitude of layers is so complex that any exact statement about the number of strata must be artificial. There are separate stratification systems for men and women. The main determinants of the male order are political rank and occupational class. The two main strata groups are chiefs and office-holders on the one hand and subjects and commoners on the other, i.e. rulers and ruled. Below them is the layer of slaves. All occupational groups are ranked, with officials, islamic teachers and wealthy merchants at the top, and butchers, mat-weavers, drummers, praise-singers and buglers at the bottom of the hierarchy.

In offices and crafts, an important distinction is between inherited (*karda*) and freely selected (*shigege*). *Karda* roles are more frequent and rank higher than *shigege*. Despite a strong emphasis on *karda*, mobility is not absent in Hausa society. As polygamy and concubinage proliferate the number of those eligible for any role, there is a form of institutionalized competition: *neman sarautu*, or clientage system. A person may become the client of an office-holder, hoping to be rewarded for his loyalty and obedience with an office. Yet there is no room in *neman sarautu* for achievement, as mobility is allowed on the basis of servitude and respect for authority but denied on the basis of competence.

Our concern in describing the three societies was with the social system, or more specifically with the system of role allocation. It was mentioned earlier that, ideally, a social orientation towards achievement is complemented by a corresponding value and motivational orientation. In fact, it was found that such a congruence exists in the three societies. In an empirical study of achievement values and achievement motivation, LeVine (1966, p. 78) concluded:

> The frequency of obedience and social compliance value themes in essays on success written by the students was greatest for the Hausa, followed by the Southern Yoruba and Ibo, in that order.
>
> The frequency of achievement imagery in dream reports was greatest for the Ibo, followed by the Southern Yoruba, Northern Yoruba and Hausa, in that order.

As the change from a premodern to a modern society implies a revolutionary change in most spheres, which all become highly problematic, we may postulate that there is only one appropriate system of role allocation: that of an open society in which roles are allocated by achievement.

We may now hypothesize that societies with a premodern emphasis on achievement have a great advantage over those societies which have to make the transition to a new system of role allocation in addition to the shift to a new system of work roles. Tentatively, one may thus formulate the following proposition:

Pre-industrial societies characterized by an achievement-based system of role allocation tend to be receptive to modernization; pre-industrial societies characterized by an ascriptive system of role allocation tend to be more resistant.

As the three largest societies of Nigeria differ widely in terms of their premodern system of role allocation, they should be highly amenable to a test of this proposition. Common sense would lead us to predict that the technologically and organizationally highly advanced Hausa and Yoruba should be very fast modernizers while the Ibo, with their relatively simple traditional economy, should be very slow. However, using the above proposition, the prediction would be very different: the Ibo with their traditional emphasis on achievement may continue to strive for higher ranking or more rewarding work roles, simply substituting new opportunities for old ones. The Yoruba, with their mixed system of role allocation, may be expected to be somewhat less receptive to change; while the Hausa, with their social contempt for individual competence and talent, are likely to be resistant to change.

Using interregional mobility, inter-generational and intra-generational occupational mobility in modern employment settings and several measures of adaptation to wage labour as modernization indicators, it was concluded, on the basis of a sample study of 509 factory workers, of a study of Wells and Warmington (1963), and of official statistics, that the Ibo modernize fastest, that the Yoruba are somewhat slower and that the Hausa have been largely resistant to change (Seibel, 1974a). Indeed, within half a century, the Ibo have reached higher levels of modernization than the Yoruba have over a full century, while the Hausa very successfully resisted any attempt at modernization until the civil war of 1967–70.

This study was also carried out in Liberia, under more controlled conditions, comparing the Kran, Kru, Bassa and Grebo (they all belong linguistically and culturally to the Kru group), who traditionally emphasize achievement, with the Kpelle, who are organized into a polycephalous associational state and place more emphasis on ascription. While the differences, in terms of criteria of role allocation, between these two groups are by far not as drastic as between Ibo and Hausa, they are pronounced enough to allow the prediction that the Kru group of societies should be more receptive to modernization than the Kpelle. Confirmation of this prediction would in fact lend considerable support to the underlying hypothesis as the Kpelle happen to be located much closer to centres of modernization than the Kru group. Measuring receptivity to modernization by a composite index of adaptation to wage labour in a random sample of 115 Kpelle and 105 Kru-group mine workers, the latter were found to adapt much faster to wage labour than the Kpelle. A replication of the study among plantation workers in Liberia confirmed these results. The proposition that pre-industrial societies that emphasize achievement are more receptive to modernization than those who are more ascriptive in their traditional system of status allocation has thus been repeatedly confirmed.

OCEANIAN SOCIETIES

Another Third World area which we would like to present as an example for the existence of very vigorous systems of self-determination, competition and achievement is Oceania, in particular Melanesia, which today largely coincides with Papua–New Guinea. This area comprises an enormous number of societies—speaking about 730 different languages—which are all more or less open societies. At the same time, we want to show that the openness of the stratification system, which we consider fundamental to the idea of self-management, is related to the environment, in particular to the problems posed by the environment. We therefore will compare the Melanesian societies, which are exposed to hostile environments, to the neighbouring Polynesian societies, who live, by comparison, under very favourable circumstances.

This difference in environmental situation between Melanesia and Polynesia was already noted by anthropologist Ralph Linton (1955, p. 179). About Samoa, one of the Polynesian islands, La

Perouse, the first European to have landed there in 1798, wrote that: 'they were so rich, and in want of so little . . .', an impression which has been confirmed later. Even the loss of the entire taro or yam crop would not produce much hardship, for planting could be continued throughout the year so that losses would be quickly recovered. In the meantime, the bounteous natural environment provided fish from the sea, wild yams and roots from the forest, and coconuts along the seashore (Lockwood, 1971, p. 11). 'So liberal was the Samoan natural environment', wrote Watters (1958, pp. 350–1), that a subsistence system was supported more easily than in most other groups of the Pacific, and little effort was required to maintain comfortable living standards. The challenge of the natural environment was on the whole only slight, and the response of the Samoan culture was accordingly small. Even diseases like malaria, filariasis and tropical phagedaenic ulcers, which are rampant in Melanesia, have spared Polynesia.

In different areas, Melanesians are plagued by a wide variety of hardships: rugged mountains and swamps, poor soils and precipitous slopes, volcanic eruptions and typhoons, leading to unpredictable droughts, crop failures, food shortages, hunger and starvation, to which epidemics, wiping out whole villages, have to be added. One of the most dramatic accounts of what a problematic situation means to Melanesian societies is the *loka* description of the Massim on Goodenough Island, presented in a stylized verbal form which betrays frequent repetition:

Omens are heard: ancestral spirits disguised as birds sing in the village. Portents are seen: the sky darkens and ash falls to smother the land. Coastal villages are swamped by tidal waves. The 'big wind' comes, toppling houses and stripping trees of their fruit. Next the 'big sun' scorches the grass and bakes the ground 'like stone'. Feasting stops and fasting begins. Taro is moved to the creeks, but these soon dry up and the plants wither. Already the old people's eyes are 'turning in their heads with hunger'. Families repair to the bush every day to search for food: roots, nuts, berries, wild yam and the despised famine foods *laiwai* and *baima*, which resemble bitter crab apples. Soon only those with lokana yams and strong *sisikwana* (anti-hunger magic) remain in the village; others live in the bush sleeping in caves or between the roots of trees. Armed sorties are made to the coast to steal fish and sago, and even the precious betel nut is cut down for its succulent heart. Seed yams have been eaten, the bush has been scoured and the gardens are still empty. The old people then die in the village while the young are dying from sickness in the bush. The strong of one village have been killing and eating the weak of another for some time; now they turn to their fellow villagers. Parents begin to exchange their children to eat . . . . (Young, 1971, pp. 173–94)

According to our theory, we would expect to find open societies in Melanesia, allowing the individual a maximum amount of participation in all affairs, emphasizing the importance of the individual through competition and achievement. In Polynesia, we would expect to find closed societies, providing a place for everyone from and through birth and discouraging any individual striving. Let us now look at the evidence.

East and west of Fidji, there are culture areas that are markedly different in religion, art, kinship structure, economic and political organization. These differences become even more pronounced when seen before the background of their similarities: both Polynesian and Melanesian societies practice agriculture with stone-age tools. With very similar technology, the same crops are planted, such as yams, taro, breadfruit, banana and coconuts, frequently supplemented by fishing.

Polynesia is known in anthropology for its differentiated forms of social strata and hierarchical structure with hereditary chieftainships and kingships. Such structures are absent in Melanesia. Thurnwald already pointed to the wide discrepancies between the small, democratic Melanesian communities and the aristocratic Polynesian societies. In life-style and consumption patterns, Melanesia appears to be egalitarian, while Polynesia is highly stratified.

In Melanesia, politically independent communities typically comprise about 70 to 300 inhabitants, in some rare cases up to 1000. In Polynesia, communities with 2000 or 3000 members are average. In areas like Tonga or Hawaii, they may even reach 10,000 or more.

Corresponding to these differences in size, there are also differences in political structure, which are very marked despite a wide range of local deviations. In Melanesia, an ethnic group, usually without a proper name, comprises a multitude of autonomous kinship groups, though kinship is used very generously as a membership criterion. Each of these groups occupies a certain territory. The political structure is segmentary. A small village or a group of hamlets form the basic unit. Each of these units is economically independent, of equal political status and structurally similar.

In Polynesia, the political geometry is pyramidal, as Sahlins (1963, p. 287) put it:

> Communities are subdivisions of larger political entities. Within a structure of differential ranks, smaller units are integrated into larger ones, with a hierarchy of chiefs as political co-ordinators. At the top of the pyramid, there is the king or paramount chief with his lineage, which is above all other lineages, which are in turn differentiated by rank among themselves. All lineages are part of an inter-generationally stable structure.

In Polynesia, leadership functions are precisely defined, and leadership roles are firmly appropriated by chiefs. In Melanesia, there exist only very loose concepts of leadership, and leadership roles are allocated only intermittently to so-called big men. At any given point in time, a large number of Melanesian men is competing to be a big man, though usually at quite different stages of the competitive game. Only a few men never in their lifetime enter that competition. In Melanesia, achievement and success are the result of hard work and intelligent investment; there is no permanent accumulation of wealth or power, and no inheritance of privileges.

In Melanesia, charisma as a magical, personal force (*mana*) is open to anyone, and everyone can build up and utilize his *mana* to enter the big-man competition. In Polynesia, a chief inherits his *mana*, which provides the basis of his power and protects him against commoners. A Melanesian big man has to possess personal abilities, such as rhetorical talents. The Polynesian chief, however, has a speaker who is especially trained in rhetoric and the chief has control over the voice of his speaker.

The same difference is found in the sphere of production. The Melanesian big man literally has to prove his productive powers all the time, while the Polynesian chief possesses them 'by nature' and without any personal effort in the form of religious control over the fertility of the land. The Polynesian chief has a right to dispose of the work and production of the households on his territory, and mobilization of economic resources is a regularly exercised practice that can be enforced. For the Melanesian big man, however, work and production have to be continuously mobilized through personal loyalties and economic obligations. In Melanesia, surplus production is the result of charismatic efforts; in Polynesia, it is routinized and enforced as a duty in regular cycles. The exchange of work services and goods tends in Melanesia towards reciprocity, in Polynesia to inequality. In Polynesia, there is an administrative staff which is dependent on the chief; in Melanesia, a big man is dependent on his followers. A Polynesian chief makes decisions because he is a chief; a Melanesian may become a big man because he frequently contributes to decisions. In his community, a Melanesian big man may have prestige, but he never has power, while the area outside his own village will always remain external territory. To the Polynesian chief, however, the area outside his community is internal territory in which he can exercise not only influence but power, and if resisted in his power, he will be legally justified in using force. In both areas, the limits to political expansion will be reached through strains on the relationship between staff and people: in Melanesia by exploiting the followers for the benefit of the wider population, in Polynesia by exploiting the people for the benefit of the staff.

At this point, a more detailed description of a Melanesian big man's rise to renown may be in order, and an example will be presented from the Solomon Islands (Hogbin, 1938).

A man is usually in his early thirties when he starts thinking of becoming a big man, a *mwanekama*. He will begin with hard work, i.e. by cultivating larger gardens. His relatives are always ready to help, but then he has to provide them with a good meal at the end of the day. At first, he therefore makes definite demands only on some of his closest relatives and neighbours. As the area under cultivation increases, more and more workers are required, but the food produced will soon exceed that given away. Most crucial for his further success is the raising of a large herd of pigs. Every time the sows belonging to the relatives have litters he begs for one or two piglets, from which he breeds. After a few years, when he has several acres in extent under cultivation, and when he has a herd of perhaps eight or ten pigs, he announces that he intends to build a large house. This amounts to publicly announcing that he aims at becoming a big man. This is actually the first hurdle, and many end up finding the drain on their energies and resources so great that they abandon their ambitions once the house is built.

If the house-building feast is successfully completed, the man of ambition has further to consolidate his position by acquiring more wealth. He will have to cultivate even larger gardens and breed still more pigs. At this point he is likely to wed some additional wives. He will prefer young widows who are apt to be better gardeners than young girls. Just like their husband, the wives of a would-be big man have to work much harder than other women, for they have to cultivate very extensive gardens and provide food for a constant stream of visitors. In exchange, they derive reflected prestige from their husband and usually have considerable influence in the community.

The process is concluded by a great public dance series with a public feast sponsored by the *mwanekama*. From the time of the feast 'to bring the performers to the dance area' until a final feast known as 'balm for the aching bones', a dance takes place every two or three weeks. At the final feast, 50 pigs may be slaughtered, and, say, 350 strings of shell discs may be given away. Once a man has held his dance he is recognized even outside his own village as a real *mwanekama*. But if he wants to maintain his prestige, he still has to be generous and provide feasts. If his wealth diminishes, as it usually does when he becomes advanced in years and less active in work, he sinks back into insignificance.

There is one further step to go, though this is not done by the average big man. The very highest renown is reached when the *mwanekama* has made himself responsible for the festival known as *siwa*. This implies entertaining a group of people from another village who have carried out vengeance on his behalf when he has lost a relative through sorcery. The sorcerer is identified, and as the mourners are prevented by mourning regulations from carrying out the killing and only another big man can carry out vengeance, a *mwanekama* from another village is requested to do the killing. Upon completion, the killing party will be lavishly celebrated, with large numbers of pigs slaughtered and as many as 5000 strings given away, a huge amount of wealth. Once a *mwanekama* has celebrated a *siwa*, he is renowned along the coast and remembered for years after his death.

While the particular forms of competitive feasting vary widely among the different Melanesian societies, the fact that such feasts are given and large numbers of pigs, sometimes several hundreds, are slaughtered, is the same everywhere, providing a social mechanism of accumulation and distribution of food upon which the survival of a whole society may depend when one of the frequent droughts and famines or other emergencies break out.

In Melanesia, roles are created by individuals, assuming a tentative shape intermittently in the process. In Polynesia, roles are structurally determined, and they are filled by designated incumbents who cannot alter their content. Polynesia is characterized by role-taking, Melanesia by role-making. The role of priest may serve as an example. In Melanesia, everyone is his own priest, and it is up to him how he shapes that role. In Polynesia, there are temples with paid priests.

In Polynesia, a happy life in the other world is guaranteed by divine descent; in Melanesia, a place in heaven is earned by economic and social success in this world, while the poor and unsuccessful are condemned to a state of unhappiness after death.

Melanesian children learn aggressiveness and individualism in their behaviour; at the same time, they also learn how to share. They are taught to develop their individual capabilities to the fullest and to utilize them. In competitive games, everyone gives his best in order to win. Polynesian children are trained to be submissive and obedient. They are punished for spontaneous, independent behaviour. The pace of Polynesian group games is determined by the slowest, and parents feel ashamed when their children are ahead of others of their group or age. The model of Melanesian education is the achievement-oriented, competitive individual; the model of Polynesian education is the reliable, dutiful servant of his master.

Melanesian societies are usually described in the literature as 'dynamic' and 'open', while Polynesian societies are referred to as 'static'. Further details have been presented elsewhere (Seibel, 1978). In particular it has been shown that the development of ascriptive, hierarchical structures in Polynesia only occurred during the last few centuries after these societies had successfully mastered the problems of settlement, which was eased by a favourable environment.

A brief note on Melanesian receptivity to modernization, which has emerged very recently, may be in order:

A new generation of leaders, who achieve status in the market economy and seek elective political office, has developed in the Highlands. Today a large coffee plantation, a trade store and a truck are the marks of economic accomplishment of ambitious Highlanders, and election to a Local Government Council or to the House of Assembly of Papua–New Guinea is the avenue they follow to modern political power. (Finney, 1968, p. 394)

THE INDIGENOUS POTENTIAL FOR SELF-MANAGEMENT

At the beginning of this chapter we have suggested that open societies are highly conducive to self-management by giving all their members opportunities for full participation in all affairs. We have then given a variety of examples demonstrating that many premodern societies are of that type. In fact, the large majority of societies that have ever existed are of that type. The reason why this has been hitherto ignored is that virtually all of them are small-scale societies which have attracted less attention than large-scale societies or empires.

We must therefore conclude that, in a great many societies in the developing world, there is an enormous indigenous potential for self-management. It is simply not true that all or most peasants in the developing countries are passive, superstitious and lazy. Maybe it is rather the laziness or ignorance and prejudice of many scholars and so-called development experts that prevent them from exploring the true nature of these societies.

Our message is that the participatory potential of the people in these societies must be utilized in all spheres of the economy and of politics. Particularly in production organizations, the participatory talents and abilities of all individuals should be mobilized by providing organizational structures for self-management.

A second, though more theoretical, finding of this chapter has been the association between environmental situation and social-political and economic structure. Traditional societies faced with severe problems tend to develop open, participatory structures. This confirms precisely the findings from Yugoslavia, where self-management originated in a situation of emergency. The system of self-management usually evolves at times of crisis. Algeria presents a very prominent example of that and many additional examples have been presented in Chapter 2.

This association between crisis situations and the emergence of self-management is of course due to the fact that only a self-management system is able to mobilize the creative potential of all members of a society to the fullest. This finding is of greatest importance to developing countries. For all of them find themselves in a state of constant crisis, permanently confronted with severe problems, particularly in the economic sphere. And for many more decades to come, they will continue to be confronted with the problem of development. We argue that a solution to the problem of development can only be found from within, by mobilizing all human resources in each developing country through self-management. And fortunately, in a great many of these societies, the potential for full participation has been already present in the traditional culture and need only to be reactivated in new ways. A variety of influences from within and without, which of course cannot all be attributed to imperialism, seem to have prevented the continued practice of participation of all, and new classes have emerged that benefit from the resulting inequality. But if development is to be speeded up, the return to, or introduction of, equality of participation has to come quickly. We hope that the Yugoslav example will convince those who are presently responsible for development that participation and self-management is not just a relic of premodern societies, but possibly the only avenue to rapid modernization.

14 Workers' Participation: Beginnings of Self-Management in the Developing World?

Many countries in Africa, Asia, Latin America and Oceania have, in their quest to industrialize, embarked on experimenting with different development models and strategies. Recently, workers' participation, a concept precursory to self-management, has begun to fascinate many developing countries, among them Zambia, Kenya, Tanzania, Chile under Allende, India and a host of others.

ZAMBIA

In Zambia, workers' participation in management was first officially debated at the Livingstone Conference in 1967. This was the most important one of a series of seminars through which the government, in particular President Kenneth Kaunda, sought to bring together labour and management for joint discussions of the industrial situation. This Conference was successful in that it indeed improved industrial relations markedly, thus preparing the ground for further discussions of workers' participation. Kenneth Kaunda was the driving force behind the idea of workers' participation, the next milestone being his speech at the Matero National Council meeting in August 1969. During this year, new industrial relations legislation was under discussion, and in this context proposals for workers' participation were made by the State House. To emphasize the role played by political leadership, it has to be pointed out that these proposals were based on working papers produced by presidential advisers.

These proposals were rather far-reaching. First of all, it was suggested that so-called works councils be established which were solely employees' bodies; and second, that these works councils were to be given considerable control over actual decisions on day-to-day personnel and industrial policy. These ideas were backed by the Zambia Congress of Trade Unions (ZCTU) and by the employees but opposed by management. The Zambian Federation of Employers voiced its concern over the implications of workers' participation. While it could not prevent the introduction of some form of workers' participation, it succeeded at least in watering down the original presidential intentions.

In 1971, the Industrial Relations Act was passed. In Part VII, it provided for the establishment of works councils in all companies of a hundred or more employees. Such works councils were to consist of three to fifteen members. Two-thirds of these were to be employees' and one-third management's representatives. As a result of the intervention of the Zambian Federation of Employers, the range of activities of these councils was largely restricted to the social and welfare sphere. The functions of the councils included participation in all health and welfare schemes of the respective company. They must also be consulted on medical, housing and recreational schemes and on pension arrangements. With regard to management and personnel decisions, which include investment policy, financial control, distribution of profits, economic planning, wage policy and appointment of senior management executives, the works councils were to be informed, but they could not participate in actual decision-making.

While the scope of actual participation was limited, this was nevertheless a first step. In fact, it speaks for limited participation during an initial phase which is to be regarded as a learning period, not only for the employees but for all parties concerned. Experience also shows that, regardless of the amount of participation granted, employees at first tend to take interest in social and welfare matters, and only in a second phase, which may follow very shortly thereafter, do they begin actually to take interest and participate in managerial decisions in the narrow sense.

However, this limited amount of participation, as provided for by the 1971 Industrial Relations Act, was resisted by the employers, and Part VII of the Act had not been introduced up to the end of 1975, suggesting that this Act was indeed felt to make a radical change in Zambia industrial relations.

It seems that the Zambian government was overzealous in bringing about workers' participation. For they introduced yet more legislation setting up so-called workers' committees alongside the works councils. The committees were made up of party, management and workers' representatives. Their main function was to advise both the government and management on industrial policy.

While this was meant to supplement the activity of the works councils on another level, it was in fact felt to duplicate workers' representation. Indeed, both management and trade unions complained that they did not know with whom to deal, the works councils or the workers' committees. As a result, there is a real danger in Zambia that workers' participation, the beginnings of self-management, remains but a piece of legislation, with the interested parties debating and contesting which provision of the legislation should be implemented.

KENYA

In Kenya, a more direct route to self-management was taken by the government by promoting workers' involvement in cooperatives. This concerns at present a rather small sector of the economy; but it has to be borne in mind that, after the viability of industrial cooperatives had been proven through the Rochdale experiments in England, economists up to the turn of the century and beyond considered an economy based on cooperatives a true alternative to both the capitalist and the state-socialist model. If Kenya would choose, therefore, to base its economy on cooperatives, this could be a direct route to self-management. However, the Kenyan government has not yet gone that far in its support for cooperatives.

In a government paper on *African Socialism and its Application to Planning in Kenya*, trade unions were encouraged to assist in establishing cooperatives:

In addition, trade unions assisted by Government should take an active role in organising consumer co-operatives, generating savings for development, promoting co-operatives and making workers aware of their contribution to the development of the nation. (Iwuji, 1979)

Legal support for the establishment of workers' cooperatives was provided by the Cooperative Societies Act. As a consequence, the Kenya Union of Commerical Food and Allied Workers, representing workers in banks, food and commercial industries, insurance companies etc., has encouraged and assisted workers in companies such as Kenya Breweries, banks, BAT, Mackenzie Kenya Ltd and Kenya Canners Ltd, to form workers' credit and savings cooperatives. A successful example of cooperative venture is Kenya Canners Cooperative Savings and Credit Limited, with a total membership of about 500, and shares valued at Ksh.985,000 as of June 1975. The Kenya Canners Cooperative Union owns shares in the Cooperative Bank of Kenya, Kenya Union of Savings Cooperative Limited, and some land in addition. Its annual profit amounts to more than Ksh.50,000, which is used to grant loans to members and to assist them in the payment of their children's school fees.

Other unions which run successful cooperative schemes include the Civil Servants Union, which operates a chain of cooperative stores and has plans to invest in cooperative housing schemes, canteens and workers insurance.

While the formation of cooperatives may be a first step in the direction of self-management, it is certainly no more than a beginning. For cooperatives form but a small proportion of the economy, and cooperatives as business ventures are not yet fully run along the principles of self-managment.

Outside the cooperative sector, the concern is more with good industrial relations than with workers' participation. The Industrial Relations Charter of 1962 and the subsequent tripartite agreements of 1964 and 1970 concern themselves with issues of a much more immediate concern, such as the alleviation of unemployment. The resulting concerted effort to fight unemployment was one of the factors strengthening the existing employers' and workers' organizations. The goal was to have the unemployed participate in work but not to have the worker participate in management.

The government is more concerned with assisting indigenous entrepreneurs to acquire and expand commercial and manufacturing business than it has been with altering the power structure between labour and capital. And the relative influence and success of unions seems to have induced union leaders more in strengthening the bargaining position of unions *vis-à-vis* government and employers than the bargaining position, or participatory powers, of workers *vis-à-vis* management. In the few exceptional cases where workers' participation in industry exists, say in the form of stock ownership, workers' councils and workers' representation on management boards, it has mainly been on the initiative of management. It seems doubtful that this is a true beginning of workers' participation in Kenya, though others are more hopeful. As one author (Iwuji, 1979) writes, 'the increasing concern for manpower development on the part of both workers' and employers' organizations can be said to augur well for possible workers' participation in management decision-making as effective participation demands of the partners knowledge of what is involved.'

TANZANIA

The core concept of Tanzania's national ideology is *ujamaa*. Its literal meaning being familyhood or brotherhood, it represents Tanzania's type of African socialism. For Nyerere (1968, p. 2), *ujamaa* is an attempt to bridge the old and the new:

> By the use of the word 'ujamaa', therefore, we state that for us socialism involves building on the foundation of our past, and building also to our own design. We are not importing a foreign ideology into Tanzania and trying to smother our distinct social patterns with it. We have deliberately decided to grow, as a society, out of our own roots, but in a particular direction and towards a particular kind of objective.

The main tenets of *ujamaa* are equality, democracy and work. According to the Arusha Declaration, agriculture is the basis of development in Tanzania. As a matter of fact, major efforts have been made to establish *ujamaa* in the rural sector, in particular through cooperatives and so-called *ujamaa* villages, where the realization of some self-management principles has been attempted.

The most important provision of *ujamaa* with regard to the industrial sector is that 'the major means of production and exchange are under the control of the peasants and workers', as stated in the Arusha Declaration (Nyerere, 1968, p. 233). The two major implications of this are: first, that major sectors of industry are to be nationalized; and second, that this provides an ideological foundation for worker participation, at some later point in time perhaps even for self-management.

A first attempt at worker participation was made in 1963 when the trade unions suggested profit-sharing as a first step. This proposal was rejected by the government right away. The opposition of management in the private sector was felt to be too strong, and the government also feared that Tanzania could not afford to increase wages by sharing profits with the workers instead of ploughing them back into development.

With the Arusha Declaration of 1967, socialist policy was proclaimed in Tanzania, and a series of nationalizations followed. Some form of organizational democracy became an ideological must. A number of options were open to the government, among them self-management, co-determination and joint managerial consultation. Self-management was ruled out. It was argued that skill levels on the one hand and the degree of political consciousness on the other hand were too low for workers to run their own companies.

After consultations between the party (TANU), the Labour Department and the central federation of trade unions (NUTA), Presidential Circular No. 1 was issued in 1970, laying down the directives for worker participation in public enterprises.

In part, worker participation was introduced out of an ideological commitment. In part, it was an attempt to mobilize the potential of the individual by giving him a say in the affairs of his company in order to increase efficiency and productivity. Clause one of the circular expresses this concern in productivity very clearly:

> Let us, therefore, have the targets for each factory worked out on the basis of what can be sold and where, let these targets be known to each worker, let them be placarded in big letters on the walls. And don't stop here, let each separate workshop or process, or group of people also have its target per year, per month, per day. . . . I believe that when our people have a clear target in front of them and when they can see how far they have exceeded or how far they fall short of it, they will respond to this challenge. . . .

It is only in the second clause that directives are given for participation:

Given a proper work environment, and proper co-operation and support from their leaders and fellows, the majority of Tanzanian workers are capable of accepting more responsibility and are willing to do so . . . top management must have an attitude which regards the workers and lower levels of management as partners in a common enterprise, and not just as tools like the machines they work.

Another major concern is discipline, which is seen as related to both productivity and participation:

. . . true industrial discipline does not exclude the workers in an industry from participating in the enterprise or from responsibility for its improvement. Indeed, true discipline in a workplace should be easier when the workers understand what they are doing, what their objective is, and when they know that they have contributed fully to the final result as fully respected partners.

The core of the new system of worker participation are workers' councils consisting of the party chairman, the general manager, the heads of departments, all workers' committee members, workers' representatives and possibly additional co-opted members. The number of worker's representatives and committee members should not exceed 75 per cent of the permanent council membership.

The main functions of the councils are advisory: to advise on wages and on the government's income policies, on marketing, on quantity and quality of the goods produced, on planning, on organizational questions, on workers' training and to discuss the balance sheet.

The councils are to meet at least once every six months, which means that the commitment to 'workers' representation and participation in planning, productivity, quality and marketing matters' (clause 4) cannot have been very profound.

In addition to councils, there are executive committees comprising the general manager, all heads of departments and workers' representatives elected by the workers' council. The function of the executive committee is to examine the recommendations of the workers' councils and to forward recommendations to the general manager and the board of directors.

On the board of directors in each parastatal organization, the workers are represented through a worker director. The worker director is appointed by the JUWATA, the trade union federation replacing NUTA. The chairman of the board is appointed by the president, and the other directors are appointed by the minister presiding over the corporation.

The directive was to be put into effect not later than December 1970. By that date, however, only about a dozen councils had been established—most of them in the subsidiaries of the National Development Corporation.

In response to this situation, TANU issued the 'TANU Guidelines' (*Mwongozo wa TANU*) in 1971. This document, popularly known as the *Mwongozo,* condemned the arrogance, high-handedness and ostentatiousness of leaders and managers and demanded instant worker participation in decision-making in the factories. Subsequently, the party and the Labour Department organized seminars for workers and managers and launched a campaign to form workers' councils. A few councils dutifully were established in other parastatal organizations but the overall effect was minimal: some councils were formed but they never met; in the remaining ones, the level of participation was very low.

Among the reasons for the failure to implement worker participation in Tanzania were the unwillingness of management to have the workers participate in what they considered their decisions, the fact that industrial relations were very strained between 1971 and 1973 and the reluctance of the government to force worker participation upon management. During this period, workers practised a negative form of self-management: they went on strike, demanding wage increases and improvements in working conditions. But participation was apparently not on their agenda. This may be interpreted as a lack of interest on the part of workers, but there was a reason for that. It was frequently alleged that workers' committees were used as managerial instruments to maintain law and order, and it was felt that the councils were mere rubber stamps of managers.

To sum up: while the issues of control of production and worker participation have been widely discussed in Tanzania, all actual attempts in this direction have been futile. It seems that the future of worker participation in Tanzania will be contingent upon more determined efforts of all three parties involved: workers, management and government.

CHILE

Chile can only serve as an example of incipient workers' participation: not only because it was brought to an abrupt end by the military take-over of 1973 but also because of internal problems during Allende's presidency.

Chile's working class is unusual in that it has been highly politicized though at the same time not very revolutionary. This was not the achievement of Dr Allende or his Unidad Popular (UP); mass participation of workers in union organizations and political parties dates back before 1970. In fact, the expansion of union membership took place under the presidency of Eduardo Frei. After a decline in membership between 1955 and 1960 and a time of very slow growth between 1960 and 1964, there was an explosion of membership between 1964 and 1970 (cf. Landsberger and McDaniel, 1978, pp. 78–80). Membership continued to grow under Allende, but it is important to note that worker mobilization had begun before.

One has to realize that support for Allende and the UP was rather tenuous. To its left was the Movement of the Revolutionary Left (MIR) which advocated a violent fight for socialism, and to the right was the National Party (NP); the middle class did not support Allende, and the workers covered a wide range of ideological orientations. Rallying the support of the workers behind the UP was therefore a key problem for Allende.

Increasing worker and union participation was a sincere ideological commitment. In 1972, Allende promised to 'strengthen popular power and consolidate it . . . by making the unions more powerful with a new awareness, the awareness that they are a fundamental pillar of the government, but that they are not dominated by it, but that, aware, they participate in, support, help and criticise its action.' Workers were to participate at two levels: at the company and at the national level, on the latter with regard to economic planning and policy formulation. However, within the UP there was only an overall ideological commitment to workers' participation, but no agreement on details.

The mobilization of the working class through participation was being used as an instrument to broaden the political base of the UP, and it was at the same time attempting to keep mobilization and participation under control. For at the same time, the UP tried not to alienate the middle class as it would have been had it taken a very rapid course towards worker participation. In 1970 and early 1971, there was still the hope of gaining the support of the middle class, and, therefore, takeovers by workers of privately owned small and medium companies were to be stopped.

The organization through which the UP tried to mobilize the workers and simultaneously keep mobilization under control was the Central Labour Federation (CUT), with Luis Figueroa, general secretary of the CUT and a key member of the UP, occupying a key position. But the workers seemed to be already too politicized, 'hypermobilized' as it was called, to be that easily controlled. There was an unprecedented rise in strikes which led Allende to state that, 'Neither revolutionary consciousness nor morality exists among the workers', a clear indication of the type of 'hypermobilization' and lack of political control over the workers.

Again, worker participation appeared as a means to regain control. 'We're letting the workers in on the problems of the plant. If they know how much is spent and produced, they'll know how much they can ask', stated the socialist president of the blue-collar union in 1972. But under conditions of galloping inflation, it was hard if not impossible to restrain the workers.

In Chile, just as in many other cases, the dilemma of worker participation was between the workers' spontaneous attempts at participation, if not self-management, on the one hand and the government's attempt to control and limit the workers' activities on the other. A major part of this conflict was carried out in the socialist sector of the economy. A core part of the UP programme was the establishment of a socialized sector of the economy comprising some 90 strategic companies. But many more were seized, 'intervened' or 'requisitioned' by workers after labour disputes, production failures or financial difficulties. In some cases, the government was involved in these take-overs, in others it was simply presented with the fact.

In a situation where the government was surprised by the vigour of workers' participation with regard to take-overs, it was yet slow in granting full participation in the management of these companies.

In the 7 December 1970 agreement between the CUT and the government, provision was made for the participation of the workers, who were to be involved in decisions within their companies as well as on the national, sectoral and regional planning level. A highly complex system of assemblies and committees was worked out, of which only a small part pertained to the company level. While the functioning of this system of participation has not yet been fully analyzed, there is agreement that it has never worked well at any level. Landsberger and McDaniel (1978, p. 88) have summarized the results of participation succinctly: 'Even on the plant level, relatively few schemes of participation were ever instituted.' According to the CUT, no more than 30 per cent of the socialized companies had created participatory committees by the middle of 1972. The estimate of Zimbalist and Stallings is even lower: they consider genuine worker involvement to have taken place in only 35 enterprises. Luis Figueroa, president of the CUT, confessed in mid-1972 that 'participation is still weak. Sometimes because the executives or "intervenors" of the firms of the socialised sector do not understand the importance of allying themselves with the workers. . . . Other times, because the union leaders think that the Councils of Administration have come to supplant their union work.' Corroborating this view, Ramón Fernandez, head of the Participation Section of the CUT, declared that participation was 'only a pretty word' and that 'all of us have some guilt here'. He acknowledged that there was no effective worker participation at the level of government planning either. Further, there was general dissatisfaction with the functioning of those systems of participation that had been formed: workers had only an advisory capacity in the management of socialized firms, always being outnumbered by management and the government's representative; and union leaders were prohibited from occupying posts in the participatory structure.

Workers reacted strongly against the failure of the government to grant them full participatory rights. They rejected any kind of institutionalized authority, and the 'breakdown of discipline' became a national problem. This 'indiscipline' included corruption, stealing, absenteeism, negligence in the use and maintenance of machines, fighting etc. Workers even left their jobs to sell the goods produced on the black market.

Attempts by the government to enforce discipline led to strikes. It is most interesting to observe that among the demands voiced by the striking workers was a request for genuine participation in decision-making.

On the whole, the participation programme failed, and this was probably one of the main reasons why the government never gained the support from the workers which it needed so badly.

In sum, the Chilean situation was characterized by a high degree of worker mobilization. The workers were ready for participation in management, maybe even for self-management. Participation was promised to them, but the promise was not carried through. Therefore, the politically divergent groupings of workers were not bound together through a powerful ideology of participation or self-management. As a result, the workers turned against a system which had failed to keep its promise of participation.

INDIA

For several decades the Indian government has made attempts to promote worker participation in industry. As early as 1947, the formation of bipartite works committees was required by the Industrial Disputes Act. Ten years later, joint management councils were instituted on a voluntary basis. Despite these efforts, there was general agreement that workers' participation was not successful. A more determined effort was therefore made under the new economic programme of 1975. On 30 October 1975, a new 'Scheme for Workers' Participation in Industry at Shop Floor and Plant Level' was issued by the Ministry of Labour in New Delhi. These provisions are different from any previous ones in that they are the first attempt at introducing participation at the shop-floor level, and that the decisions taken are final and not just recommendations. The functioning of the works committees remains unaffected by this resolution. The resolution was published in November 1975, and by early 1977, 1187 public and private enterprises had introduced schemes for worker participation in management on the shop-floor level.

Taking cognizance of the facts that various forms of participation were already in existence and that local conditions in a country the size of India varied widely, the government resolution tried to permit as much flexibility as possible instead of providing a rigid legal framework. After a period of experimentation, more specific legislation is intended.

The present scheme is to be instituted in the first instance in manufacturing and mining companies with 500 or more workers. It provides for shop councils at the shop or departmental levels and for joint councils at the enterprise level.

Shop councils consist of an equal number of representatives of employers and workers. The employers' representatives are nominated by the management and must consist of persons from the shop or department concerned. Similarly, the worker representatives must be chosen from the unit concerned.

In consultation with the union or with the workers, as the case may be, the employer decides on the number of shop councils and departments to be attached to each council and on the total number of members, which usually should not exceed twelve.

One provision peculiar to participation in India is that all decisions of a shop council are to be on the basis of consensus and not of voting; but either party may refer matters in dispute to the joint council.

Every decision of a shop council has to be implemented within one month unless otherwise stated in the decision. Compliance reports have to be submitted to the council. Shop decisions affecting other shops or the company as a whole are referred to the joint council for decision.

A shop council is instituted for a period of two years. It meets at least once a month.

The chairman of the shop council is nominated by the management, the vice-chairman by the workers from among themselves.

The shop council is to attend to the following matters: assist management in achieving monthly and yearly production targets; improve production, productivity and efficiency; identify areas of low productivity and take necessary corrective steps at shop level; study absenteeism and recommend measures to be taken; take safety measures; assist in maintaining general discipline; improve the physical conditions of work, such as lighting, ventilation, noise and dust; take measures for the reduction of fatigue; adopt welfare and health measures; ensure adequate two-way communication between management and workers, particularly on matters relating to production figures, production schedules and progress in achieving the targets.

In addition to shop councils on the department or shop level, there is in every company a joint council which is formed for periods of two years. The chairman of the joint council is the chief executive (general manager) of the company, while the vice-chairman is nominated by the worker-members of the council. One of the members of the council is appointed as its secretary. The joint council meets at least once every three months. Decisions of the joint council are on the basis of consensus and not by voting. They are binding on employers and workers and are to be implemented within one month unless otherwise stated in the decision.

The joint council deals with the same matters as the shop councils in so far as these matters pertain to more than one department or to the company as a whole. It also takes up matters that could not be resolved within the shop councils, and it may assign specific tasks to a shop council. In addition, the joint council is in charge of worker education and training, preparation of schedules of working hours and of holidays, and awarding of rewards for valuable and creative suggestions received from workers.

It is stressed that situations and conditions are so diverse that no uniform constitution for shop councils and joint councils is presented by the resolution. Instead, the management in consultation with workers, is to evolve the most suitable pattern of representation.

It is particularly emphasized that special care is to be taken as to the development of a suitable and effective system of two-way communication and exchange of information between management and workers.

Finally it is pointed out that the scheme is not statutory. The central and state governments are to promote the implementation of the scheme in as large a number of companies as possible. (Cf. Ghosh and van de Vall, (1978.)

How does worker participation as instituted by the October 1975 resolution function in practice? It is of course too early to reach any final conclusion. But two case studies have been presented by Leberman and Leberman (1978) which may throw some light on the conditions under which worker participation may or may not function.

The first case study was done in a private chemical company with about 1250 workers. Prior to the introduction of the participation scheme, industrial relations in that company were very strained. While the scheme was initiated and organized unilaterally by management, the commitment of management was at the same time ambivalent. Due to the type of work performed, the educational level of the workers was generally low. No trade union was recognized.

Council meetings were dominated by management. In both shop and joint council meetings, management prepared the agenda and structured the discussions. For the most part, meetings consisted of lectures presented by management in which they informed on topics as they saw fit. Discussions tended to be broad and unspecific, and no effort was made to arrive at new solutions to a problem. The overall impression was one of lack of interest from both sides.

The performance of the joint council in terms of decision-making was poor. In three bi-monthly meetings, only three positive resolutions were reached from a total of 33 discussions, and those three involved insignificant matters. The joint council moved with excessive caution, reflecting apprehension over the worker-participation scheme.

Decision-making in the shop councils was somewhat more effective. In 95 meetings, 710 items were discussed by 12 production shop councils, and almost 23 per cent came to a positive resolution. The most important substantive decisions were taken in the fields of physical working conditions, safety and production.

It was found that in the shop councils, the extent of participation practiced depended very much on the chairman: the more positive the chairman's attitude towards participation and the higher his leadership ability, the better the council's performance. As the company decided not to appoint a vice-chairman, which would have to be chosen from among the workers, there was a tendency for the workers who sought active participation to feel alienated and for the chairman to be isolated.

On the whole, the company's approach to worker participation remained rather similar to the preceding scheme of consultative *panchayats* ('councils of five'). The present scheme is operated by management as a token gesture, with the intention of distracting the workers from any effort towards unionism. While workers and managers are brought together, the councils are far from functioning effectively as participative structures.

The second case study was done in a public electrical equipment company employing about 4100 workers. Work was predominantly of a skilled nature, and the educational level of the workers was accordingly high. Two trade unions were recognized, and industrial relations had been harmonious for several years prior to the introduction of the new scheme.

Management appeared committed to the idea of participation, and the scheme for participation was characterized by a relatively balanced partnership of management and trade unions. During the critical phase of initiating the scheme, unions and management cooperated closely. As union leaders nominated the council members and coordinated the workers' participation on different platforms, the workers did not feel that the scheme was imposed on them by management.

The co-chairmen (vice-chairmen) in the councils of this company were vested with considerable authority, and the positions were usually filled by union leaders. Because of their dual role, the co-chairmen became the spokesmen for the council members, which had an adverse effect on the attendance of the other worker members. A similar process occurred with regard to junior managers who tended to defer to senior management and view their role on the council as perfunctory. As a consequence, the councils became typical bipartite platforms similar to those in collective bargaining.

Fortunately, industrial relations in that company were harmonious so that the polarity of interests did not usually become antagonistic. While both parties put high expectations in the participation scheme, the workers were somewhat frustrated as the unions occupied too strong a position.

As a manifestation of the concern for permanency of the participation scheme, most of the council meetings during the first year, particularly those of the joint councils, were concerned with working out a viable and effective organizational structure. In quantitative terms, the efficiency of decision-making in the joint councils was impressive, three out of every four items discussed reaching a positive resolution. The two joint councils discussed a total of 129 items in 17 meetings, and over 75 per cent were positively resolved. This is remarkable if one considers that decision-making is by consensus and not by vote. Most decisions taken concerned council procedure, production, raw materials utilization and product quality.

The shop councils were almost as effective. They arrived at positive resolutions from close to 60 per cent of the items discussed. The shop council decisions pertained predominantly to physical working conditions, safety and production.

At the time of study, implementation procedure were still in the developing stage.

Based on the two case studies, several practical suggestions have been worked out which seem important for effective participation, not only in India but probably also in other countries (cf. Leberman and Leberman, 1978):

A participation scheme has to be initiated and worked out jointly by management and workers.

Council members, including both managers and workers, have to engage in training programmes pertaining to industrial operations as well as participation procedures. In addition, special programmes should be available for council chairmen and vice-chairmen.

Vice-chairmen should be appointed from among the workers and given actual responsibility.

The work of the shop councils and of the joint council has to be coordinated. This must include the distribution of minutes and documents.

For each meeting, a detailed agenda has to be worked out and distributed well in advance to assure adequate preparation by the council members.

The chairman and vice-chairmen should feel responsible for developing an orientation towards effective decision-making; alternative solutions have to be presented, and the discussion must aim at reaching a decision.

Procedures have to be instituted which are directed at the implementation of council decisions and at the monitoring of such implementation.

On the whole, it seems to be worthwhile to observe the Indian approach to worker participation closely over the next few years. One should then examine carefully: first, whether the Indian system is effective and flexible enough to serve as a model for other countries in the Developing World; second, whether this model of worker participation may serve as a basis for further development towards self-managemenrt; and third, what aspects of the Yugoslav experiment may be incorporated in such a newly emerging scheme.

15 Self-Management and Workers' Participation in Algeria: Origins and Development

ORIGINS OF SELF-MANAGEMENT

Self-management in Algeria originated in a situation of complete breakdown when the economy was left in shambles. It cannot be said with any degree of certainty whether or not, the spontaneous emergence of self-management was rooted in cultural or historical traditions, but some possible factors should be briefly discussed.

France conquered Algeria in 1830. Rather than impose its colonial authority on an intact social and economic system, the existing society and economy were destroyed as thoroughly as possible. Instead of shipping the population to the Canaries or Azores as suggested by some, it was decimated from nearly six million in 1830 to two and a half million in 1852. A city like Oran was reduced from some 40,000 inhabitants in 1831 to about 1000 in 1838. Resistance and rebellion were the response, but they were brutally crushed, the final uprising occurring among the Berber tribes in the Kabylic mountains in 1870–1.

Beginning in 1848, when Algeria legally became part of France, it was settled by French deportees, unemployed and impoverished peasants and by refugees from the Balkans, Spain and other countries. By 1876, there were 344,000 European colonizers in Algeria, of whom 153,000 were of non-French origin. The only thing that unified these diverse elements was their hostility to the indigenous population and the defence of their privileges. The Muslim population was left in near-total destitution, and in 1950, 90 per cent of them were still illiterate.

Every uprising led to land confiscation, which at the end was heavily concentrated in the hands of a few magnates. Of the indigenous masses, the large majority barely survived on subsistence agriculture. There was a small proletariat of 542,000 Muslim workers, of whom 434,000 were seasonal or day-labourers.

Algerian nationalism was dominated by two ideologies: that of complete assimilation, with equal rights for the Muslim population, and that of armed struggle, signifying a political division that has continued to shake Algerian politics until today.

In 1954, the armed struggle began, and it ended in 1962. Overnight, the French settlers fled Algeria. Not only did they leave the country without any technical and administrative cadres, they also employed the scorched earth technique, destroying machines and equipment, buildings and communications networks, files and administrative records. The economy came to an abrupt standstill. It was in this situation of total catastrophe that self-management emerged. When there was no other alternative and at the same time no authority keeping the workers from taking the initiative, they took over the plantations and industries and set up their own administration. The first factor explaining the origin of self-management is therefore to be seen in this situation of emergency.

A second factor may be seen in the experience of eight years of resistance and guerilla warfare. As Frantz Fanon has described in detail, it was this experience that returned to Algerians, after a long period of colonial emasculation, their pride and sense of independent and individual action. Thus, in this state of economic chaos, the Algerians did what they had learned during their war for independence; they took their own initiative, they improvised, they took full responsibility, they acted on their own behalf. As spelled out in the Tripoli Programme of June 1962, the first political document of the independent Algerian government:

> The analysis of the social context of the liberation struggle shows that, in general, it is the peasants and workers who are the active base of the movement and have given it its essentially popular character. . . . Ideological combat must follow the armed struggle; the democratic and popular revolution will follow the struggle for independence. The democratic and popular revolution is the conscious construction of the country

according to socialist principles and with power in the hands of the people. (Clegg, 1971, p. 42)

And a recent (FLN) paper dealing with the origins of self-management is even more specific:

In an upsurge of revolutionary enthusiasm, workers and peasants alike were quick to react and they demonstrated a firm determination to re-establish the rights which they acquired as a result of their fierce struggle. They occupied closed factories and businesses and many of the rich agricultural estates which had been abandoned and they began to reopen them at once. Fully conscious of their new responsibilities, they organized themselves with admirable control and elected their *directions collégiales* [management committees]. In this way, the system of *autogestion* [self-management] emerged quite naturally as the logical conclusion of a continuing development of thought and action and the revolutionary accomplishment of the working class. (Clegg, 1971, p. 46)

A third factor points back to the tribal traditions in Algeria, to an indigenous political system where decisions were made by a council of elders. When workers' councils sprang up in the various agricultural and industrial enterprises deserted by their owners and managers, they may have been inspired, at least in part, by the cultural tradition of political decision-making through councils in the tribes.

But one factor was definitely absent in the emergence of self-management: initiative from the top, by the political leadership. For the Tripoli Programme of June 1962 made no reference to self-management as the organizational model for the Algerian economy. With regard to industry, it announced central planning and industrialization through the development of heavy industry under state control. With regard to agriculture, the new principle was to be: the land to those who work it! The land deserted by the settlers was to be distributed in part to landless peasants; the rest was to be converted into state farms, with some participation in management and distribution of profits to go to the workers. But at that time, self-management proper was still an alien concept to the politicians.

SELF-MANAGEMENT IN AGRICULTURE

Self-management in Algeria did not start as a type of industrial democracy as it did in Yugoslavia. In Algeria, the number of industrial companies was rather small; and even if one adds transportation and similar companies, they are still outnumbered by agricultural enterprises. For the French had made Algeria one huge export-oriented plantation. Hence the stronghold of self-management in Algeria has been centred in agriculture.

By October 1962, about 1,000,000 hectares of land were administered by workers' councils. (This figure went up to approximately 2.3 million hectares in 1966, comprising a total of 200,000 workers on 1876 estates and producing about 75 per cent of the gross agricultural product and 60 per cent of total exports.) (Lazreg, 1976, p. 88)

Before the end of 1962, self-management had become a reality that could no longer be ignored by the political leadership. After the deserted land had been declared 'free land' by a decree of 24 August 1962, self-management was first officially recognized by the first decree of 22 October 1962, which provided for the appointment of so-called management committees in 'free' agricultural, industrial and mining enterprises with more than ten employees. The committee members were to be under the supervision of the Bureau National pour la Protection et Gestion des Bien Vacants.

In a second decree issued on the same day, the Minister of Agriculture referred to self-managed farms as state farms on which veterans, widows, orphans and other groups were to be settled. It seems that the meaning of self-management was not yet fully understood by the politicians at that time. For until March 1963, it was still assumed—and positively suggested—that the former owners would return to their property.

It has to be made quite clear that self-management had developed in Algeria before the new state had formed its structure and ideology. Self-management was an accomplished fact when it came to the attention of the political leaders.

In March 1963, full legal recognition was granted to self-management by Ben Bella's government. From the so-called March decrees onwards, self-management was to be the keystone of Algerian socialism.

The structure of self-management described by the March

decrees was heavily influenced by the Yugoslav model, which at that time was of a type which we have described as representative self-management. That means, the power of the workers was limited by the power of the state which kept control over the running of the companies. Hence, there was essentially a dual structure, one of true self-management borne by the workers, and one representing the interests of the state through the position of the director who was given considerable power. All the subsequent history of self-management in Yugoslavia is one of a power struggle between workers' self-management and the state's control over the workers.

The March decrees provided for the following model. Legally, all power was vested in the general assembly of workers (*assemblée générale des travailleurs*), comprising all full-time workers of a company. The general assembly was to be convened at least once every three months.

By secret ballot, the general assembly elects the workers' council (*conseil des travailleurs*), comprising between 10 and 100 members. In order to prevent white-collar dominance, at least two-thirds of the members had to be engaged in production. The workers' council was to meet at least once a month.

There is a management committee (*comité de gestion*) which is elected by the workers' council, comprising between three and eleven members of which again two-thirds have to be chosen from production. In companies with fewer than 30 employees, the management committee is the only representative organ, and it is directly chosen by the general assembly.

From its members, the management committee elects a president for a period of one year. The president thus represents the top of the self-management pyramid, though it has to be kept in mind that this is a pyramid where the power is legally vested in the base, the real distribution of influence notwithstanding.

Finally, there is the office of the director who represents the state.

It is the function of the general assembly of workers to examine and accept all actions and plans submitted by the various organs. In particular, it approves the annual development plan, major acquisitions and production and marketing programmes, and it approves all regulations and accounts.

The workers' council controls the internal organization and examines the accounts before they are presented to the general assembly; it decides on long- and medium-term credits, on the purchase and sale of machines and on the recruitment and dismissal of workers.

The management committee works out the annual development plan regarding investments, production and marketing in accordance with the tenets of the national development plan. It purchases raw materials, determines the way programmes are carried out, regulates the organization of production, decides on short-term credits and prepares statements of accounts.

The president convenes all meetings of the organs of self-management and presides at the sessions. He also countersigns all documents.

Unlike the president and the members of the self-management organs who are elected by and from the employees of the respective company, the director is elected by the local commune administration. Being a representative of the state, he examines the lawfulness of all economic and financial transactions and signs all documents. He examines the feasibility of decisions, and he has the power of veto in all matters unless otherwise provided for by law. He approves all bills and has control over considerable financial resources. He is an intermediary between state and company, and his main function is to ensure the proper realization of the national development plan on the enterprise level.

With regard to every organizational scheme, a distinction has to be made between formal and real structure and functioning, and one has to examine carefully how wide or narrow the gap is between the formal and the real. While the Algerian model appears to be an excellent example of self-management on paper, it has lagged behind its ambitious claims, not from its inception, but from the moment the state gave legal recognition to it. Its shortcomings are, to a large extent, a result of a power struggle between workers' self-management and the state bureaucracy in which the latter has gained more and more control over the former. As a result, the functioning of the organs of self-management is severely restricted.

The general assembly of workers has, in theory, ultimate authority in a company; in reality, it meets rarely and is limited to formally accepting the production plan, without having any influence on, or even knowledge of, its details. The government points out that the workers' assembly is too large to be effective, but as the majority of enterprises in Algeria are rather small, this argument cannot be taken seriously.

Given the powerlessness of the general assembly, the next organ of authority should have been the workers' council. Under its jurisdiction were decisions on long-term credits and purchase and sale of machines; but in reality, neither credits nor machines were usually available, and the preceding decisions therefore turned out to have been futile. Decisions on hiring and firing could have remained as falling under its competency; but this was not particularly emphasized in the decrees. On the whole, the functions of the workers' council are not precisely enough delimited, a fact criticized in a more recent government publication:

The decree of 22 March 1963 does not explicitly specify what the central role of the workers' council is. If one refers to the terms of the decree, the workers' council very much appears to be a restricted council approving or disapproving the propositions presented to it by the management committee. . . . The decree of 22 March 1963 provides for the workers' council to elect and control the management committee, but this control is not at all precisely defined, neither in terms of procedures nor in terms of limits. As a consequence, the management committee has absolute power in all affairs pertaining to management. (Ministry of Information and Culture, 1970, pp. 27–8)

In short, the failure to provide precise definitions for the assembly and the council and the tendency of the administrative bureaucracy of the state to control the economy as tightly as possible has two major effects. The general assembly met so rarely that it was of no practical significance, and the workers' council practically ceased to exist after the election of the management committee.

The remaining organ of self-management is the management committee with its president. This committee was to consist of the most able members of the workers' council. But it seems questionable whether the members of this committee ever acquired the necessary technical competence, at least in the eyes of the government this appears to be very doubtful. One consequence of the lack of competence seems to have been the tendency to shed responsibility. However, it is not quite clear whether it was in fact the management committee assigning its responsibilities to the director and thus indirectly to the administration, or whether it was the administration via the director usurping the responsibilities of the management committee.

The government denies the workers the very competence they obviously did have in 1962–3:

> After all, the management committee and its president have no competence whatsoever in assuming the management of an estate; for they are incapable of comprehending the economic side of it. During the days of the settlers, the worker was a worker in the true sense of the term, i.e. a labour force and not an associate of production. (Ministry of Information and Culture, 1970, p. 30)

Self-managed enterprises in agriculture were under the administrative authority of the Office National de Réforme Agraire (ONRA) (cf. decree of 3 July 1963), which belonged to the Ministry of Agriculture. The most important positions in ONRA were the so-called delegates. Placed under the authority of a commissioner, they were the ones who took influence on the enterprises through the directors as their intermediaries within a given area for which they were responsible. They also coordinated the activities of so-called production consultants. While the director was in charge of organizational matters, the production consultant inspected the quality and the calculation of proceeds. It was up to the production consultant to determine the efficiency of an enterprise and to suggest its nationalization in case of inefficiency. The granting of credit, the purchase of equipment and the sale of produce was always under the control of ONRA, and it has been alleged that this control was frequently used to bring the enterprises to the point where they had to be converted into state enterprises. 'A series of deviations led the self-management sector towards gradual although undeclared State takeover,' states the Ministry of Information and Culture (1973b, p. 17) laconically. 'An analysis of the development of the self-management sector until 1966 leads to the observation that the bodies representative of the workers were left without responsibility and were replaced by a myriad of State bodies operating in an anarchic fashion.' In 1967, ONRA was dissolved, either because it had achieved the goal of nationalizing many self-managed enterprises as claimed by some, or because it interfered with self-management as alleged by the government.

Subsequently, the agricultural self-management sector was to be 'decentralized' as codified in the 30 December 1968 ordinance. It seems that from the very beginning the government had no intention of granting the self-management organs full command over their enterprises, as indicated by the power vested in the director as a representative of the community administration and the state. The situation in Yugoslavia, however, was the same at that time. But in Yugoslavia, the subsequent development was towards more, and ultimately direct, self-management, while in Algeria the reverse process took place. If it had not been for a certain lack of commitment and active involvement on the part of the Algerians participating in self-management, the development might have been different. But again, the Yugoslav political leadership actively encouraged and supported the transition from paternalistic to direct self-management, while the Algerian politicians interfered with it, to say the least. From that one may conclude that self-management can only succeed when the base is actively supported by the political leadership. At least, there has been no known case in history where the workers or peasants succeeded in the long run in building self-management against the will of the political leaders. This may be interpreted as a violation of the spirit of genuine self-management, which should not be contingent upon any leaders; but, so far, history does not seem to present any other examples.

It should be added that at present a few estates are still left under genuine self-management, and are not the property of the state.

SELF-MANAGEMENT THROUGH COOPERATIVES

With the 8 November 1971 ordinance on the agrarian revolution, cooperatives were designated as 'one of its pillars'. The land was to be owned by the state, which is a deviation from the usual model of a cooperative, but the organization of the participating peasants was to be that of a cooperative. Compared to self-management, cooperatives were conceived of as a similar but alternative mode of organization: 'Just as self-management, co-operation is a form of democratic association and advancement for the farmers.' (Ministry of Information and Culture, 1973b, p. 27.) A qualifying note has to be added. Cooperatives also employ workers, and the self-management principles apply only to the participating peasants, not to the workers.

Being an 'economic and social institution of producers, freely constituted and democratically managed by the farmers and breeders' (7 June 1972 decree), a true cooperative may indeed be considered as an organization formed along the principles of self-management, except with regard to the above qualification. In fact the model organization for cooperatives is very much akin to self-management in smaller enterprises where the management committee and the workers' council are fused into one.

The ultimate authority in cooperatives is vested in the general assembly, which includes all members. It determines the plan of activity and decides on all measures required for its implementation.

In cooperatives of more than ten members, business is effectively run by a management council which is elected by the general assembly for three-year periods. One-third of its members are up for election every year. It executes the decisions of the general assembly and prepares its sessions. All decisions are made by the management council on behalf of the general assembly.

The management council elects a chairman who is responsible for running the cooperative. He is its outside representative.

There is a director who manages the cooperative in accordance with the decisions of the management council. He is chosen from a list provided by the Ministry of Agriculture.

There is an auditor who represents the state, controlling the appropriateness of the financial operations. He is also chosen from a list provided by the Ministry of Agriculture and approved by the Ministry of Finance.

This organizational model of cooperatives seems to replicate rather exactly the dual structure of the so-called self-managed enterprises, one structure being formed along the lines of self-management proper, the other one, which includes the director and the auditor, representing the state administration. All shortcomings and conflicts of the system of self-management seem to be carried over into the cooperative system.

Within the cooperative sector, a special case deserves mentioning that may be unique to Algeria: the case of army cooperatives. They were first initiated by Colonel Aouchiche and his associates, and in financial terms they are today the strongest among Algerian cooperatives. While the land is owned by the army, the members of the cooperative are veterans and other army members. As in other cooperatives, self-management principles seem to be realized to a considerable extent.

PARTICIPATION IN INDUSTRY

In 1962, the spontaneous take-overs of companies by workers took place in agriculture as well as industry, but the number of industrial take-overs was much smaller than those in industry because of the relatively small size of the industrial sector in Algeria. There are no reliable figures, but Lazreg (1976, p. 88) estimates that in July 1962 some 700 companies were under self-management. For Spring 1964, figures given by various government agencies vary between 370 and 550, but these include some companies which were counted twice. Laks' (1970, pp. 17–32) own estimate for June 1964 is 432 companies under self-management, of which 46 per cent were located in the region of Algiers, 34 per cent in Oran and 20 per cent in Constantine. Clausen (1969, p. 67) suggests that of a total of 1600 industrial companies in 1964, about 500 were under self-management, employing about 15,000 workers. Most of the self-managed companies are rather small: of the 500 firms, 421 employ less than 20 persons, 74 have between 20 and 100 employees and only 5 employ more than 100.

At the beginning, the self-managed companies in industry functioned along the same lines as those in agriculture: after a grassroots system of self-management had evolved in 1962, it was given legal backing through the March decrees of 1963. The subsequent development was one of increasing government control over self-management until a moderate form of worker participation had replaced self-management.

Eventually, in the 16 November 1971 ordinance which laid down the rules of the socialist management of industry, the concept of worker participation was substituted for self-management. While the workers were taken as 'producers who assume responsibilities for the management of the enterprise', limitations were imposed on them to prevent them from taking sole responsibility.

Ultimate control resides in the presiding Ministry, which is represented in the company by the director-general. However, according to the new 'revolutionary system', he was to share responsibility with the workers. Workers' participation in these enterprises is to be based on the workers' assembly, which is not identical with the workers' collective. The workers' assembly is an elective body of active trade union members. Nominations are collected by an *ad hoc* committee composed of representatives of the party, the UGTA and the presiding ministry. It is through the intermediary of his assembly that the worker is considered to participate in management. The workers' assembly is consulted on general policy matters and may give recommendations on the draft development plan for the company, on estimated receipts and expenditures, on the draft programme of production, supply and marketing and on draft investment programmes. The law also gives the workers' assembly control over management, which means it may consult any documents and request explanations as it sees fit. The workers' assembly has decision-making power with regard to the adoption of its own rules and the distribution of profits within the confines of the law. The workers' assembly can only be suspended or dissolved by a ministerial decree or by executive order.

There are five permanent committees which are in charge of day-to-day business. The economic and financial committee participates in every management decision and in contract negotiations. It deals with supply and marketing, controls the use of public funds and examines questions of productivity.

The social and cultural affairs committee is in charge of social and cultural programmes.

The personnel and training committee takes part in hiring and firing, salary questions and training programmes.

The disciplinary committee is consulted on all matters concerning personnel discipline; its suggestions are then submitted to the director. A government publication points out what the limits of the committee's activities are: ' . . . the workers are subject to the power hierarchy of the management which alone can take final decisions in the field of employment, advancement or dismissal, the rights of workers being guaranteed first and foremost by law.' (Ministry of Information and Culture, 1973a, pp. 30–1)

The hygiene and safety committee is in charge of safety regulations and workers' education in safety matters.

In the discipline and safety committee, half the members are named by management and half by the workers' assembly. In the other three committees, all members are designated from among the members of the workers' assembly.

Actual management is in the hands of the management council, which is presided over by the director-general. It convenes at least once a week. Only one or two of its members are elected by the workers' assembly. It therefore seems that on the highest level of management, participation of workers is severely limited.

At the top of the enterprise is the director-general.

The director of the enterprise remains in sole charge of the running of the enterprise. He exercises a power of hierarchy over the personnel and makes propositions to the ministry concerning personnel to be hired to assist him in his task. He represents the enterprise in all acts of a civil nature. (Ministry of Information and Culture, 1973a, p. 32)

In the socialist sector of industry, no provision is thus made for self-management. However, participation exists on two levels. Workers' participation in the form of consultation is found on all levels; in a few limited spheres, the workers have decision-making rights. On the management level, a form of participative management is practiced which involves first of all the professional management; workers participate on that level through one or two representatives. As the highest authority rests with the director as a representative of the state, the basic structure of the enterprise remains that of a pyramid in which power is vested in the top and not in the base. But as legal provision is made for workers' participation, the further process towards more or less participation may very much depend on the workers' actual involvement.

Outside the socialist sector, self-management exists in two other spheres of industry. First, there exist some army cooperatives, akin to those in agriculture, which incorporate the principles of self-management; in construction such army cooperatives are dominant.

In private industry, a few companies are left under full self-management. However, these are usually rather small subcontractors for larger, mostly state-owned, companies, and there are a few bus companies that are under self-management.

This shows that some vestiges of self-management still exist in industry, and one has therefore to be careful in predicting the future of self-management in Algeria (for further references on self-management in Algeria, cf. Clausen, 1969; Clegg, 1971; Laks, 1970; Lazreg, 1976; Mahsas, 1975; and Viratelle, 1970).

16 Is there a Chance for Self-Management in the Developing World?

Self-management as a social, economic and political model of participation is designed to mobilize the potential of every individual to the fullest. In one country, this model has been tried out as a large-scale historical experiment, namely in Yugoslavia. For a period of over thirty years, self-management has grown to remarkable strength and vigour and, starting in industry, it has gradually spread to all other types of organizations. There, the mobilization of individual potential and participation has proved to be highly successful: it was under self-management that Yugoslavia moved from an underdeveloped to a developed country.

What does this mean for the Developing World? It is quite clear that the Developing World badly needs the full participation and mobilization of individual potential to tackle the task of development. It is equally clear that human potential in the Developing World is presently grossly underutilized. In this situation, the success of the self-management system in Yugoslavia should be inducement enough to examine it very carefully as a model for development. There are of course alternative models: capitalist countries have developed, and so have socialist countries. At this point, we do not want to enter the debate as to the relative efficiency of the three models. We have tried to show that self-management is efficient; but for a rigid comparison, the available data, and particularly the available historical experience, may not be sufficient. Political values will certainly play a major role in determining what development path a society will follow. But for those countries in the Developing World which are disenchanted with either capitalism or socialism, self-management does present a viable third way.

Despite an urgent need for more participation in the Developing World, however, self-management has not got very far. The most prominent and most promising example was Algeria, where self-management emerged spontaneously in agriculture and industry upon the conclusion of the French–Algerian war. Not only was there a mass movement towards self-management originating from the base, but subsequently this was even legally backed by the enactment of laws which made self-management the legal system of work organization. In the ensuing conflict between base and centre, between workers and administrative bureaucracy, the old story repeated itself, as we learned it from various other countries: the centre won and the base lost. Many feel, therefore, that Algeria is also one of the saddest examples of experiences with self-management. While there are still a very few well-functioning self-managed enterprises, self-management in the rest of the economy either exists only on paper or not at all. The revolutionary zeal from which self-management grew in Algeria has been quenched and new endeavours would have to be made in order to make self-management again a reality. At the same time, the Algerian case has not lost all its promise. For the decline of self-management has not been primarily due to lack of interest, support, qualification, ability etc., from the base, the claims of the administration notwithstanding. And this is very important for an evaluation of the potential of self-management as it must always rest on the participation of the base. At the same time, the Algerian experience shows that without support from the top self-management is doomed to failure. This may be sad, but it is a reality. And this reality places a heavy burden on the political leadership of the countries in the Developing World: the burden of responsibility for the success or failure of self-management.

It is frequently said that what militates against the potential success of self-management in the Developing World is the inexperience and lack of education of the workers. Since the workers and even many of their representatives are often not well educated, they find it difficult to follow the complex task of management let alone carry out the actual task of managing or participating in decision-making. This may be, however, very much an excuse, for Algerian peasants were hardly any better educated in the early 1960s than people in the other developing countries. Learning comes first of all by doing: given the opportunity for self-management, practice and experience will follow. Education does play a crucial role in this process: but only after the opportunity for self-management has been granted. Once self-management has been, or is about to be, initiated, training for self-management must begin. For guidelines, one may look to the Yugoslav workers' and people's universities. As the potential for self-management is there, as has been amply demonstrated by our examples, all that it takes is the opportunity for practice, and specialized training for self-management tasks has to be added to that.

What militates most against the introduction of self-management is the management style practiced in developing countries. In his book on *Theories of Management and the Executive in the Developing World*, Damachi (1978, p. 113) has characterized this style as 'authoritarian paternalism'. It is questionable whether this style is rooted, in any significant way, in the traditional culture. As far as foreign entrepreneurs or managers are concerned, it is certainly easier to detect authoritarian than paternalistic patterns in their style of management; and *vis-à-vis* workers, this is equally true of most indigenous businessmen or managers. Only when it comes to filling positions in management may the latter show some signs of benevolent paternalism. Damachi (1978, pp. 113–14) writes:

> Any form of delegation of authority is usually to relatives or close friends. The delegation of authority is therefore limited because of managers' mistrust of those not related by ties of kinship or ethnicity. . . . The African manager relies heavily on ascriptive practices in personnel selection. He gives first preference to his relatives and then those of friends. Despite his ascriptive practices, he insists on competence. If the new recruits are not initially competent, he believes that they can be trained to be.

It may be more important to point out that the authoritarian patterns of authority practiced in industry as well as in other complex organizations in developing countries are the direct and immediate result of the importation of such patterns from the industrialized countries. In fact, this management style is the only one known to political and business leaders in the Developing World. It is not surprising that they do not know any better; for the structuring of organizations in the form of authoritarian hierarchies (sometimes euphemized as 'functional hierarchies') is one of the few points on which bureaucratic state socialism and capitalism agree.

In the light of such management practices, is there a chance for self-management in the developing countries? First of all, it should be pointed out that self-management started in Yugoslavia when the prevailing management pattern was autocratic; but at the same time Yugoslavia found itself in an exceedingly difficult situation. While the ties with the East had been cut and ties with the West were not yet established, it could only rely on itself—and invented self-management. In most of the developing countries, the economic situation should be dire enough, at least at some time or other, to warrant the introduction of self-management. It is in such situations that the political leaders in the Developing World should be aware of the existence and feasibility of self-management as a third model.

Yet, before starting to develop any optimism, one has to be aware that there are usually very powerful vested interests against the introduction of self-management. It is probably no accident that self-management was first introduced in Yugoslavia at a time when such vested interests happened to be largely absent, at the end of a world war. It is interesting to note that self-management was not introduced by one of the big, rich, powerful nations. In wealthy and well-established societies, there are powerful forces, social classes or interest groups at work to preserve the status quo. As any major change may threaten their privileges, they are likely to use their power to prevent a major change. New structures are thus more likely to be tried out in societies that have not yet developed a firmly established power and interest structure. This also explains what writers from Marx to Mandel have observed as the law of uneven development: in no single society has development taken place unilineally from the beginning to the end of the universal continuum. For example, capitalism was first introduced in England; but it was in the United States where it reached the height of its development. Yet, the United States did not make the transition to socialism. The country which did it first, the Soviet Union, does not appear to be one which will carry socialism to the height of its development. Similarly, democracy was first introduced in the United States on a large scale, but it was in Yugoslavia where it was first extended to business and other organizations. Societies lose their innovativeness to an extent as the rich and powerful gain control over the system of role and reward allocation, the social basis of a society's or organization's problem-solving capacity, innovativeness and creativity.

Are the vested interests in developing countries so strong that there is no chance for self-management? For some, this may certainly be the case, but less so in others. If a real economic or political disaster occurs, which, unfortunately, is not too rare an occurrence in the Developing World, such vested interests may simply be wiped away. In the highly industrialized countries this is much less likely to happen and, accordingly, there is much less of a chance for self-management in these countries. Maybe, in the long run, we will see once again the law of uneven development in action, when self-management will spread in the still under-developed world.

As we have shown in Chapters 12 and 13, there is also an indigenous potential for self-management in many of the developing countries, rooted in traditional culture: in the former small-scale societies in the form of grassroots' democracy and active participation by all in the political and economic sphere, and in other societies in the form of premodern cooperatives for which self-management has always been constitutive. If those countries go back to their own cultural traditions, which many of them prefer to ignore in favour of imported alien concepts, the chance for self-management may be greatly enhanced.

To the extent that the indigenous cultural potential for self-management is there and that the population could readily learn to utilize their potential to participate, it all hinges upon the leadership in the Developing World. One of the main pillars on which the continued success of the Yugoslav system has rested has been the dedication of the Yugoslav political leadership to the idea of self-management. These leadership qualities have become a model for the average Yugoslavs to emulate; for they were soon convinced of the sincerity and determination of their leaders to involve them in self-managed national development. Consequently, they too became determined to give their best to developing their country. It is because of this determination by both the leaders and the citizens and especially the sincerity of the leadership that self-management became a success.

In most developing countries, however, the situation seems to be very different. Leaders tend to have two codes of ethics, one for the citizens and the other one for themselves. Quite frequently, leaders in developing countries conjure concepts and programmes in which they themselves do not actually believe: they are meant to ingratiate them with the public. At times they do not even give the concept or programme a chance to be implemented. Unfortunately, this seems to be true in many of the cases where works councils or other forms of worker participation or self-management are introduced. Such actions are of course apt to confuse and disillusion workers and management alike. As a result they can never be sure whether the leadership is serious in its endeavour to establish workers' participation in management or not. The eventual result of such attempts is, at best, limited success, at worst, utter failure. Moreover, the style of management in most countries makes it difficult to adopt any form of self-management. Since most of the private employers are eager and anxious to protect their entrepreneurial or managerial prerogatives, and since even the political leadership is reluctant to share power and authority (their professed ideology notwithstanding), the prospects for self-management seem limited.

But one thing is apparent. In any production process, it is not only technology and management but also the workers' skills and attitudes that determine the rate of work and the quality of production. In short, the workers are responsible for the actual mechanics of production. This does not mean that the professional managers' contribution will become superfluous. The Yugoslav experience shows quite clearly that it is the combination of professional management and workers' participation in management which really optimizes productivity. If managers in developing countries could be convinced of this fact, if they could be assured that the introduction of worker participation in their respective plant or industry would increase productivity, they may be persuaded to try it at that level.

Self-management at the national or political level in developing countries is likely to remain a dream for some time to come. Even in countries that purport to be socialist, the political leaders are reluctant to share power and decision-making with the people. Even where workers' committees or tripartite bodies exist, the government holds sway over the decision-making process.

There may be a certain, though perhaps limited, chance for developing countries to introduce workers' participation in management at plant or industry level. How and when this will come about cannot be said yet. We only know that self-management is a highly flexible system. Hence, the respective structure of self-management may be just as unique in every country as the circumstances of its emergence. The responsibility for the introduction of self-management and the shape it takes will rest with the leadership of each country. As they are the ones who can prevent self-management from developing, they must also be the ones to implement it. As far as the masses are concerned, they will surely participate.

Bibliography

Adizes, Ichak (1971), *Industrial Democracy: Yugoslav Style: The Effect of Decentralization on Organizational Behavior* (New York: The Free Press).

Almond, Gabriel A. and James S. Coleman (eds) (1960), *The Politics of the Developing Areas* (Princeton, N. J.: Princeton University Press).

Babeau, André (1960), *Les conseils ouvriers en Pologne*. Cahiers de la Fondation Nationale des Sciences Politiques, 110 (Paris: Librairie Armand Colin).

Bajec, Milan (n. d.), *Yugoslavia: Self-Management in Action* (Belgrade: *Yugoslav Review*; London: David Harvey; Frankfurt: Europäische Verlagsanstalt).

Blair, Thomas (1969), *The Land to Those who Work It: Algeria's Experiment in Workers' Management* (New York: Doubleday).

Blum, Emerik (1970), 'The Director and Workers' Management', in M. J. Broekmeyer (ed.), *Yugoslav Workers' Self-management*, pp. 172–92 (Dordrecht, Holland: D. Reidel).

Blumberg, Paul (1968), *Industrial Democracy: The Sociology of Participation* (New York: Schocken Books, 1973).

Bottomore, T. B. (1965), *Classes in Modern Society* (London: Allen & Unwin).

Bourgin, Georges (1971), *La guerre de 1870–1871 et la commune* (Paris: Flammarion).

Broekmeyer, M. J. (ed.) (1970), *Yugoslav Workers' Self-Management*, Proceedings of a Symposium held in Amsterdam, 7–9 January 1970 (Dordrecht, Holland: D. Reidel).

Burt, W. J. (1972), 'Workers' Participation in Management in Yugoslavia', *International Institute for Labour Studies Bulletin*, vol. 9, pp. 129–72.

Chaliand, Gérard and Juliette Minces (1972), *L'Algérie indépendante* (Paris: Maspéro).

Clausen, Ursel (1969), *Der algerische Sozialismus. Eine Dokumentation* (Opladen: Leske Verlag).

Clegg, Ian (1971), *Workers' Self-Management in Algeria* (New York: Monthly Review Press).

Coates, Ken (1973), 'The Quality of Life and Workers' Control', in Eugen Pusić (ed.) *Participation and Self-Management, 3: Workers' Movement and Workers' Control* (The University of Zagreb: Institute for Social Research).

Constitution of the Federal Peoples Republic of Yugoslavia (1946) (Washington, D.C.: Embassy of the Federal People's Republic of Yugoslavia).

Constitution of the Socialist Federal Republic of Yugoslavia (Constitution of 1963), Constitutional Amendments (1969) (Belgrade: The Secretariat of Information of the Federal Executive Council).

Constitutional Amendments XX–XLII (1971) (Belgrade: The Secretariat of Information of the Federal Executive Council).

Constitution of the Socialist Federal Republic of Yugoslavia (1974) (Constitution of 1974) (Belgrade: The Secretariat of the Federal Assembly Information Service).

Coser, Lewis (1956), *The Functions of Social Conflict* (New York: The Free Press).

Damachi, Ukandi G. (1976), *Leadership Ideology in Africa: Attitudes toward Socioeconomic Development* (New York: Praeger).

—— (1978), *Theories of Management and the Executive in the Developing World* (London: Macmillan).

——, Guy Routh and Abdel-Rahman E. Ali Taha (eds) (1976), *Development Paths in Africa and China* (London: Macmillan).

——, H. Dieter Seibel and Lester Trachtman (1979), *Industrial Relations in Africa* (London: Macmillan).

Djilas, Milovan (1957), *The New Class: An Analysis of the Communist System* (New York: Praeger).

—— (1969), *The Unperfect Society: Beyond the New Class* (New York: Harcourt, Brace & World).

Djonlagić, Ahmet, Žarko Atanacković and Dušan Plenča (1967), *La Yougoslavie dans la seconde guerre mondiale*, trans. Novak Strugar (Belgrade: Medjunarodna Stampa Interpress).

Federal Institute for Statistics (1973–1976), *Statistical Pocket-Book of Yugoslavia* (Belgrade).

Festinger, Leon (1957), *A Theory of Cognitive Dissonance* (Stanford University Press).

Finney, Ben R. (1968), 'Bigfellow Man Belongs Business in New Guinea', *Ethnology*, vol. 7, pp. 394–410.

Fürstenberg, Friedrich (1969), 'Workers' Participation in Management in the Federal Republic of Germany', *Bulletin of the International Institute for Labor Studies*, 6.

Garson, G. David (1973), 'The Politics of Workers' Control: A Review Essay', in Gerry Hunnius, G. David Garson and John Case (eds), *Workers' Control: A Reader on Labor and Social Change*, pp. 469–88 (New York: Vintage Books).

Gertzel, Cherry (1979), 'Industrial Relations in Zambia', in Damachi, Seibel and Trachtman (1979).

Ghosh, Pradip K. and Mark van de Vall (1978), 'Workers' Participation in Management—Applied to India', *Indian Journal of Industrial Relations*, pp. 55–68.

Giap, Vo Nguyên (1962), *People's War, People's Army* (New York: Bantam Books).

Gorupić, Drago (1970), 'The Development of the Self-Managing Organization of Enterprises in Yugoslavia', *Yugoslav Survey*, vol. 11, pp. 1–16.

Gorupić, Drago and Ivan Paj (1970), *Workers' Self-Management in Yugoslav Undertakings* (Zagreb: Ekonomski institut 9).

Hogbin, H. Ian (1938), 'Social Advancement in Guadalcanal, Solomon Islands', *Oceania*, vol. 8, pp. 289–305.

Horvat, Branko (1969), *An Essay on Yugoslav Society* (White Plains, N. Y.: International Arts and Sciences Press).

—— (1971), 'Yugoslav Economic Policy in the Post-war Period: Problems, Ideas, Institutional Developments', *American Economic Review*, vol. 61, pp. 69–169.

——, Mihailo Marković and Rudi Supek (1974), *Self-Governing Socialism: A Reader* (White Plains, N.Y.: International Arts and Sciences Press).

Iwuji, E. C. (1979), *Industrial Relations in Kenya*, in Damachi, Seibel and Trachtman (1979).

Jenkins, David (1973), *Job Power: Blue and White Collar Democracy* (New York: Doubleday).

Jerovšek, Janez (1969), *Samoupravljanje u radnim organizacijama s gledišta efikasnosti i demokratičnosti*, Naše teme 11.

—— and Stane Mozina (1970), *Self-Management in Working Organizations from the Point of View of Efficiency and Democracy* (Varna: Seventh World Congress of Sociology).

—— (1979), *Radnički Štrajkovi u SFRJ* (Belgrade: Zapis).

Jovanov, Neca (1971), 'The Organization of Workers' Self-Management in the Bor Mines and Smelting Works', *Yugoslav Survey*, vol. 12, pp. 12–32.

—— (1972), 'Das Verhältnis des Streiks als Gesellschaftskonflikt zur Selbstverwaltung als Gesellschaftssystem' (Belgrade: Kommission für Selbstverwaltung des Rats des Gewerkschaftsbundes Jugoslawiens (unpublished mimeograph)).

Kamušič, Mitja (1970), 'Economic Efficiency and Workers' Self-management', in M. J. Broekmeyer (ed.), *Yugoslav Workers' Self-management*, pp. 76–116 (Dordrecht, Holland: D. Reidel).

Kolontay, A. (1921), *The Workers' Opposition in Russia* (Chicago: Industrial Workers of the World; English trans., n.d.).

Kostin, L. (1960), *Wages in the Soviet Union* (Moscow).

Laks, Monique (1970), *Autogestion ouvrière et pouvoir politique (1962–65)* (Paris: EDI).

Landsberger, Henry A. (1958), *Hawthorne Revisited* (Ithaca, N.Y.: Cornell University Press).

—— and Tim McDaniel (1978), 'Hypermobilisation in Chile, 1970–1973', in Everett M. Kassalow and Ukandi G. Damachi, *The Role of Trade Unions in Developing Societies*, pp. 67–97 (Geneva: International Institute for Labour Studies).

Lane, David (1971), *The End of Inequality? Stratification under State Socialism* (Harmondsworth: Penguin).

Lazreg, Monique (1976), *The Emergence of Classes in Algeria* (Boulder, Col.: Westview Press).

Leberman, Susan M. and Robert L. Leberman (1978), 'Two Case Studies on Workers' Participation in Management', *Indian Journal of Industrial Relations*, pp. 467–510.

Lemân, Gudrun (1976), *Das jugoslawische Modell: Wege zur Demokratisierung* (Frankfurt: EVA).

Lenski, Gerhard E. (1966), *Power and Privilege* (New York: McGraw-Hill).

LeVine, Robert A. (1966), *Dreams and Deeds: Achievement Motivation in Nigeria* (University of Chicago Press).

Likert, Rensis (1961), *New Patterns of Management* (New York: McGraw-Hill).

—— (1967), *The Human Organization: Its Management and Value* (New York: McGraw-Hill).

Linton, Ralph (1936), *The Study of Man* (New York: D. Appleton-Century).

—— (1955), *The Tree of Culture* (New York).

Lockwood, Brian (1971), *Samoan Village Economy* (Melbourne: Oxford University Press).

Luhmann, Niklas (1964), *Funktionen und Folgen formaler Organisation* (Berlin).

Mahsas, Ahmed (1975), *L'autogestion en Algérie* (Paris: Editions Anthropos).

Marković, Mihailo (1965), 'Socialism and Self-management', *Praxis*, vol. 1, pp. 178–95.

Marrow, A. J. (1964), 'Risks and Uncertainties in Action Research', *Journal of Social Issues*, vol. 20, pp. 5–20.

——, D. G. Bowers and S. E. Seashore (eds) (1967), *Strategies of Organizational Change* (New York: Harper & Row).

Marx, Karl (1921), *The Civil War in France*, also known as: *Address of the General Council of the International Working-Men's Association: To All the Members of the Association in Europe and in the United States* (London: The Labour Publishing Company).

—— (1938), *Critique of the Gotha Programme* (New York: International Publishers).

Matejko, Alexander (1973), 'The Sociotechnical Principles of Workers' Control: Industrial Democracy: Myth and Reality', in Eugen Pusić (ed.), *Participation and Self-management, 3: Workers' Movement and Workers' Control*, pp. 25–55 (University of Zagreb: The Institute for Social Research).

Meister, Albert (1970), *Où va l'autogestion Yugoslave?* (Paris: Editions Anthropos).

Middleton, John and David Tait (eds) (1958), *Tribes without Rulers: Studies in African Segmentary Systems* (London: Routledge & Kegan Paul).

Mihyo, Paschal H. (1979), 'Industrial Relations in Tanzania', in Damachi, Seibel and Trachtman (1979).

Miller, Delbert C. and William H. Form (1964), *Industrial Sociology: the Sociology of Work Organization* (New York: Harper & Row).

Ministry of Information and Culture (1970), *L'Autogestion, The Faces of Algeria*, 8 (Algiers).

—— (1973a), *The Socialist Organization of Enterprises, The Faces of Algeria*, 22 (Algiers).

—— (1973b), *The Agrarian Revolution, The Faces of Algeria*, 23 (Algiers).

Mlinar, Zdravko and Niko Toš (1971), *Neizkori Ščeni Potenciali za Družbeni Razvoj* (Ljubljana: Kommunist: Tema dneva 8).

Mozina, Stane, Janez Jerovšek, Arnold S. Tannenbaum and Rensis Likert (1970), 'Testing a Management Style', *European Business* (Autumn).

Nikolić, Miodrag (1973), 'Changes in the Structure of Industrial Production, 1952–1972', *Yugoslav Survey*, vol. 14, pp. 33–42.

Nyerere, Julius K. (1968), *Uhuru na Ujamaa* (Freedom and Socialism) (London: Oxford University Press).

Obradović, Josip (1970), 'Participation and Work Attitudes in Yugoslavia', *Industrial Relations*, pp. 161–9.

Paj, Ivan (1971), 'The Organization of Self-management in Enterprises', *Yugoslav Survey*, vol. 12, pp. 31–50.

Pašić, Najdan (1970), 'Integration Based on Self-management and the Political System', *Socialist Thought and Practice*, vol. 39, pp. 12–29.

Peterson, Richard A. (1973), *The Dynamics of Industrial Society* (Indianapolis: Bobbs-Merrill).

Polajnar, Tone (ed.) (1973), *Pomembnejčni podatki za občino Škofja Loka* (Škofja Loka: Podatke je pripravila in izdala uprava skupščine občine Škofja Loka).

Pusić, Eugen (1968), *Samoupravljanje* (Zagreb).

—— (ed.) (1972), *Participation and Self-management* (Zagreb).

Reynolds, Lloyd G. and Cynthia H. Taft (1956), *The Evolution of Wage Structure* (New Haven, Conn.: Yale University Press).

Robert, Ernie (1973), *Workers' Control* (London: Allen & Unwin).

Roethlisberger, J.F. and W. J. Dickson (1947), *Management and the Worker* (Harvard University Press).

Rus, Veljko (1967), 'Institutionalization of the Revolutionary Movement', *Praxis: Revue philosophique*, vol. 2, pp. 201–13.

Sahlins, Marshall D. (1963), 'Poor Man, Rich Man, Big-Man, Chief: Political Types in Melanesia and Polynesia', *Comparative Studies in Society and History*, vol. 5, pp. 285–303.

Schneider, Dieter Marc (ed.) (1971), *Pariser Kommune 1871, I· Bakunin, Kropotkin, Lavrov* (Reinbek: Rowohlt).

—— and Rudolf E. Kuda (1961), *Mitbestimmung: Weg zur industriellen Demokratie* (München: Deutscher Taschenbuch Verlag).

Schröder, Günter and Hans Dieter Seibel (1974), 'Ethnographic Survey of Southeastern Liberia: The Liberian Kran and the

Sapo', *Liberian Studies Monograph Series Number*,3 (Newark, Del.: Liberian Studies Association in America, University of Delaware).

Seibel, Hans Dieter (1973), *Gesellschaft im Leistungskonflikt* (Düsseldorf: Bertelsmann Universitätsverlag).

—— (1974a), *The Dynamics of Achievement: a Radical Perspective* (Indianapolis: Bobbs-Merrill).

—— (1974b), 'Self-Management as a Model of Development: The Yugoslav Case', *SSIP-Bulletin*, no. 40, pp. 99–109.

—— (1975), 'Problemlage und Schichtungssystem. Eine allgemeine Theorie der Entwicklung', *Kölner Zeitschrift für Soziologie und Sozialpsychologie*, vol. 27, pp. 731–54.

—— (1976), 'Problemlage und Schichtungssystem in der Sowjetunion', *Kölner Zeitschrift für Soziologie und Sozialpsychologie*, vol. 28, pp. 212–38.

—— (1978), 'Offene und geschlossene Gesellschaften. Überprüfung einer Hypothese im interkulturellen Vergleich: Melanesien und Polynesien', *Zeitschrift für Soziologie*, vol. 7, pp. 272–98.

—— and Michael Koll (1968), *Einheimische Genossenschaften in Afrika. Formen wirtschaftlicher Zusammenarbeit bei westafrikanischen Stämmen* (Düsseldorf: Bertelsmann Universitätsverlag).

—— and Andreas Massing (1974), *Traditional Organizations and Economic Development: Studies of Indigenous Cooperatives in Liberia* (New York: Praeger).

Simmel, Georg (1922), *Soziologie* (München: Duncker & Humblot).

Sixth Congress of the Socialist Alliance of Working People of Yugoslavia (1966) (Belgrade: Medjunarodna politika).

Smith, M. G. (1959), 'The Hausa System of Social Status', *Africa*, vol. 29, pp. 239–52.

Socijalistička Federativna Republika Jugoslavija, Savezni zavod za statistiku (1973, 1976), *Statistički Godišnjak Jugoslavije*, 20, 23 (Belgrade: Izdaje i štampa Savezni zavod za statistiku).

Starčević, Stevan, *et al.* (1972), *The Second Congress of Self-managers of Yugoslavia* (Belgrade: Medjunarodna politika).

Strong, Anna Louise (1937), *Spain in Arms* (New York: Henry Holt).

Sturmthal, Adolf (1964), *Workers Councils: A Study of Workplace*

Organization on Both Sides of the Iron Curtain (Cambridge, Mass.: Harvard University Press).

Sweezy, Paul (1964), 'The Transition from Socialism to Capitalism?', *Monthly Review*, vol. 16, pp. 569–90.

Tannenbaum, Arnold S. (1968), *Control in Organizations* (New York: McGraw-Hill).

Teutenberg, Hans Jürgen (1961), *Geschichte der industriellen Mitbestimmung in Deutschland* (Tübingen).

Tinbergen, Jan (1970), 'Does Self-management Approach the Optimum Order?' in M.J. Broekmeyer (ed.), *Yugoslav Workers' Self-management*, pp. 117–27 (Dordrecht, Holland: D. Reidel).

Tittel, Roland (1971), *Mitbestimmung* (Köln: Deutsches Industrieinstitut).

Todorović, Mijalko (1970), 'Self-management: Historical Aspiration of the Working Class', *Socialist Thought and Practice*, vol. 40, pp. 3–27; vol. 41, pp. 39–63.

Tomasevic, Nebojsa (n.d.), *Facts about Yugoslavia* (Belgrade: Yugoslav Review).

Toš, Nico (1969), *Poročila 'Slovensko javno mnenje 69'* (Ljubljana: Fakulteta za Sociologijo, Politične vede in Novinarstvo, Univerze v Ljubljani, Center za Raziskovanje Javnega Mnenja in Množičnik Komunikacij).

—— (1971), *Poročila 'Slovensko javno mnenje 71'* (Ljubljana: Fakulteta za Sociologijo, Politične vede in Novinarstvo, Univerze v Ljubljani, Center za Raziskovanje Javnega Mnenga in Množičnik Komunikacij).

Vanek, Jaroslav (1970), *The General Theory of Labor-Managed Market Economies* (Ithaca, N.Y.: Cornell University Press).

—— (1971), *The Participatory Economy: an Evolutionary Hypothesis and a Strategy for Development* (Ithaca, N. Y.: Cornell University Press).

Veljković, Ljubo (ed.) (1968), *Economic Development in Yugoslavia*, Studies, no. 25 (Belgrade: Medjunarodna štampa Intcrprcss).

Viratelle, Gérard (1970), *L'Algérie Algérienne* (Paris: Editions Economie et Humanisme).

Wachtel, Howard M. (1973), *Workers' Management and Workers' Wages in Yugoslavia: the Theory and Practice of Participatory Socialism* (Ithaca, N.Y.: Cornell University Press).

Watters, R. F. (1958), 'Cultivation in Old Samoa', *Economic Geography*, vol. 34, pp. 338–51.

Wells, F. A. and W. A. Warmington (1963), *Studies in Industrialization: Nigeria and the Cameroons* (London).

Wesołowski, W. (1966), *Changes in the Class Structure in Poland*, pp. 7–35, in J. Szczepanski (ed.), *Empirical Sociology in Poland* (Warsaw: Polish Scientific Publications).

Wlotzke, O. (ed.) (1973), *Betriebsverfassungsgesetz* (München: Deutscher Taschenbuch Verlag).

Young, Michael W. (1971), *Fighting with Food: Leadership, Values and Social Control in a Massim Society* (Cambridge: Cambridge University Press).

Name Index

Subject Index